HAMLYN CHILDREN'S HISTORY OF
# BRITAIN

# HAMLYN CHILDREN'S HISTORY OF
# BRITAIN
## FROM THE STONE AGE TO THE PRESENT DAY

## Neil Grant

DEAN

# Contents

**Illustrations by:**

Colin Andrew; Mike Bell; Shirley
Bellwood; John Berry; Brian
Bysouth; Mike Codd; Donald
Harley; Mick Hodson; Sue Hunter;
Jack Keay; Angus McBride; John
Marshall; Edward Osmond; Pat
Owen; Edwin Phillips; Kristin
Rosenberg; Ivan Lapper; Patrick
Leeson; Michael Turner; Gerald
Witcomb.

First published 1977
by The Hamlyn Publishing Group Limited.
This edition first published 1992 by
Dean, an imprint of Reed Children's Books Limited,
Michelin House, 81 Fulham Road, London SW3 6RB, and
Auckland, Melbourne, Singapore and Toronto.
Reprinted 1993

ISBN 0 603 55075 4

British Library Cataloguing-in-Publication Data.
A catalogue record for this book is available from the
British Library.

Printed in the Slovak Republic

# Foreword

*History is the old coin your grandfather gave you; the castle you explored on your last holiday; the iron beaker in the British Museum; the old cotton mills of Oldham; the Van Dyck painting in the National Portrait Gallery; and a million other things belonging to the past. History is the story of the past, of how things happened and why they happened (or why they did not happen), and everything that belongs to the past belongs also to history.*

*History is interesting because the world today and we who live in it are the result of what has happened in the past, the result of history. If we know something about the past, it is easier to understand the present. It is not true that history repeats itself: no event is exactly the same as another. Yet if we know what happened in the past, we can make a better guess at what is likely to happen in the future.*

*This book does not try to tell the whole story of Britain's past. That would be impossible. It gives a general picture which spans more than 2,000 years; one that will encourage readers to take an even closer look at the fascinating story of their national heritage.*

# Chapter 1

## People of Ancient Britain

Long ago, the British Isles were not isles at all. Britain was part of the European continent: the English Channel did not exist and East Anglia merged into the Netherlands. Then, about 10,000 years ago – when the last Ice Age had ended, when the bones of the last mammoth had sunk into the mud of the Thames valley, when the climate grew warmer – new rivers and seas were formed and Europe was slowly moulded into its present shape.

The people of Britain, like their cousins on the continent, were simple hunters who lived on the flesh of wild animals, which they shot with flint-tipped arrows or caught in traps. They killed fish in the estuaries and shallow rivers with spears made from the antlers of deer. They gathered wild fruit, nuts and honey, and probably ate snails, caterpillars and other grubs. They did not

*Home life in the Stone Age: making a spear and grinding grain.*

build permanent houses, but moved from place to place, sheltering in caves in cold weather.

The people of Britain lagged behind the people of certain warmer lands in their development. While they were still living in caves and scratching about for insects to eat, the Egyptians were building pyramids and writing literature.

Of all the stages between the cave and the skyscraper, perhaps man's greatest leap forward was taken when he became a farmer. The Stone Age farmer of about 5,000 years ago had to clear patches in the forests which covered most of Britain that was not barren heath or swamp. He cut down trees with stone axes, burned off the scrub, and tilled the ground with a stone-headed hoe. He kept half-wild cattle and pigs in the forest, where they could find their own food, and in treeless parts, like northern Scotland, he kept sheep. The people who grew grain in southern England had flint sickles to reap the harvest.

By the end of the Stone Age, about 2,000 BC, metal was already being used. The Beaker people, who are named after the clay mugs, or 'beakers', they made, also used bronze knives. They came to Britain from northern Europe, and started the building of the stone monuments at Stonehenge and Avebury.

A simple plough also appeared about this time. It was little more than a spike to rip up the ground: the field was ploughed twice, the second time at right angles to the first. These improvements allowed people to settle in villages, where they stored food for the winter in underground larders. In a few places, like the Orkneys, houses were built of stone, and their remains can still be seen, complete with stone shelves and bedsteads.

Mining and trade were growing during the Bronze Age (roughly 2,000 to 500 BC). Copper was imported from Ireland and tin from Cornwall – the two metals from which the harder alloy, bronze, was made. Amber was imported from the Baltic and pottery from the Mediterranean area. Carts were made for moving heavy goods.

The people of the Wessex culture (southern England) developed the most advanced society Britain had seen. They used ornaments of gold and had complicated funeral ceremonies, with burials in round 'barrows', or mounds. Building continued at Stonehenge, which was a kind of temple, perhaps having some connection with the changing seasons. The stones seem to be lined up with the sun at different times of the year, and some experts have suggested that the whole building was a kind of astronomical clock.

About 500 BC, the inhabitants of Britain were learning how to smelt iron. Iron ore was easier to obtain, as it often lay close to the surface and was far more common than copper or tin. Although good tools were made of bronze, iron tools were much cheaper.

The beginning of the Iron Age coincided with the arrival of new people from the continent, mainly from France. They were the Celts. Archaeologists have discovered at least three Celtic groups, whom they call A, B and C people. The C people, the last and most advanced group, were the people known to the Romans as the Belgae (they did indeed come from roughly the area of Belgium). They were not 'pure' Celts, having some German blood. In fact there was less difference between Celtic and Germanic people in ancient times than some modern 'Celts' would like to think.

*Miners bringing up flints at Grime's Graves, Norfolk, over 4,000 years ago.*

9

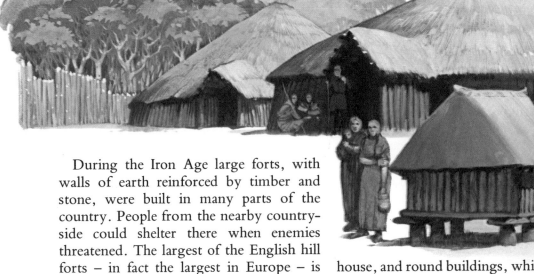

During the Iron Age large forts, with walls of earth reinforced by timber and stone, were built in many parts of the country. People from the nearby countryside could shelter there when enemies threatened. The largest of the English hill forts – in fact the largest in Europe – is Maiden Castle in Dorset. Standing on its great earthen ramparts, on a silent wintry afternoon if possible, some faint sense of Iron Age Britain can still be felt.

An Iron Age house was found by archaeologists at Little Woodbury, in Wiltshire. It was built on the plan of two circles, one inside the other. The family lived inside the smaller circle and the farm animals were stabled in the outer ring. The men of the family smelted their own iron, from which they made sickles for harvesting. The women made clothes, spinning and weaving their cloth, and clay cooking pots. They probably also pounded grain into flour.

We know of many types of Iron Age house, and round buildings, which are simpler than walled houses, have been found in many places. The mysterious round stone towers of northern Scotland called *brochs* belong to the late Iron Age.

In spite of the evidence of the hill forts and stone towers, life in prehistoric Britain was not always violent. The arrival of new immigrants must have caused problems, but they usually came in smallish groups and soon mingled with the native population. It was never a case of the natives being overwhelmed by more aggressive and more advanced invaders. The Celts, who were of mixed race themselves, married natives whose ancestors had also been immigrants from northern Europe and from Spain.

*The Celts made elegant house objects, like this gilt-bronze shield (late 1st century BC), bowl (1st century BC) and mirror (early 1st century AD).*

*A Celtic chieftain watches while a smith forges his sword blade. The stream has been dammed to make a pool into which the red-hot blade will be plunged at the right moment.*

Britain was unknown to the more civilized parts of Europe until it was visited – 'discovered' in fact – by Pytheas, an educated merchant from Marseille, in about 320 BC. Pytheas wrote the first description of the people, whom he called Celts. They were gentle folk, he said, and welcomed visitors.

The opinion of Pytheas is surprising. The next educated visitor to Britain described the British as a fierce race – savages who dyed their skin blue with woad. But that visitor, who was probably wrong about blue-skinned Britons anyway, came in no friendly spirit. His name was Julius Caesar.

# Britain conquered by the Romans

In 55 BC Britain was invaded by Julius Caesar, a Roman general and governor of Gaul (France), soon to be, in all but name, the first Roman emperor.

At that time the city of Rome was about 700 years old, but the Roman empire was much younger. As late as 211 BC Rome had narrowly escaped destruction by the Carthaginian general, Hannibal. But Hannibal's defeat left Rome without a serious rival, and by Caesar's time it controlled an empire that stretched from Spain to the Near East.

Two places more different than imperial Rome and Celtic Britain could hardly have existed. Roman society was urban, with grand public buildings built of marble. Britain was a country of mud huts, with no settlement large enough to be called a town. An upper-class Roman lived in greater comfort than any Britisher before the 15th century. His house even had central heating.

The Romans, as heirs of the civilization of Ancient Greece, were interested in art, philosophy and history (Caesar himself wrote good military history in simple prose). The British could neither read nor write. They were not savages, and in some ways Celtic art was superior to Roman, or so it seems to us, but the Romans naturally thought of them as hopelessly primitive barbarians. To the Romans – and to many non-Romans too – there was but one worthwhile form of society, and that was their own. The only useful function of other peoples was to contribute to the glory of Rome.

Britain was a mysterious isle to the Romans. But Caesar knew it contained valuable minerals, and he knew also that the British were helping their cousins in Gaul against Rome. He decided on invasion.

Caesar had another motive – personal glory; yet his invasion nearly ended in disaster. Landing on an open beach near Deal, the Romans fought their way ashore, beat the assembled British, and accepted tributes from some of the chiefs. But a storm wrecked their ships and they had to scramble back to Gaul, having advanced little farther than the Kent coast.

Next year Caesar came again, this time with a much larger expedition – five legions (about 25,000 men) and 800 ships. The British tribes sank their differences, uniting under the leadership of Cassivellaunus, and it took some time for Caesar to work out a way of dealing with the British chariots. The Romans were not used to this form of warfare, as chariots were obsolete in Gaul.

But Cassivellaunus failed to stop the attack. Caesar advanced through Kent, crossed the Thames at London, and marched through the thick forests of Essex towards Colchester. When an attack on the Romans' naval camp failed, the British decided to come to terms. Caesar took hostages and imposed an annual tax (we do not know for how long the British paid it). Then he sailed back to Gaul.

The British had been defeated but not conquered, and for nearly a hundred years

A Roman soldier equipped for battle. The soldiers came from all parts of the empire, and few of them were actually 'Roman'.

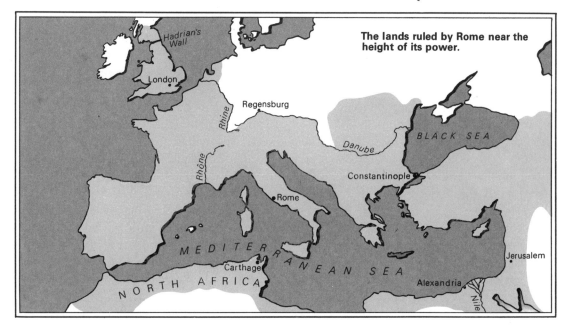

The lands ruled by Rome near the height of its power.

afterwards no Roman army appeared in Britain. Caesar's expeditions had shown that Britain would not be conquered easily.

Between 54 BC and AD 43, the date of the Roman conquest, Lowland Britain prospered. The country enjoyed the benefits of trade with the great Roman empire without the disadvantages of Roman rule. The British came to know the Romans well. Roman merchants travelled to Britain, and Roman influence was strong. Many British leaders were pro-Roman. In some respects, Britain was 'Romanized' before the Roman conquest.

In AD 43 the Romans landed at Richborough, Kent, and advanced steadily north and west. They were chiefly interested in the fertile south-east, but they soon found that the minerals they wanted (lead, copper, etc.) lay in the mountainous parts. They found, too, that having conquered part of Britain it was hard to draw a line and say: *that* is where we stop.

The British were still not united, and the main opponent of the Romans, a clever and determined king of the Catuvellauni named Caratacus, was unable to create a national coalition. He did his best, and when defeated in central England he retired to south-east Wales, where the Silures resisted the Romans more fiercely than any other people. Then, as Roman strength built up in the West Country, Caratacus fell back to Snowdonia, where the Ordovices kept up the struggle. After a hard battle, the Romans captured their stronghold near Caersws, and all of Caratacus's family were taken prisoner. He fled to Brigantia (northern England), but the queen of the Brigantes favoured Rome and had him arrested. He was sent in chains to Rome. There, he was triumphantly displayed before the people as a symbol of the Roman victory. Caratacus looked in wonder at the rich and powerful city. 'Why', he asked his captors, 'with all these great buildings, do you still want our poor huts?'

The Romans brought their campaign in Wales to a conclusion by conquering the Isle of Anglesey, off North Wales. Anglesey was a centre of the cult of the Druids, a class of priests (or witchdoctors) who had great influence among the British and knew that Rome's victory would mean their deaths. The Romans, who were tolerant of most local customs, were determined to destroy the Druids, as they disliked their ritual of human sacrifice.

As the Romans looked across the Menai Straits, they saw a hoard of hostile warriors, urged on to battle by mad-looking women in black and by the robed figures of the Druids, lifting their bloody hands to heaven to call down curses on their enemies. Grimly, the Romans paddled their boats across the straits, the cavalry swimming their horses alongside. They cut their way through the rabble opposing them and slaughtered the Druids among their own altars.

At this moment (AD 61) a dramatic revolt broke out on the opposite side of the country. The king of the Iceni had died, and the Romans refused to recognize his daughters as his successors. The Roman soldiers in East Anglia were not well led (their governor was in Wales, of course), and they behaved stupidly towards the local people.

They swaggered brutally through the country, stealing what they fancied. They raped the king's daughters and gave their mother, Queen Boudicca, a whipping.

Suddenly the country was in flames. Boudicca's people were joined by others, including many who had first welcomed the Romans but had since suffered from their greed and pride. A wild army swept down upon Colchester. London and St Albans fell to the rebels, who killed all the Roman colonists. Meanwhile, the governor hastily gathered his troops and, with 10,000 men, he met Boudicca in battle north-west of Towcester. The rebels were defeated. Boudicca died soon afterwards, and the revolt fizzled out.

Probably, the Romans could have conquered all of Britain if they had been determined to do so. But Britain was on the fringe of their empire; it was small, and

*The battle of Maiden Castle, Dorset: Vespasian, the Roman general, watches his troops advancing in 'tortoise' formation, with shields protecting their heads, to attack the Celtic stronghold.*

expensive to govern. Some Romans thought it was not worth the cost.

Julius Agricola, the best of the governors of Britain, came near to completing the conquest before he was recalled to Rome. He advanced north across the Forth and the Tay, and in AD 84 he defeated the Caledonians of northern Scotland at the great battle of Mons Graupius (probably a few kilometres east of Inverness). Roman historians say that 10,000 Caledonians were killed, and only 360 Romans.

But soon afterwards the Romans decided to retreat. After some serious setbacks in the north, the Emperor Hadrian marked the frontier with a great wall across Britain between the Tyne and the Solway (Newcastle-Carlisle). Built in the 120s, the wall was the largest structure in the Roman empire.

Although Hadrian's Wall was such a vast engineering project, the Romans were never certain that it was in quite the right place. In 142 a second wall was built farther north, between the Clyde and the Forth (Glasgow-Edinburgh). Serious outbreaks continued; the Picts attacked from Scotland and the Brigantes from Yorkshire. In a revolt at the end of the 2nd century all the

Hadrian's Wall, with a coin of the same emperor, which was made to commemorate his visit to Britain in 122.

forts from York northward were destroyed.

Eventually, the Romans withdrew to Hadrian's Wall, which marked the real frontier of their power, although Roman patrols ranged far beyond it and Roman peace prevailed in the Scottish Lowlands.

In the third century, Roman Britain was already being attacked by Saxon pirates from Germany, and forts had to be built along the 'Saxon Shore', from the Wash to the Isle of Wight. In 367 the Saxons, the Picts and the Scots (aggressive Irish immigrants who were beginning to settle in south-west Scotland) attacked together. Although order was eventually restored, Roman power was waning fast and in 406 all troops were recalled from Britain to defend Rome from the attacks of the Goths. The legions never returned.

# The Roman Province of Britain

The Romans were in Britain for over 350 years – a very long time in the history of any country. In the north and west they remained an occupying army, keeping a grip on an often hostile people; but Lowland Britain (most of England) was thoroughly Romanized. The effects of the occupation were surprisingly small in the long run, but Roman rule certainly changed the lives of the British.

The greatest blessing of Roman rule was the *pax Romana*, 'Roman peace'. Tribal wars in Lowland Britain stopped, and the attacks of outsiders, like the Picts from the north and the Saxons from overseas, were resisted. The Romans set up law courts and enforced justice, though their idea of justice was not the same as ours and their punishments, which included execution by crucifixion, were cruel.

The Romans built the first towns. London was the largest, with about 30,000 people. Colchester and St Albans each had about half as many, but most Roman towns had only 3,000 or 4,000.

The typical Roman town was surrounded by a defensive wall, and was entered through stone-towered gateways. Streets were laid out in squares, and many of the ordinary houses and shops were made of timber and plaster. Larger, stone houses belonged to local leaders, government officials or merchants. The centre of the town was the marketplace, or forum, and nearby were a town hall, several temples, public baths (the Romans were fond of bathing and even had a type of sauna), and an inn or two. Some buildings, such as the amphitheatre where plays were performed, were outside the defensive walls.

Roman towns in Britain were less grand than towns nearer the heart of the empire, but they included fine marble buildings decorated with sculpture, and advanced engineering works, like the water supply and drainage system of Lincoln.

Lincoln's water was pumped – uphill – from a spring two kilometres away, through a pipe protected by concrete, to a reservoir inside the wall. There was enough water to provide a sluice or flush for each house. A drain carried water into the sewers, stone tunnels large enough for a child to walk along, which ran under the main streets, with manholes at regular intervals.

As well as the first towns, the Romans built the first English country houses, or villas. We know the sites of about 600 villas (many can be visited), and more will undoubtedly be discovered. Unlike the Roman villas of southern Europe, which were weekend retreats for the rich, villas in England were usually working farms. The old Celtic leaders did not like the new-fangled idea of towns, and preferred to live on their estates.

Some villas were small farmhouses and others were grand palaces, like Fishbourne in Sussex (which is well worth visiting). The illustration shows one of the larger villas, which had two floors and were built around a courtyard. The Romans, more sensible than later builders, usually chose good, sunny places. The villa had glass windows, something not seen again for a thousand years, and was decorated with paintings, mosaics and sculpture. Although a 20th-century family would miss some comforts, like electricity, few people today live in so pleasant a house.

Large villas were for the wealthy few. We should not forget that the estate was run by slaves, and that at one villa archaeologists found the skeletons of seventy new-born babies – unwanted slave children put outside to die.

Of all the relics of Roman Britain, the roads lasted best. Their routes can still be seen from the air, and many modern roads follow them. Roman roads were built

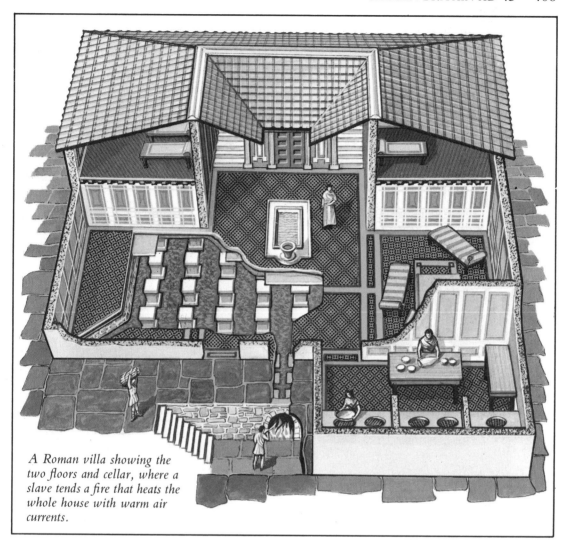

A Roman villa showing the two floors and cellar, where a slave tends a fire that heats the whole house with warm air currents.

straight, going over hills rather than around them, because their purpose was the swift movement of soldiers. They were also built to last, with massive stone foundations. The Romans built everything that way, thinking their empire would continue for ever.

Like all imperialists, the Romans were interested in their colony for what they could get out of it. Metals were Britain's most important product from a Roman point of view, and Britain provided lead (from which silver was obtained), copper, and other useful metals. There was even a gold mine in Wales. Britain also exported jet and pearls, which came from oysters (the fish-and-chips of ancient times), bearskins and sealskins, corn, and slaves. British hunting dogs (the ancestors of our bulldogs and greyhounds) fetched good prices in Rome.

But in Roman times, as now, Britain probably had an 'unfavourable balance of payments', meaning more imports than exports. Though the British were great beer-drinkers, wine was a big import item, and so was olive oil. Most luxury goods came from abroad because British products were inferior. The rich man's silver, bronze-ware, glass and pottery came from older parts of the empire, although such things were made in Britain too. Egyptian papyrus (for writing on), spices and incense were the kind of goods that *had* to be imported.

The Romans brought new developments to British farming. They built watermills for grinding corn, and used iron ploughs (Celtic ploughs were wooden, though iron-tipped). They were the first to claim fertile land from the Fens by digging canals for drainage – and transport. New crops were introduced: rye, oats, flax, cabbages, parsnips, turnips and many other vegetables. (Most of the vegetables we eat today were first grown either by the Romans or the American Indians.) The Romans brought larger horses and cattle, new fruit trees, perhaps including apples, and many flowers that we think of as typically British, like the rose. They were the first bee-keepers in Britain, and the first to eat home-reared roast goose.

The Romans also brought their gods to Britain. There were an immense number of them, and they often became merged with local Celtic gods. Especially popular with Roman soldiers was the worship of Mithras, originally a Persian god, one of whose temples was found a few years ago buried in the heart of London. Another new religion was Christianity. Christians were intolerant of other religions, especially the Romans' worship of their emperor, and until 313 they were persecuted in Rome. The British also disliked emperor-worship, which was one of the causes behind Boudicca's revolt, and Christianity seems to have been established in Britain by about 150.

One of the greatest conflicts in the early Christian Church began in the British Isles as a result of the teaching of Pelagius, an Irish monk born about 360. Pelagius attacked the idea of original sin – the belief that a person's acts do not affect his destiny, which depends on god's favour. Pelagianism was kinder and more tolerant than official Christian doctrine, but the Church nervously stamped on such signs of individualism. Still, Pelagian ideas did not disappear.

In spite of all the Roman improvements, the mass of the British may have been worse off under Roman rule. Tribal wars in Lowland Britain could have ended without the *pax Romana*. Towns did not suit the simple British economy, and the villa was a Mediterranean house, which was not ideal for Britain's colder, wetter climate. Farmers may have grown more food, but they had to pay imperial taxes, which ate up their profits. Public buildings and roads were all very well, but their cost – in labour as well as cash – was heavy. Mining expanded, but Cornish tin-mining, Britain's greatest industry in pre-Roman times, was stopped because the Romans did not want it to compete with Spanish tin production.

Britain existed to serve Rome. In doing so, it gained benefits but also suffered disadvantages. Were the benefits greater than the drawbacks? The answer would depend on whether you were a prince or a peasant.

*A busy street in a Roman garrison town in Britain. Other than roads and walls, little remains of the Roman occupation.*

# Britain after the Romans

The decline of the Roman empire was a long process. In a way, it began before the conquest of Britain, when some of the old Roman virtues were already disappearing. By the 3rd century, there could be no mistaking the decadence of Rome. Ordinary people seemed to care for nothing except 'bread and circuses' (food and cheap entertainment). The aristocracy had grown lazy and soft through living on the work of slaves. Standards of education had fallen, and inflation was ruining the economy.

The slow breakdown of Rome coincided with the restless stirrings of more vigorous people. The fierce Huns were expanding westwards from central Asia, and others – Vandals, Goths, Franks, etc. – moved west ahead of them. Among them were the Saxons who came to Britain.

Roman civilization in Britain was dying for many years before the legions departed. Some towns, like Bath, were ruined and deserted before the Saxon invaders reached them. Coins and pottery, which provide such valuable clues for archaeologists, were becoming scarce before 400. Written records disappeared almost entirely. Looking back, we seem to see a gloomy northern mist falling on Britain. Through it we hear the cries and sounds of battle, while now

*This beautiful silver dish was found near Mildenhall, Suffolk, by a farm worker. It is the central piece of a famous collection, now in the British Museum.*

and then some menacing figure looms dimly through the mist, bent on plunder.

However, Roman civilization did not suddenly disappear in 406, the year that the Roman legions suddenly disappeared for good. The Mildenhall treasure, discovered in Suffolk in the 1940s, is a dazzling witness to the wealth of some households at the time when Roman rule was collapsing. British leaders thought themselves better Romans than the citizens of sinful Rome for, influenced by Pelagius, they were critical of the Roman 'establishment' in both Church and State.

Without the legions Britain was almost defenceless against its various enemies, and Saxon raids increased. A British king, Vortigern (a title not a name), allowed some of the raiders to settle in Kent about 430. He hoped these people, who were probably Jutes, would prevent further raids, but he soon fell out with them himself. Almost the last direct word we hear from Britain for over a hundred years is a letter of about 446, which speaks of 'the groans of the Britons', whom 'the barbarians are driving to the sea'.

This was an appeal for help to Rome (never answered), and it probably exaggerated the plight of the British. With so little historical evidence, we tend to think that Roman-British society was quickly wiped out. But that did not happen. We now know that cities like St Alban's and Silchester were still inhabited in the 6th century, and that there was a revival of Celtic art, probably resulting from the weakening of Roman influence in the late 4th century. We know too that the British succeeded, at least for a short time, in halting the Germanic invaders.

In the late 5th century, the British were led by a shadowy figure called Ambrosius Aurelianus (note the Latin, i.e. 'Roman', name). He harassed the Saxons by fast-striking attacks at fords and crossroads. When he died, some time after 500, the leadership was taken over by his chief general, whose name was Arthur.

We are now in Round Table country: the stories of King Arthur, his Queen Guinevere and his noble Knights of the Round Table are well-known. But these beautiful stories are legends – made up by poets in the later Middle Ages. It was once thought that they were total fiction. But we now know that Arthur was a real general or king.

He must have been a good commander, for he beat the Saxons twelve times before his greatest battle at Mount Badon, somewhere in the West County, about 516. Arthur's victory there not only stopped the Saxons, it persuaded some of them to go back to Germany.

About twenty years later Arthur was killed, probably in a civil war. The Saxons advanced again, and before the end of the 6th century they had spread throughout Lowland Britain.

*King Arthur's Round Table, which hangs in the Great Hall of Winchester Castle. The table was round, so that no knight would appear more important than another. It was once said to be Arthur's own table, although it is probably no older than the 13th century.*

# Chapter 2

## The arrival of the Anglo-Saxons

The Germanic invaders of Britain, who were to become the English, came from north-west Europe, between the mouth of the Rhine and the Baltic Sea. By Roman standards they were uncivilized people. They had never known Roman rule, and when they reached Britain they were startled by the Roman buildings. Only a race of giants, they thought, could have built them. They avoided the towns, preferring their own simpler settlements. That is why many Roman sites – St Alban's is a good example – are separated from the modern town.

At first the Anglo-Saxons arrived in small groups. Then, liking the country, they came in larger bands, and began to move inland, finding their way to the heart of England up the Thames and other rivers. The England they found was not much like the England of modern times. To judge from Anglo-Saxon poetry it was a grim, cold place. Thorny forests and barren heaths covered much of the land, swamps and marshes covered more. Rivers were not neatly confined within banks but oozed over the fields. Bears, wolves and wild boar roamed the forests. There were pelicans in Somerset and golden eagles in Surrey.

When immigration was at its height in the 6th century, the Anglo-Saxon bands numbered many hundreds, perhaps thousands. But it was never a mass migration. The Saxons that Arthur defeated at Mount Badon were probably less than 1,000-strong. Few large battles took place, but the Anglo-Saxons did not gain the land without violence.

Not only did they fight the British, they fought among themselves. Saxons and Angles battled for possession of the Midlands, Saxons and Jutes for Surrey and Hampshire. Gradually, family groups came together to form larger, stronger tribes, and then kingdoms. By about 600, the newcomers controlled all England except the extreme north-west and south-west, plus south-east Scotland; but they did not hold Wales.

What, meanwhile, happened to the Celtic British? Here and there archaeologists have found evidence of the two peoples living side by side – or dying side by side – for at York there were Roman-style coffins buried next to Germanic funeral urns. Yet there are few signs of Roman or Celtic influence in Anglo-Saxon England. The British were driven back, into the more remote and mountainous parts of Britain which the Anglo-Saxons, like the Romans before them, hardly entered.

Although there is almost no evidence for such a thing, we can be sure that many of the ancient British remained. Certainly they had little in common with the newcomers, and failed, for example, to convert them to Christianity. But it does not seem likely that the whole native population was killed or driven away. Many of the British must have become slaves of the Anglo-Saxons, and many British women must have borne the children of Saxon fathers. But as far as history is concerned, in the regions settled by the Anglo-Saxons the old British society ceased to exist.

*An Anglo-Saxon settlement: the stockade will keep out dangerous animals as well as human enemies.*

23

# The England of the Anglo-Saxons

Anglo-Saxon England settled into a pattern of seven kingdoms. The three largest, Northumbria, Mercia and Wessex eventually came to dominate the country, each at different times. First it was Northumbria (the only time in English history when the centre of power has been in the north). Northumbria stretched as far as Edinburgh and for a time included part of the kingdom of Strathclyde, in south-west Scotland.

During the 8th century, Northumbrian leadership was replaced by the midlands kingdom of Mercia. The greatest of Mercian kings, Offa (757–796), corresponded with the mighty Charlemagne, emperor of the Franks; he minted his own coins – the first nationwide currency since Roman times. He is remembered also as the builder of Offa's Dyke, an earth rampart over 190

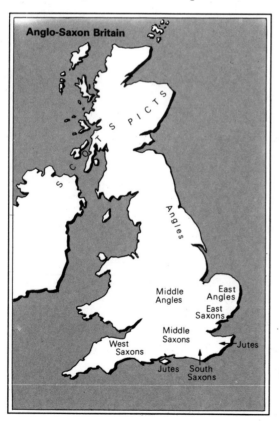

kilometres long which marked the border of Mercia with Wales. It can still be seen, but it was much higher in Offa's time.

On his coins, Offa called himself 'king of the English', and his power stretched far enough for him to have a rebellious king of East Anglia beheaded, and to give estates to his subjects in Sussex. He even had some influence in Northumbria.

However, neither Northumbria nor Mercia succeeded in making their kings the rulers of all England. That honour was to fall to the House of Wessex, made great by King Alfred.

But what was this office of kingship, and how did it work in Anglo-Saxon England?

The idea of kingship was not invented in England. The Anglo-Saxons knew it in Germany. Kings grew from simple tribal chiefs, who were leaders successful in war, and therefore conquest of land. As time went by, the king became a grander, more exalted figure, and when England became Christian again in the 7th century reverence for kingship was encouraged by the Church.

The king was elected; he did not gain his crown by right of inheritance. Or not at first. In time it became the custom to elect a member of the royal family. Still the king's power was not total. He ruled with the advice of his council – the great men of the kingdom. He had no permanent capital and was always on the move. It must have been quite difficult for visitors hoping for a royal interview to track him down.

The later Anglo-Saxon kings received a constant stream of visitors, from overseas and from other parts of Britain. In 973 King Edgar was visited by no less than eight sub-kings at the same time. They manned the oars of his boat as a gesture of loyalty.

Such visitors brought expensive gifts, or tributes. But for his regular income the king relied on the profits of his own estates, which were large and widely scattered, and on rent, usually paid 'in kind' – i.e. as goods, not cash. Receipts from tolls of vari-

*An Anglo-Saxon warrior; Anglo-Saxons first came to Britain as pagan raiders about 400.*

those responsible for his death. Sometimes *wergild* was refused by the injured family, who preferred violent revenge. Then tremendous feuds began, with one act of vengeance following another. We know of one feud in Northumbria which began in 1016 and was still going strong nearly seventy years later. But kinship also meant co-operation in everything within the clan, looking after orphans, and even protecting the interests of a young woman who married outside the family.

The amount of a man's *wergild* was a sign of his position in society. A nobleman's *wergild* was larger than a peasant's.

To be classed as a nobleman, or thegn, a man had to have at least five hides of land (a hide was the amount needed to support one household). The nobleman lived in a windowless, barn-like hall, built of wood, surrounded by smaller houses and protected by a stockade. (Stone buildings appeared in the 9th century.) The furniture was simple – trestle tables, benches, and straw mattresses on the floor. In this hall, much heavy drinking and telling of stories took place after a day's hunting. Anglo-Saxon poetry is full of fighting, feasts and falconry – the main

ous kinds and fines from the law courts added something. His subjects gave him free labour and military service: in an emergency that meant every male who could swing a sword. Special expenses, like bribing the Vikings not to attack, were met by special taxes, and various persons or places owed special duties to the king. Norwich, for example, supplied a bear and six dogs for the sport of bear-baiting.

Anglo-Saxon kings were less worried by money problems than their successors in medieval and modern times, but from Alfred's time maintaining the fleet became a costly business.

In return for the support of his subjects, the king gave them protection and rewarded them with grants of land.

Besides their loyalty to the king, men were also bound by obligations to their own relations: the bond of kinship. If someone were murdered, it was the duty of his relations to avenge him: to die unavenged was a terrible thing. Fear of family vengeance helped to prevent crime at a time when there was no better way of enforcing the law. Everyone had a *wergild* ('man-price'), the sum payable in compensation to his family by

*Anglo-Saxons till the soil; they became a settled, farming people.*

*A thegn's hall, showing the timber framework. This was the largest building in the village.*

activities of the thegns. Before Alfred's time, few could read.

Running the household was the woman's job. But an Anglo-Saxon household was nothing like a suburban semidetached. It was almost self-sufficient, doing its own baking, brewing and so on. The woman's job was not mere housework, more like managing a business. Anglo-Saxon women were not oppressed. Divorce was easy (Christianity made it harder), and a divorced woman was entitled to half the household goods. She could hold property in her own right – impossible in later times.

The *wergild* of a churl, or peasant, was one-sixth that of a nobleman. The churl normally held at least one hide of land, and lived in a simple thatched hut with no window or chimney – just a hole in the roof. The better kinds of tradesmen – goldsmiths, sword-makers, falconers and small merchants – were also classed as churls. The churl was free but poor, and he depended on the nobleman for protection. In time, he often came to sell his service to the nobleman and so, gradually, he became less independent.

The third class in society was the slave, or unfree peasant. He had no rights and no

*wergild*, though if you killed him you had to pay compensation to his owner (about £1 – the price of eight oxen). Unlike the churl, the slave could often improve his position and even buy his freedom.

Although Anglo-Saxon settlements were nearly self-sufficient, trade in goods like salt, fish and metals went on inside the country and overseas. The contents of the Sutton Hoo burial ship proved that an early East Anglian king owned luxuries imported from Europe. England's chief exports were wool and slaves (although the slave trade declined in Christian times because of Church opposition.) Trade led to towns growing up at harbours and crossing places. London and Winchester were the largest; few others had more than 5,000 people.

Although several kings issued written laws, a lot of Anglo-Saxon law was simply custom, passed on by word of mouth from one generation to the next. There were no professional lawyers, and the nearest thing to a law court was the folk moot, a public assembly where quarrels were settled, local problems discussed and crime punished. (Later, some noblemen had private courts on their own estates.)

An accused man sometimes had to prove

his innocence by ordeal. One form of ordeal – probably not so common, though we hear a lot about it in books – was by water. The accused was thrown in, and if he floated he was guilty. The trouble was that if he sank, although he might be proved innocent, he was likely to be drowned. However, not many crimes carried the death penalty. The Church disliked capital punishment, though the alternative it preferred – chopping off a hand or an ear – seems savage enough to us.

Among the treasures buried in the Sutton Hoo ship were this king's helmet, shoulder-clasp (below) *and purse-lid* (above).

*The Sutton Hoo ship, in which a king was buried. It was probably built specially for the king's funeral, and was never meant to be launched on the water.*

# The Christian Church in Britain

In the Roman slave market one day, Pope Gregory noticed some pretty fair-haired Yorkshire children for sale. He asked who they were and was told they were *Angli*, English. '*Angli* who look like *Angeli* (angels)', the Pope replied, making a famous pun.

If this old story is true, the Pope's interest in Britain was aroused on that day, and he decided to send a missionary to convert these attractive heathens to Christianity. In 597, St Augustine landed in Kent. After 150 years of silence, England's contact with Rome was restored.

St Augustine landed very near the spot where the Roman legions had waded ashore, but unlike them he came in peace, and with the agreement of the king of Kent. His message was gratefully received: on Christmas Day 10,000 people were baptized at Canterbury, where a Christian church was still standing.

Beyond Kent, Christianity spread less rapidly. King Edwin of Northumbria, after consulting his council, accepted Christianity in 626; but he was killed a few years later and the new churches were destroyed in a pagan reaction. Although Christianity was soon restored, it was not by missionaries from the Church of Rome.

For Christianity had never disappeared from the British Isles. The British, when they retreated from the Anglo-Saxons, took their religion with them. More than thirty years before St Augustine landed in Kent, an Irish monk, St Columba, founded the monastery of Iona, Scotland's Holy Isle, which became the centre of British Christianity. It was to Iona that the new king of Northumbria sent for a bishop in 635, and the man appointed was St Aidan, who settled at Lindisfarne. He soon made that island a Northumbrian counterpart to Iona.

The Ruthwell Cross, Dumfries, dates from the late 7th century. It stands six metres high and is one of the best preserved crosses that survive from the Anglo-Saxon period.

While out of touch with Rome, the British, or Celtic, Church had developed differently from the continental Church. Even the date of Easter was different, so that in places where both Churches were represented, half the people were mourning the crucifixion of Christ while the other half were celebrating his resurrection.

In 663 a synod (a meeting of clergy) was held at Whitby in Yorkshire to decide the matter of the double Easter. At least, that was the main point on the agenda; but what the synod really decided was a much wider question: was the Church of England to be British or Roman? The King of Northumbria, who presided, decided that English Christians should not cut themselves off from fellow Christians in the rest of Europe. But although the Romanists won the argument, Celtic influence remained strong. The Church in England was always to remain different in spirit from the Church in Italy or France, and the influence of Celtic Christianity, gentler and less grand than Roman, was one of the chief reasons for it.

The Celtic Church was a Church of missionary monks, while the Roman Church was organized under bishops, whose headquarters were in large towns. The Roman Church was supported by a mass of learned laws and, from a political point of view, it looked like a more orderly, stable institution. For that reason kings preferred it. The bishoprics in England covered larger areas than Italian bishoprics, and that helped to encourage the system of parishes, with a priest living in each parish.

Monasteries were also a vital part of Roman Christianity. St Augustine himself was a monk (he founded the monastery of St Peter and St Paul at Canterbury), and monastic influence was strong in early Christian England. All kinds of people became monks, including several kings, and many of them deliberately chose a monastery far away from home, to cut themselves off more thoroughly from ordinary life.

Devout Christians went on pilgrimages if they possibly could, mostly to Rome though one or two bold people went to Jerusalem. King Alfred was taken to Rome as a child. But a pilgrimage, or any journey, was neither safe nor simple. Storms and pirates made the Channel crossing a fearful experience, and on land bandits and swindlers waited to trap the innocent traveller. One archbishop, on his way to Rome, was frozen to death crossing the Alps. Sensible people made their wills before they set out on a pilgrimage.

Irish monks were working as missionaries in Europe before 597, and this tradition was continued by early English Christians. Most of northern Europe was converted to Christianity by English missionaries. Charlemagne's chief assistant in his programme of educating the people of his empire was a Yorkshireman, Alcuin.

Christianity was a great civilizing influence. To begin with, it introduced more education. Its teaching was narrow, as it was simply designed to make native Englishmen fit to be priests, but it did produce scholars who knew Greek as well as Latin and had read some Classical – i.e. pre-Christian – literature. Among them was the 'father of English history', Bede.

Bede, who is sometimes called 'the Venerable', though such a dusty title does not suit him, spent all his life in the Northumbrian monastery of Jarrow. He wrote many books, but the most famous is his *Ecclesiastical History of the English People*, finished in 731. It is the only worthwhile history of England in the earliest period. Bede had a remarkable sense of history – of the passing of time – as well as a rare scholarly attitude to facts. His book, in English translation, still makes good reading.

*A drawing of Bede, the monk of Jarrow, at work on his history of the English people.*

Although books were written in increasing numbers, a far greater number were imported from the continent. Up and down the country monks were kept busy copying them, and often decorating them with beautiful miniature illustrations. The Lindisfarne Gospels in the British Museum (produced about 700) are a magnificent example of their work.

All these books were written in Latin. But English too was being written. According to Bede, the first Anglo-Saxon poet was a peasant named Caedmon, who was inspired by a dream to write about the Creation. Anglo-Saxon is, of course, almost a foreign language to us. Caedmon's poem, for instance, runs like this:

*Nu scylum hergan hefaenricaes uard,*
*metudaes maecti end his modgidanc . . .*

(Now we must praise the guardian of heaven, the powers of the Creator and his thoughts . . . ).

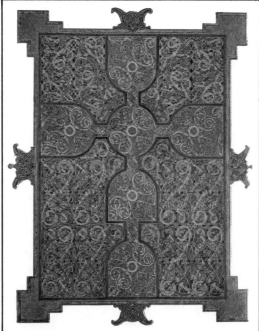

*An ornamented page from the Lindisfarne Gospels, produced by the monks of the island monastery in about 700.*

The most famous Anglo-Saxon poem is *Beowulf*, the saga of a hero who saves his people from a series of evil monsters. Like many Anglo-Saxon stories, it is on the grim side.

The objects – works of art, tools, weapons, etc. – that survive through the centuries do not always give a perfectly accurate picture of the works of an ancient people. Most Anglo-Saxon art that has survived is Christian, for people went round smashing pagan idols after they were converted. We also have examples of sword-hilts, drinking horns and jewellery, but not

*The Church of St Peter and St Paul at Canterbury, first headquarters of St Augustine, who was welcomed to the town by the king of Kent.*

much to show us the fine quality of early English needlework, because cloth does not last as well as metal or stone. We know that English needlework was of a high quality through letters that speak of cloaks of purple silk embroidered with gold; but only the beautiful stole, embroidered with figures of Christian saints, which was found in the coffin of St Cuthbert, has been preserved.

Anglo-Saxon art was similar to Celtic art in design and inspiration; at least, it was more like Celtic than Roman art. Patterns of decoration were often abstract, or semi-abstract, based on animals and plants. Christianity brought foreign influences with it, in particular the tradition of realistic art inherited from Ancient Rome. In Northumbria the two styles merged to produce sculpture, like the stone cross at Ruthwell, Dumfries, made in the 7th century, which experts once believed to have been made 500 years later.

# Invasions of the Vikings

Before the end of the 8th century, the British Isles were raided again by another non-Christian people, from Scandinavia. In 793 the Vikings, as we call them, destroyed the monastery of Lindisfarne, drowning some of the monks and stealing precious objects.

The Vikings were a sea-going people; they had the best boats yet seen in Europe, powered by oar and sail. They crossed the Atlantic, founding a colony in Newfoundland 500 years before Columbus discovered America; they rounded Lapland and sailed up the rivers of Russia; they raided Europe from the Baltic to the Mediterranean. Norsemen sailed around Scotland and down the west coast of Britain as far as the Mersey; they established colonies in northern Scotland and created a Scandinavian kingdom in Ireland. Danes raided the east coast of England, burning and killing, exulting in violence. Nothing stopped the Vikings, not even the northern winter.

These long-haired warriors wore coats of mail, carried hefty battle-axes and long shields. No one had the ships to match them at sea, and when they landed they moved so fast – rounding up all the horses in the neighbourhood – that they could destroy a town, burn a church and slaughter the people before a force could be raised against them. When they were brought to battle, they were often too strong for the motley group of poorly armed peasants who confronted them, and when they were defeated they were back again, stronger than ever, a year or two later.

What began as raids for quick plunder soon developed into something more. The Danes descended on England in ever-larger bands and raided steadily farther inland. In 851 a Danish host spent the winter in Kent. A few years later they wintered near London. The English were in no position to prevent them. Northumbria was feeble, with rival kings fighting for the crown. In Mercia another royal argument was going on, and the midland kingdom was squeezed between the Danes from the east and the forces of the Welsh prince, Rhodi Mawr, from the west.

That was the situation in 865, when a Danish army larger than any before arrived in England. This time the Danes came not merely for plunder, and they had no plans to return in the autumn or the following spring. They meant to conquer England.

York fell in 866, and the rival kings of

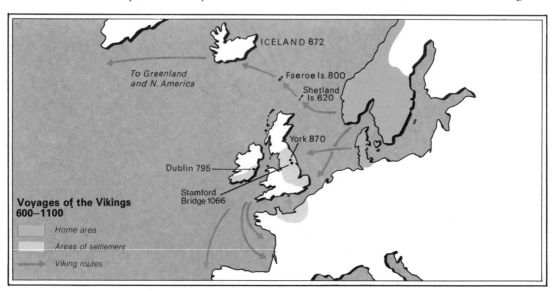

Voyages of the Vikings 600–1100
ICELAND 872
To Greenland and N. America
Faeroe Is. 800
Shetland Is. 620
York 870
Dublin 795
Stamford Bridge 1066
Home area
Areas of settlement
Viking routes

Northumbria were killed. East Mercia was overrun and the rest of the kingdom saved, for a short time only, by a truce bought with Mercian gold. In 869 King Edmund of East Anglia (St Edmund of Bury) was savagely murdered while a prisoner. Essex was conquered. By 870 only Wessex was left to resist the barbaric Danes, whose main camp at Reading was well placed to receive reinforcements up the Thames.

Soon after the Danes turned against Wessex, the West Saxons gained a new king, who was only about twenty-two years old. His name was Alfred (849–899), and we know him as 'the Great'. He is the only English king who has earned that title.

After one stirring victory, Alfred was forced on to the defensive, and for a few years it looked as though Wessex too would soon be submerged. By 878 Alfred was a fugitive, hiding in the wintry marshes of Somerset. (It is from this period in his life that legends later grew – stories like the tale of the burning cakes which the king was supposed to be watching while the farmer's wife was out of the kitchen.)

But Alfred's West Saxon peasant-warriors, or most of them, remained loyal. With the spring, he surged out of the marshes to harass the Danes. In May, the men of Wiltshire and Hampshire met him in the forest near Southampton. They told him they were 'glad to see him'. Two days later, Alfred's Christian army smashed the Danes at the battle of Edington. 'The turn of the tide!' Alfred exclaimed.

Under their able commander, Guthrum, the Danes fell back to Chippenham. Alfred swept the surrounding country bare of food and horses, and in two weeks the Danes were forced to surrender. They promised to leave the country. Guthrum accepted Christian baptism, with Alfred acting as godfather.

What made Alfred a great man was not just his military victories but his statesmanship. After years and years of bloody

*A sight to strike terror into peaceful farmers: a Viking warrior.*

conflict, he saw the futility of trying to destroy the Danes by force. He believed that a man who grows content will cease to be a dangerous enemy, and he was determined to reach friendly agreement with the defeated Danes. This he did. His treaty with Guthrum gave the Danes a large part of eastern England, where Alfred hoped they would settle down as peaceful farmers.

Alfred's statesmanship showed itself also in his ability to learn from his enemies. When new groups of Vikings resumed the attack some years later, they found England far better prepared. Having studied the defenceworks of Guthrum's camps, Alfred set up a system of strongly fortified burghs in southern England. (Traces of his fortifications can still be seen at Wareham in Dorset, among other places.) He also built warships on the Danish pattern and, as the English were not experienced sailors, he hired men from the coastal districts of the Low Countries to man his navy. We know that more than once Viking raiders were defeated at sea by Alfred's ships, and prevented from landing.

# The England of Alfred the Great

The first duty of the king was to lead his people in war. That Alfred had triumphantly done. But he was no old-fashioned Saxon war-lord, and he knew that there were better things in life than fighting. By settling the Vikings in eastern England Alfred had, for a time, ended the danger of conquest. But to maintain peace a country needs good laws also, and so he set himself the task of revizing English law.

Alfred collected old laws from other kingdoms, from the Bible and Jewish law; threw out what seemed unsuitable and kept what seemed sensible. His councillors – some of them bearded veterans of battles against Guthrum, others intelligent priests with a knowledge of foreign countries – gave their approval, and at last a new code of laws was produced. When he published it, Alfred explained how he had compiled it, and he added an interesting statement. Some of these laws, he said, might cease to be useful in the future, and should then be changed. This may seem obvious to us, but it was an extraordinary thing for a 9th-century man to look into the future or even to realize that times are bound to change.

We know more about the king himself in Alfred's time than any other Englishman – we even have a biography of him written by his friend Bishop Asser – and that may be part of the reason why Alfred seems to stand

*After the Danes forced him to flee, Alfred gathered his thegns in a forest clearing to plan a new campaign.*

not in the original book but were, Alfred thought, worth publishing. It is through Alfred that we know of the voyage of Othere, a Norse merchant, in the White Sea, which the king put into a Spanish history book he happened to be translating at the time when Othere told him the story.

Alfred's desire to raise intellectual standards was strengthened by his knowledge that Anglo-Saxon society had once been more civilized than it was in his own time. He complained that in the old days foreign scholars had come to England but now English scholars were forced to go abroad to pursue their studies. He looked back longingly to the golden age of Northumbria in early Christian times, when Bede was writing his *History*.

Historians are especially grateful to Alfred because he began the *Anglo-Saxon Chronicle*, a year-by-year history of England which begins with the Roman conquest. It gives us a detailed picture of events in the 9th century, although it is not so useful for earlier periods. The only thing the *Chronicle* could find to say about the year 671, for instance, is 'This year there was a great death among birds'.

out from his time like an oak tree in a field. But there is no doubt that he was an extraordinarily intelligent man, who was kind and honourable, as well as a brilliant leader and governor. He suffered most of his life from some kind of illness, but it never hindered his efforts to raise the standards of English society.

Alfred was determined that his people should have the benefits of Latin culture, but as few people except priests could read or write, that was not easily done. The king tried to ensure that every free-born boy should at least learn to read English, but all the educational books of the time were written in Latin, so Alfred set out to have them translated. He often did the translating himself, sometimes adding in stories that were

*This precious object in the Ashmolean Museum, Oxford, bears the words, 'Alfred had me made'. It is known as the Alfred Jewel, and could really have been ordered by Alfred the Great.*

# Alfred's Wars against the Danes

Though Alfred saved England, he did not stop the attacks of the Danes. Luckily, his immediate successors were strong rulers like himself. His son, Edward the Elder, and his daughter Aethelflaed, 'the Lady of the Mercians', defeated the Danes time and again. Following their father's example, they built a chain of fortified burghs across England, which acted as launching pads to strike against Danish outbreaks.

Edward continued the work of centralizing the kingdom. Aethelflaed, a splendid lady, as loyal as she was tough, always supported him, and when she died Edward swiftly merged Wessex and Mercia into one. He reorganized his kingdom into districts which ignored the borders of the old Anglo-Saxon kingdoms. Each new district, or shire, took its name from the town that governed it: Wiltshire was governed from Wilton, Hampshire from Southampton.

Edward was recognized as overlord by kings from Wales and Scotland, and his son Athelstan (924–939) called himself grandly 'king of the English and of all the nations round about'. His three sisters were married to the greatest rulers of Europe, and Athelstan's kingdom was certainly a great one, even if he were a little unsure of its size.

The status of the English kings did not mean that they could sit back and enjoy the luxury of peace. There was always fighting, and though most of the Danes of the northeast had settled down, the *Danelaw*, as the region was called, provided a friendly base for new Danish raiders.

After Athelstan, troubles increased. A strong kingdom required a strong king, but by bad luck England had several young and inexperienced kings in the 10th century. They gave land away too easily, and the estates of their provincial governors began to look like little independent kingdoms.

Edgar was succeeded by his eldest son Edward. He had another son, Ethelred, by another wife, Aelfryth. When Edward went to visit Ethelred and Aelfryth at Corfe Castle, in Dorset, in 978, it was a perfectly friendly visit, but as he rode into the courtyard, the thegns of Ethelred came to greet him, and a sharp quarrel broke out. When it ended, the young king lay dead. Was it a planned political assassination? We do not know. Edward himself, who, though later acclaimed as a saint, had a vicious temper, may have been to blame.

Ethelred's reign began unhappily under the shadow of Edward's murder, and things never really improved. Ethelred is often called 'the Unready', and though his Anglo-Saxon nickname, *Unraed*, really means 'ill-advised', he does seem to have often been unready for the Danes. As one chronicler complained, when the Danes attacked in the east, Ethelred and the army were in the west; if the Danes attacked in the south, the army was in the north.

Other disasters – a harvest failure causing famine, a freak tide causing floods – no man could prevent. And the Danes seemed as unstoppable as the floods. Ethelred bought them off with large payments of gold – *Danegeld* – but they soon came back for more. They used bases in Normandy, where the people were descendants of Viking settlers, and they were helped by English opponents of Ethelred. Finally, the Danish king decided on total conquest, and in 1013 Ethelred was forced to flee. Cnut was acknowledged as king and Ethelred's death in 1016 left him in command. Cnut's personal empire included Norway and Denmark, besides England.

But the Danish royal house did not last long. Cnut himself was a capable ruler, though he let the great earls grow still greater, but his sons were a savage couple. Fortunately the House of Wessex was restored in 1042 when Edward the Confessor, a son of Ethelred, was elected king.

# The Kingdom of Scotland unites

When the Vikings attacked Scotland (then known as Alba) at the end of the 8th century, they found a country which, like England, was not yet united in its own defence. In the next hundred years or so The Norsemen captured Orkney, Shetland, the Western Isles and a large part of the northern mainland.

At that time Scotland was divided into four, including Lothian, which was part of English Northumbria. In the south-west was the Celtic kingdom of Strathclyde, stretching into Cumbria. Northern and central Scotland, the largest territory, was the land of the Picts, another Celtic people who had perhaps arrived in Scotland at the same time as their fellow Celts were settling in England. The fourth kingdom was Dalriada, which occupied Argyll, Kintyre and nearby islands. The people of Dalriada were the Scots, who had come from Ireland, bringing with them the Christian religion which St Columba and other missionaries spread to the rest of the country.

In spite of their common religion, the four kingdoms were constantly fighting, especially the Scots and the Picts, whose rivalry lasted for centuries and caused terrible bloodshed. The result of this contest was to decide which race should dominate Scotland. In the early 9th century the Viking attacks in the north weakened the Picts, and this gave the Scots, who had been partly under Pictish control, their chance.

The king of Dalriada, Kenneth MacAlpin, also had a claim to the Pictish crown. In 843, he made himself king of the Picts and, for the first time, all Scotland north of the Forth was united under one ruler. As for the Picts, once the most numerous people in Scotland, they disappeared from history, and to this day they remain a shadowy people of whom we know little.

**The height of the Norse conquests.** The shaded areas are those that were overrun.

Kenneth MacAlpin and his successors were not satisfied with the union of the Scots and Picts, and tried to expand the kingdom farther. Their chief ambition was to gain Lothian from the English. Viking attacks, which had made victory over the Picts possible, also weakened Northumbria, and Kenneth MacAlpin hoped to repeat his success there. However he failed to capture Lothian despite several campaigns and those who came after him were no more successful.

Sometimes the Scots fought with the Norsemen against the English. But England under Alfred and his successors had also become a united and much stronger country. In 937 the Scots and the Norse were defeated by Athelstan at the great battle of Brunanburh, on the Mersey. Not until 1018 did King Malcolm II finally gain Lothian from the English.

Malcolm's grandson, Duncan, had a claim to the independent kingdom of Strathclyde, and although his claim was not strong, when the King of Strathclyde died without an obvious heir in 1018, Duncan was able to enforce his claim. In 1034 he also succeeded his grandfather as king of the Scots, uniting the whole of Scotland, plus part of Cumbria, under him.

37

# Chapter 3

## The Norman Conquest of England

Edward the Confessor was half-Norman by birth; he had spent most of his life in Normandy; and he appointed Normans to important positions in the state (partly to balance the power of great English earls like Godwine of Wessex). England was already half 'Normanized' before the Norman Conquest of 1066.

Edward had no children, and as he died he recognized Harold, son of Godwine, as his heir. Across the Channel in Normandy, a loud protest was heard. According to Duke William, Edward the Confessor had made the same promise to him; what was more, Harold had already accepted William's claim during a visit to Normandy two years before.

Such arguments are usually decided by force. William swept across the Channel with his army and landed near Hastings. Harold was in the north, where he had just defeated a Norse invasion, but he hurried south and, brave but foolish, offered battle. His men were tired and he would have done better to have starved the Normans out. Still, his position on a hill was a strong one, until the Normans, pretending to run away, lured the English down the hill.

When Harold was killed, the battle – and the kingdom – was lost. Duke William, the most formidable empire-builder of his time, marched directly to London, where the nervous and disunited English lords fell over themselves in their eagerness to surrender.

We know King William I as 'the Conqueror'. But he wanted no talk of conquest. He had come, he told the English, to restore the good laws of King Edward and to uphold the constitution. All conquerors talk like that, and William was an expert politician as well as a good general. Yet he was probably sincere.

At first he moved gently, and tried to disturb Anglo-Saxon institutions as little as possible. England already possessed better government machinery than Normandy, so that was only sensible. But rebellions against the Normans provoked him into harsher action. In the north, his soldiers swept through the country like fire. Between York and Durham they left hardly a building standing.

Although Norman influence was strong in England before 1066, that date is still the most famous one in English history, and the Conquest certainly did cause quite a number of great changes. For one thing, it tied England more closely to Europe. William ruled Normandy as well as England, and for the next 500 years English kings also held land in France.

The Conquest caused sweeping changes among the leading land-holding families. There were Norman landlords before 1066, but most were Anglo-Saxon or Danish. Within twenty years, all William's chief tenants (strictly speaking, no one 'owned' land except the king) were Normans. As a sign of the change, stone castles rose threateningly at every strongpoint, and work was started on the great cathedrals in the cities. In the early stages of construction, the two types of building looked alike – a sign of the alliance in Norman England of the powers of Church and State.

*The Normans landing on the coast of Sussex, 1066.*

*The Bayeux tapestry tells the story of the Norman Conquest in pictures and captions, like a comic. It took many hands and many months to make. The words on this piece say 'King Harold is killed'. It was once thought that the third figure from the left represented Harold, and that Harold was killed by an arrow in the eye. But probably the falling man further right is the king.*

REX·INTERFEC
TVS:EST

# The Empire of the Normans

The late 11th and 12th centuries in Europe were a time of good order, prosperity and progress. An age when war was treated almost as a sport, as something all upper-class men were expected to practise, was not always peaceful. But increasing trade, growing towns and safer travel were signs of better times. The Norman rulers of England were not responsible for these improvements, but they did something to make them possible.

Kings of England enjoyed one great advantage over other rulers. England was a united kingdom, accustomed to royal government. This was the achievement of Alfred and his successors. In more recent times, with the rise of the great earls, the kingdom had shown signs of breaking up into smaller pieces, but that development was prevented by the Norman Conquest.

William the Conqueror did not have to invent centralized government. The system already existed, and a very thorough system it was, right down to the courts of justice in every shire and hundred (a hundred was a division of a shire). The English people were used to regular taxation – one good result of the *Danegeld* – and together with the huge estates that William kept as royal property, the Norman monarchy could count itself rich.

All that was needed was a strong man at the top. William was such a man, and so were his sons, the rough, red-faced William Rufus (shot in a hunting accident at the age of forty) and the cool, clever Henry I.

William the Conqueror was, above all, a military leader. His army had gained the kingdom for him, and his army had to keep it. The first essential was to make sure of the loyalty of his chief followers, which he did by rewarding them for their service with land. William had about 200 tenants-in-chief, or barons as they were later called, to whom he gave large estates. He made sure that their estates were scattered in different parts of the country, as he did not want to run the risk of creating dangerous centres of power for some future rebel.

The tenants-in-chief carried out certain duties in return for their lands. They were the king's representatives in the provinces, and they had to attend his court and give advice if needed (the king did not have to follow their advice). Most important of all, they had to provide military service, not only by bearing arms themselves, but also by bringing with them a certain number of knights (the number depended on the size of

The Norman Empire. The Normans also established a dynasty in Sicily.

their estates), properly armed and mounted.

As a rule these knights were sub-tenants – men who held land from the barons just as the barons held it from the king. Many of them found it very tiresome to spend an agreed forty days a year on military service, as they were more interested in their farms. The custom grew up of paying *scutage*, 'shield money', instead – the medieval way of buying yourself out of the army.

The idea of land rented for military service was not new to England. But the businesslike Normans made it the foundation of society, a matter of strict contracts and official agreements.

The organization of the country in this military way certainly did not suit everyone. The poor peasant farmer was struggling to keep his independence in Anglo-Saxon times; under the Normans he often became a serf, or villein – not a slave (slavery was disappearing), but definitely 'unfree'. He had to work for the local lord; he could not leave the village or get married without the lord's permission. Of course, he might have been no better off if the Norman Conquest had never happened. He might even have been worse off, for not all peasants went down in the world after 1066, and although he had so many duties to his lord, the lord also had some duties towards him.

All the same, the English were a conquered nation after 1066. William I might insist that no 'conquest' had taken place, but many an Englishman, hiding from Norman soldiers in his ruined house, must have laughed bitterly at such a notion. Hardly any Englishmen were left in positions of power, and although William Rufus might speak affectionately of 'my Englishmen, strong and true', the law made it plain that Englishmen were different from Normans. If a man was found murdered in any place and his murderer not discovered, the local inhabitants had to pay a fine – unless they could prove that the dead man was an Englishman, and not a Norman. (Clearly, it was not wise for a Norman to walk unguarded into an English village.)

When we look at the magnificent buildings of the Normans – majestic cathedrals like Durham, superb castles like the Tower of London – we think of the skills of the stone-mason and the vision of the master-builder. We forget the pain and exhaustion of the labourers who were forced to haul the great stone blocks into place. When we read about the efficiency of the Normans, we think of orderly government and enforcement of law. It is easy to imagine that the Normans brought 'civilization' to Anglo-Saxon England, as the Romans brought it to Celtic Britain. But when we ask exactly what this 'civilization' meant for ordinary people, we often find it meant terror, distruction and death.

Eventually, the Normans and English merged into a single nation, but there were few signs of reconciliation until the reign of Henry I (1100–35). At the beginning of his reign Henry issued a charter of English liberties, which promised to restore the 'good laws' of Edward the Confessor. He married an English princess, a descendant of

*Most of the great English cathedrals were begun by the Normans. Durham has more of the original Norman work than any other cathedral.*

*A mason at work, based on an illustration on a medieval manuscript.*

King Alfred, but gave her a French name (Matilda) to make her sound more respectable to his Norman subjects. They were scornful of Henry's pro-English policies and in private called the king and queen simple old Anglo-Saxon names, Godric and Godgifu, which was like calling Elizabeth II and Prince Philip 'Phyllis and Phil'.

When a business company takes over another firm, its directors want to know as much about the new firm as possible. When the Normans 'took over' England, one of their problems was that they did not know a great deal about the country. If William gave an estate in – for example – Gloucestershire to some French knight (not all his men came from Normandy), the man must have had a hard time finding out where the place was.

Of course, many English were willing to help: within a year or two of the Conquest, William was using English soldiers against English rebels. But there were no records to compare with the records kept by a modern business company, let alone our modern civil service, and William, as a good manager, wanted to know more.

Twenty years after the Conquest, when the country was fairly peaceful, William organized a government inquiry into the state of England. Its results were recorded in the *Domesday Book*.

The purpose of the Domesday inquiry was to discover, in every shire and hundred, who occupied the land, what were the local rights of landlord and tenant, what were the local law courts, how much land was cultivated, was there a working watermill, or fish pond, and so on. The government wanted to know the exact number of cattle and pigs kept, even chickens, and it wanted an answer for the situation at present (in 1086), and for the situation twenty years earlier, in the time of Edward the Confessor. At each place a 'jury' of witnesses was assembled, who gave their answers under oath.

The king did not carry out this huge inquiry just for curiosity. He was interested in taxes, and taxation only works if the government knows what there is to tax. The survey also told him how many knights he could call on to fight a Danish invasion (which he was expecting), and it provided evidence to settle the many arguments over land ownership which had arisen since 1066.

But for historians, the *Domesday Book* has a greater value. It gives a detailed picture of everyday affairs in Norman England, and it also shows what changes had taken place as a result of the Norman Conquest.

*A page from the Domesday Book. The results of William I's famous survey, down to the last pig or chicken, are contained in two large volumes. London and the north (not yet conquered) were not included.*

After 1066 Norman castles were built at every spot where William felt opposition from his new subjects. This picture shows the 'keep' (the central tower-like part) of a castle, cut away to show the inside. At the top there were the battlements where soldiers kept guard and below them were the dormitories. People ate in the Great Hall, where there was a huge, open fire. Below this was the guardroom, then the store-rooms and dungeons.

# Anglo-Norman England

In 1100 the population of England was less than 1·5 million – about the size of the present population of Birmingham and Coventry. Only about 100,000 of them lived in towns, and few places were large enough to match our idea of what a town should be. (The word 'town' originally meant a homestead – just one house.) London was, as always, an exception. When William I began to build his White Tower overlooking the Thames, about 20,000 people lived there, all of them inside the walls of the old Roman city. York, Norwich and Lincoln were the next largest, though probably none had more than 5,000 people.

Towns were nevertheless growing fast under the Normans, and they went on growing until the early 14th century. Landowners soon noticed that towns were profitable places, and they were eager to start one, or, more often, to increase the size of a town that already existed. This was something that only rich landlords could do, as it did require some expense to get a town going, though nothing like the expense of building new towns today.

Landlords were not concerned with 'town planning'. New parishes were added

*Knocking down acorns for the pigs, which were closely related to the wild boar of the forests.*

on higgledy-piggledy: you have only to look at a city like Norwich, where there are twenty medieval parish churches within five minutes' walk of one spot (not counting the cathedral, which alone might have held the whole population) to see the chaos – but attractive chaos – of the growth of a medieval town.

Nine out of ten people in England lived in the country, the majority in small villages. There were isolated farms in some parts, where people lived a pioneer life far from the nearest neighbours, like farms on the frontier of the American West in the 19th century. But Norman England was mostly a country of small villages.

Driving through the English countryside today, the villages seem very close together, but 800 years ago they seemed much farther apart. There were no roads then, only muddy tracks, and a journey of only a kilometre or two could be difficult in winter. In any case, people did not travel. Most of them probably did not want to, and they would very seldom have had the opportunity. The English peasant was born, lived and died in the same place.

*Ploughing: oxen were the best draught animals.*

In the English village, the houses and other buildings were all in a group, with the fields stretching away beyond. If possible, they were built on a hill, but sometimes they had to be in a valley to be near a supply of water. The fields were the big open fields of Saxon times, farmed in strips. But in some places small hedged fields were already in use. They became more common as time passed.

As everyone lived together in the village, it was a long way to walk to the farthest field; but that was a small drawback compared with the advantages. People had to share tools and services: there was only one mill, one brewery, perhaps only one oven for baking, and not many villages were lucky enough to have a plough for each household. In Norfolk, one of the most heavily populated counties, one plough had to be shared among five households. It was also easier for the lord of the manor to keep an eye on his tenants in a village, and harder for robbers to attack.

The amount of land in use was far smaller than it is today. About half the country was forest, marsh or heath, where nobody lived. But all through the 12th century the English were busy colonizing their country. This was a process that had been going on since the Stone Age, and it has not quite stopped even now; but probably more progress was made between about 1100 and 1200 than in

*Cows being driven home for milking.*

any other century. From the Tyne to the Channel, woodland was cleared, marshes were drained, and dykes were built to keep out the sea. It was all done without the help of machines and with only the simplest tools. Monasteries often took the lead. At Glastonbury Abbey a man was hired full-time as an expert on drainage, and the Somerset fens, where Iron Age people had built their houses on stilts and Alfred had taken refuge from the Danes, began, slowly, to dry out.

Hundreds of square kilometres were still covered by forests. Perhaps 'forests' is not the right word, for they were not dense jungles like the forests of tropical countries but open woodland, with grassy glades among the oak, beech and elm. The forests were not exactly waste land because they were reserved for a definite purpose – hunting. This was the favourite sport of all English kings, and savage penalties, like the chopping off of a hand, waited for any peasant who was caught poaching the king's deer.

The king was jealous of any reduction of his forests, large as they were, and it was not always easy for a village to get permission to enlarge its fields by clearing trees. But as time went by more and more woodlands were sold off to meet the royal need for cash. By the 16th century, England was actually short of timber, and house-builders had to change from timber to brick.

*Harvesting: the corn was straggly and had a low yield compared with modern types.*

*A Norman manor house: the main floor was usually the first floor and was approached by an outside staircase. Windows were high up, where they were less draughty.*

Parts of England in the 12th century were already gaining an appearance that we would recognize. Some counties looked then much as they look now. Parts of rural Dorset, for example, have not changed greatly, and the traditional sheep-farming regions of England and Wales would not seem strange to someone from the 12th century. But he would certainly notice some changes, not least in the sheep themselves. Medieval sheep looked more like skinny poodles than the fat beasts we know.

Although the Normans liked to organize things systematically, there was no such thing as a 'typical' village in Norman England. Kent, for example, remained a county of independent peasant farmers. But the most common arrangement, at any rate in the Midlands and southern England, was the manor, with the village grouped around the manor house, peasants cultivating their own strips in the open fields, grazing their animals on the common pasture, and working partly for the lord of the manor.

The manor house was the true centre of all village affairs. Looking like something

and one of a two-storey manor house in Cambridge (it is the building now known as the School of Pythagoras). We can see what the later type of medieval hall looked like – carved wooden screen at one end, raised stage at the other – in many of the colleges of Oxford and Cambridge or (a splendid one) at Hampton Court.

The furniture, as in Saxon times, was simple; mainly tables, benches and chests, though fireplaces and chimneys were replacing the open fire. The walls were hung with tapestries.

No peasants' houses have lasted intact to the present, and that is not surprising as they were often little better than tents or earth dug-outs, roofed with thatch or turf. (Perhaps the closest idea we can get of what life was like in such dwellings is the type of hut put up by men repairing a road.) Better houses were built on a timber frame, often using a single curved post to form wall and roof support. The walls were made of wattle and daub – a kind of loose basketwork plastered with mud – which is much harder-wearing than it sounds. This type of building later developed into the half-timbered house, which is still a common sight in old towns and villages (*see the picture on page 92*).

between a church and a barn, it was basically the same as the old Saxon hall, with one large room and perhaps a few smaller ones – bedrooms and offices – built off it. But the use of stone, instead of wood, brought some changes. In some manor houses, the church-like look of the place was increased by aisles, dividing the hall into three. Others had two floors, with the main hall on the upper floor.

Very few manor houses of Norman times have survived to the present, but there is a famous example of an aisled hall at Oakham

*Plan of a Norman village, with fields in strips.*

# The struggle for the English Crown

Henry I had a great many children, most of them by ladies to whom he was not married. He had only one legitimate son, and in 1120 this young man was drowned when his ship sank in the Channel. That left only a daughter, Matilda, who was married to a vigorous French prince, Geoffrey, count of Anjou.

Henry made his barons swear loyalty to Matilda as his successor. In fact, he made them give this oath on more than one occasion, which showed that he was afraid they would not accept a woman as their ruler (England had never had a ruling queen). Not only was she a woman, a serious drawback when monarchs were expected to lead their people in war, but her husband was the enemy of the many barons who held land in Normandy as well as England.

Henry's fears were justified. When he died, his nephew, Stephen of Blois, was accepted as king by many of the barons, as well as the leaders of the Church and the city of London. But Stephen's position was far from secure. He had to buy support by granting to the Church, to the towns, and to many powerful subjects certain rights

which a strong king would never have forfeited. Meanwhile, as usually happened when the English government was weak, the Scots attacked in the north, forcing Stephen to give up Cumbria, and the Welsh, whom the Norman kings had brought under control, threw off English rule. The soldiers of Geoffrey of Anjou overran Normandy and, in 1139, Matilda herself landed in England with an army commanded by one of Henry I's illegitimate sons, Robert of Gloucester.

In the civil war that followed, many innocent people who did not much care who wore the crown were killed or made homeless. However, medieval wars were not so terrible as modern ones, and in fact no big battles were ever fought between the supporters of Stephen and Matilda. More serious was the breakdown of law and order in some parts of the country, where unruly knights seized the chance to pay off old scores and villainous barons robbed the helpless, using mercenary soldiers to kidnap and torture unarmed villagers and townsfolk. More responsible barons, however, kept control of their estates and, as far as possible, they ignored the warring monarchs.

Although Stephen was Matilda's prisoner for a time (she rather foolishly exchanged

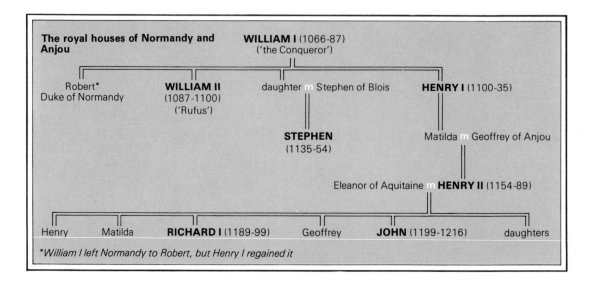

The royal houses of Normandy and Anjou

WILLIAM I (1066-87) ('the Conqueror')

Robert* Duke of Normandy — WILLIAM II (1087-1100) ('Rufus') — daughter m Stephen of Blois — HENRY I (1100-35)

STEPHEN (1135-54)

Matilda m Geoffrey of Anjou

Eleanor of Aquitaine m HENRY II (1154-89)

Henry — Matilda — RICHARD I (1189-99) — Geoffrey — JOHN (1199-1216) — daughters

*William I left Normandy to Robert, but Henry I regained it

*A model of a contemporary ship: she had a single square sail, 'castles' for archers fore and aft, and was steered with a paddle.*

('Angevin' is the adjective from 'Anjou'), was the king of France himself, Louis VII, whose sister was married to Stephen's son. In 1152, Louis made a serious political mistake. He divorced his queen, Eleanor. She was a lady of many remarkable qualities, but what was most important from the political point of view, she held the great duchy of Aquitaine, in southern France. Henry immediately married Eleanor himself, adding Aquitaine to the Angevin empire, which was now much larger than the lands controlled directly by the king of France.

A year later, King Stephen's son died, leaving him without an heir. That made the final agreement possible. Stephen kept the crown, but he recognized Henry as his heir. Soon afterwards, in 1154, Stephen himself died, and Henry II came into possession of the largest European empire that any king of England (except, for a short time, Henry V) has ever held.

*Matilda had to make a quick getaway from Oxford when attacked by her cousin's forces.*

him for Robert of Gloucester, who had also been captured), he never lost control of the south-east, and life there went on much as usual. We read of dreadful suffering in the chronicles of the time: 'men said openly', one of them recorded, 'that Christ and his angels slept'. But the chroniclers, even the oldest of them, could not remember a time when there had been no strong central government. If they had lived in almost any other part of Europe, they would have been more hardened to the scenes of brutality, robbery and violent death which so distressed them.

Still, the reign of Stephen was a miserable period. What finally brought the conflict to an end was the fortunate deaths of some of its chief figures. Geoffrey of Anjou died in 1151 and, thanks to his conquests, he left to his son, Henry (the future Henry II), a large part of France (Anjou itself, Normandy and Maine). English barons with French estates began to feel quite strongly that to support Stephen against Matilda and Henry in the face of such a power might not be in their best interests.

The most dangerous rival to the new Angevin power of the young Henry

# The Work of the Monasteries

Monasteries were important institutions in Britain even before the days of Bede, but in later Anglo-Saxon times they almost disappeared. Then came the revival in the reign of Edgar (944–975), whose archbishop of Canterbury and chief counsellor, St Dunstan, was himself a monk. In spite of the reaction against them at Edgar's death, monasteries went on growing. By 1066 there were forty in England, as well as twelve nunneries.

These were all 'black monks', or Benedictines, who followed St Benedict's Rule for religious orders, compiled about 500 years before. The three principles of the Order were Obedience, Poverty and Chastity: monks should obey their abbot, have no property, and no women. The rules were not always strictly kept, and in later times they were often totally ignored.

The monasteries, like the villages, were self-contained, with their own brewery, bakery, fish ponds, and so on. They were usually richer than ordinary villages, thanks to gifts from pious people. The chief duty of the monks was worship, and much of their time was spent in prayer.

Besides prayer, the monks were skilled in various useful crafts. We remember them best for their copying and decorating of books, work they did with great skill and endless patience: a man might spend his whole life on one book. Nearly all literature and art in the early Middle Ages came from monasteries, which also provided most of the English bishops and many royal advisers. The monks also did some teaching. Their pupils were usually boys who would eventually become monks themselves, but sometimes noblemen sent their sons to be educated at a monastery.

The year of the Norman invasion also marked the beginning of another invasion, which continued for over a hundred years: an invasion of monks. The first to arrive were Normans who were brought over to take charge of English abbeys.

They were followed by a host of new religious orders, like the Cluniacs from Burgundy, or the 'black' and 'white' canons; some women's orders also came over. The Carthusians came from Chartreuse, where they developed the magical – and powerful – green liqueur still made there. Other orders founded hospitals, perhaps the first hospitals in England, in the growing towns. These hospitals knew nothing about medicine, but they did provide care and sympathy for the sick and the old.

Far the most important of the new religious orders which arrived in England in the 12th century were the Cistercians, or 'white monks'. They were founded by St Bernard (1090–1153), the abbot of Clairvaux, who was probably the greatest European of his age. Like the Benedictines, the Cistercians followed the Rule of St Benedict although in a stricter manner, so they said. The first Cistercian houses were founded in Yorkshire by 1150, and they rapidly spread over England and Wales.

The Cistercians were more energetic than the older orders and, unlike the Carthusians for instance, who were practically hermits, they had a great effect on English society. Their monasteries were often built in out-of-the-way places, and Cistercian monks took the lead in the land-clearing that was going on all over the country. They were interested in farm work, and to help them they took in local peasants as lay brethren.

By 1200 there were about 600 religious houses in England alone. Monasteries owned a good part of the land, and monks were a sizeable minority in the population. They were never really popular but many people must have been thankful for the monasteries, where they could get food if they were starving, a bed if they were travelling, and nursing care if they were sick.

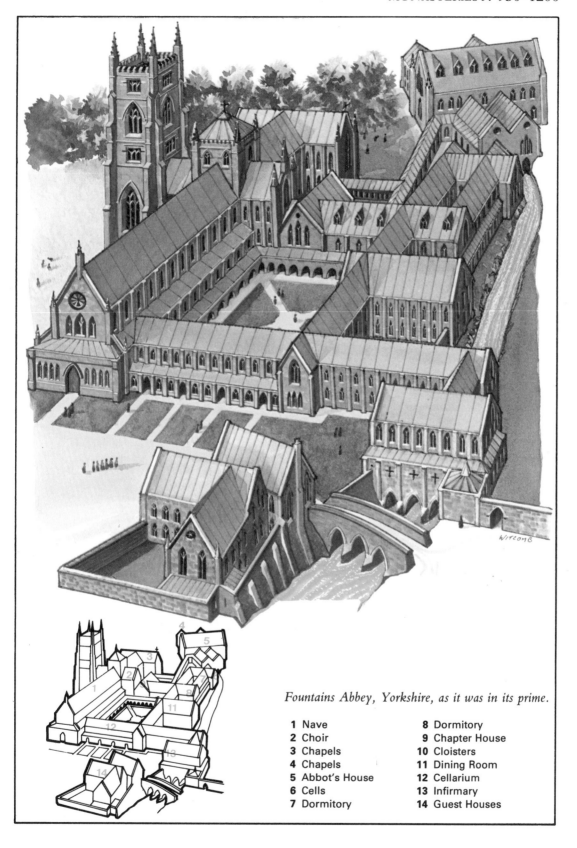

*Fountains Abbey, Yorkshire, as it was in its prime.*

| | | | |
|---|---|---|---|
| **1** | Nave | **8** | Dormitory |
| **2** | Choir | **9** | Chapter House |
| **3** | Chapels | **10** | Cloisters |
| **4** | Chapels | **11** | Dining Room |
| **5** | Abbot's House | **12** | Cellarium |
| **6** | Cells | **13** | Infirmary |
| **7** | Dormitory | **14** | Guest Houses |

# Chapter 4

## The England of Henry II

The development of England into a united nation, with a strong central government headed by the king, had received a setback in the chaotic reign of Stephen. But the setback was not so severe as it looked to people like the monks who wrote the chronicles of the time. The system had not been destroyed. During the reign of Henry II, law and government in England were restored and strengthened.

Monarchs are always interesting people – because they are monarchs. Historians have been fascinated by the character of Queen Victoria, but if she had been the daughter of a banker or a fishmonger no one would have noticed her. In the Middle Ages, when monarchs were far more powerful than they were in the 19th century, their personalities and talents were more important. England today might be a different place if Henry II had not reigned from 1154 to 1189.

Henry was about medium height, heavily built, with slight bow legs from spending so much time on horseback. He had reddish hair and a big freckled face, with grey eyes that grew bloodshot and glowed when he was in a rage. Like all his family, he had a fierce temper, and would roll on the floor, biting the rushes that covered it. But normally he was a kind, even humble man, and less cruel than most men of his time. His favourite sport was hunting, and vigorous exercise helped prevent him growing fat.

His energy was extraordinary. In a time when travel was difficult he once went from

Ireland, via England, to France – about 1300 kilometres including two sea crossings – in a month. He often ate his meals standing up.

His energy was not only physical. He tackled all problems, like changes in law and taxation or a new issue of coins, in the same spirit. He knew four or five languages and he was so widely recognized as a wise judge that two Spanish kings asked him to decide a dispute between them. He might sometimes chatter in church, but he would spend half the night puzzling out a tricky legal case.

Henry's empire was so large that only a man of great ability could have held it together. Yet his many responsibilities prevented him becoming a dictator. He could

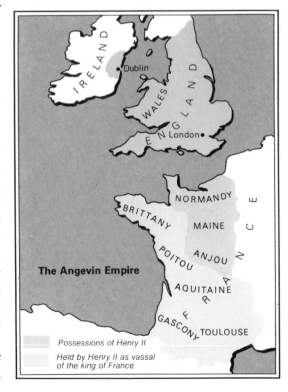

**The Angevin Empire**

Possessions of Henry II
Held by Henry II as vassal of the king of France

not afford to use the royal power too severely for fear of a rebellion.

No one thought of Henry's possessions as an empire. The Holy Roman Emperor and the Pope were two figures who commanded some authority in Europe beyond personal loyalties, but otherwise everything depended on the bond between a man and his lord. Henry's rights and powers were different in each of his possessions. His lands in France were held from the king of France, and Henry was therefore the vassal of Louis VII, just as the king of Scots, who held estates in England, was a vassal of Henry along with the English barons. That did not, of course, prevent Henry fighting the French or the English fighting the Scots.

Henry's power was greatest in England, where his rule was most successful. He made the barons pull down the castles they had built during the reign of Stephen, and he regained the land the Crown had lost since the death of Henry I. But his greatest gift to England was his work in law and government.

Words like 'reform' and 'change' meant nothing to a medieval ruler, and Henry did not regard himself as the inventor of new laws or the reformer of government. His intention was not to change but to restore, and although that sometimes meant introducing new laws, Henry always thought – or said – they were merely the good laws of earlier times stated anew.

The custom of sending travelling judges around the country had begun in the reign of Henry I, if not earlier. Henry II made it a permanent system, and it has lasted, with many changes, to the present. Nor was the use of juries new. Juries of a kind had been known in Anglo-Saxon England. They had been consulted about local conditions for the *Domesday Book*, acting more like witnesses than jurymen. But by the end of Henry II's reign, it was becoming common for juries to be consulted in criminal cases – to say if a man were innocent or guilty. Henry disliked the old system of trial by ordeal (*see page 27*): it was already going out of fashion in France while he was a young man.

The centre of law and government was the king's court or household. The court was to begin with a court of justice, where disputes between subjects were settled. But it was also a kind of super-cabinet, where all government action was decided, and a council of advisers, attended by the king's chief vassals. Everything revolved around the person of the king or, when he was abroad, around his appointed deputy, always one of the greatest barons, who was called the Justiciar.

This system had some disadvantages, which grew worse as time went by. The chief difficulty was not just that the king was simply too busy, but that he was always on the move, carrying the whole government with him. Gradually, separate departments of the government were formed. At first they were still attached to the royal household, but eventually they became separate institutions with permanent headquarters. A great step forward in this direction was taken when the Exchequer – the department that dealt with government income (which made it, from the king's point of view, the most important) – became established at Westminster. The choice of headquarters for the Exchequer ensured that the capital would be – where it still is – in the city of Westminster.

Henry II brought peace and order swiftly to England, but he was not quite so successful in forcing the Scots and the Welsh to accept English order.

Under King David I, Scotland had made great strides towards becoming, like England, a unified nation with a strong central government. David had been educated in England and when he became king of Scots in 1124 he gave many Scottish estates and bishoprics to Normans, men whom he had come to know in England. With their assistance, he created an efficient state on the

*A travelling judge sentences a prisoner. Juries of a kind existed as far back as Anglo-Saxon England.*

Anglo – Norman pattern. But only in the Lowlands: the Celtic chiefs of the Highlands paid little or no attention to the royal government.

David I died in 1153 (the year before Henry II inherited the English crown) and he was succeeded by the fourteen-year-old Malcolm IV, known as Malcolm the Maiden. Malcolm's short reign was troubled, and the Scottish-held parts of Northumbria and Cumbria were lost to the English; but with William the Lion (1165–1224) the Scots again had a strong king. William served in France with Henry II, but later turned against him, encouraged by Henry's rebellious sons and by the French. (The 'auld alliance' between France and Scotland can be dated from William's reign.) He was defeated at Alnwick, captured by the English, and forced to acknowledge Henry as his overlord; some Scottish castles were manned by English troops. But what William failed to do by force he later gained with cash. A large payment in gold to Richard I (Henry's son) secured Scottish independence and regained the lost lands in Northumbria.

During the reign of Stephen the Welsh had run wild and captured several English castles. Wales was not easily subdued, partly because of its mountainous country and partly because of the help the Welsh received from Ireland. Henry II fought several quick campaigns in Wales without much success, and finally he decided to leave matters to the Marcher lords. These semi-independent princes were mostly Norman in origin, but they had intermarried with Welsh princely families. One of them, known to history as Strongbow, undertook the conquest of Ireland in 1169–70. His success brought Henry II new territorial responsibilities which he could well have done without.

Henry's last years were harassed. In 1180 Philip Augustus came to the throne of France: he proved a tougher and more cunning opponent than his father. Henry was faced with successive rebellions in France in which his own sons played leading parts. Not only was that a miserable experience for a father (though Henry had not been the best of parents), it made the situation more dangerous: a revolt supported by a royal prince always gathered more support. Worn out and railing against God, Henry lost his eager energy. As he lay sick, he was told that John, his favourite among his surviving sons, had joined the rebels. He turned his face to the wall, muttering, 'I care for nothing in the world now', and died soon afterwards.

Richard I, who inherited the crown, was more of a French knight than an English monarch. He gained a glorious reputation in Europe as a Crusader in the East, where he defeated the great Saladin and just failed to capture Jerusalem. He deserved his nickname *Coeur de Lion*, 'lion-hearted'. But during his ten-year reign he was only in England for a few months, and then mainly to raise money.

*Hunting was the sport of kings and noblemen. Deer and wild boar were favourite game.*

# Quarrels between Church and King

Besides the power of kings and governments, there was another authority in medieval Europe which all men acknowledged – the Church. The head of the Church was the pope, in Rome. All priests and bishops were subject to him and, in a sense, kings were too, as they also were members of the Christian Church. The pope had no armies and ruled no great territories; his influence was spiritual, a matter of influence rather than force. But that did not make him powerless. It was the pope who, in the 11th century took the lead in organizing the First Crusade – an international expedition which aimed to regain the Holy Land from the Muslims and succeeded, for a short time, in creating a Christian kingdom of Jerusalem. Later Crusades were less successful, but the Crusading ideal lived on into the 15th century, inspiring militant Christian knights like Richard I.

In an age when religion was so strong that men lived and died for it, the influence of the Church was a force for kings to reckon with. Besides that, the Church was a great land-owner. To William I bishops were powerful local governors little different from his other barons. He treated them as his lieutenants, responsible for maintaining royal authority in their bishoprics.

It is not hard to see how problems were certain to arise when the aims of a political ruler, like the king of England, disagreed with the aims of the Church, represented by the pope. Where did the first loyalty of bishops lie? With the king or the pope? As long as there was no conflict between the two, everything went smoothly. But whenever there was, the awkward question about loyalty cropped up again. In England the question was never really answered until the Reformation, when Henry VIII's government rejected the authority of the pope and set up a national Church, governed by the king.

The most famous quarrel between the Church and royal government in England occurred in the reign of Henry II.

There were several different kinds of courts of justice in England, including the royal courts, which Henry did so much to strengthen, and the Church courts, where clergymen who committed crimes had the right to be tried. Henry did not object to this system, but what did annoy him was the failure of the Church courts to inflict proper punishments on criminal priests. An ordinary person who committed a murder had his hand cut off, or was put in prison and fined (Henry did not like the death penalty). A priest who committed the same crime was 'defrocked' – banned from being a priest – but not given any other punishment.

Henry thought that was absurd. He proposed that when a priest was convicted in a Church court, he should be handed over to the royal courts for punishment. But this proposal ran into opposition as solid as the columns of Canterbury cathedral itself. The Archbishop of Canterbury – the pope's deputy in England – would not hear of it.

*Thomas Becket falls before the altar of his cathedral: he became England's best-known saint.*

was barred from all services of the Church, and the interdict, which would bar the whole country, so that no one would even be able to receive Christian burial.

Louis VII of France tried to act as peacemaker. He brought the two men together in his own country, and agreement seemed to have been reached. Henry held Becket's stirrup for him to dismount, saying with tears in his eyes: 'My lord archbishop, let us return to our old friendship and forget our hatred completely'. But when Becket said goodbye before sailing to England, he said, 'My lord, I think I shall never see you again in this life'. Nor did he.

That Christmas Henry was in Normandy, in a sulky mood. News came from England that Becket was as proud as ever. He had excommunicated the bishops who had taken the king's side in the quarrel and had preached a hostile sermon on Christmas Day. Henry flew into one of his rages. 'What idle and miserable men I have encouraged and promoted in my kingdom, faithless to their lord, who let me be mocked by a low-born clerk!' (Becket's father had died a poor man.)

Hearing this outburst, four of Henry's knights took the hint and slipped away, probably without Henry's knowledge. When he found they had gone he guessed why, and sent a messenger to stop them. But it was too late. They reached Canterbury and savagely cut down the archbishop on the altar steps.

Henry was genuinely shocked. He also realized that the murder was a political disaster: no one could imagine a more dreadful act and the king was to blame. Becket was a martyr: his tomb became a shrine; miracles were soon being reported from Canterbury. Henry walked barefoot to the cathedral to show his sorrow, and later had himself flogged by the monks. And in a way, Becket had won the argument by his martyrdom in 1170; for Henry dared take no more action to control the Church.

*Pilgrims at the tomb of Becket: the king was one of the earliest.*

The archbishop's name was Thomas Becket. He was an old friend of the king, and Henry had appointed him to Canterbury because he believed that Becket would support him in any argument over the power of the Church. He was wrong.

Church courts were not the only cause of disagreement between the king and the archbishop: Becket defended the Church at every point against the royal government. He was a stubborn man. But so was Henry.

The king decided to ruin Becket, and charged him with dishonesty and fraud in his previous office of chancellor. Becket held out for a time, but in 1164 he was forced to go into exile. That still did not end the quarrel, which dragged on for another six years.

The pope naturally supported Becket, but he was in an awkward position because there was a rival pope in existence whom Henry, if driven too far, might decide to recognize as the true pope. At the same time, Henry dared not force the pope into using his chief religious weapons – excommunication, which would mean that Henry

# King John and Magna Carta

Government in the Middle Ages depended on co-operation between the king and the barons. As they often quarrelled, it is easy to suppose that they were opponents at heart; or at least that they had different interests, like employers and trade unionists. But when the royal government was strong and successful, the king usually had no trouble with the barons, just as employers and trade unionists get along better when business is good. As a rule, the barons liked a strong royal government, even if that meant some restrictions on themselves. Like most peo-

ple, they preferred law and order to chaos.

To keep the barons loyal and helpful, the king had to be a man worthy of their respect. King John (1199–1216) fell far short of that standard. Although he was not an evil man, John could be vicious and treacherous. Though clever, he was lazy. Though he had a sense of humour, his jokes could be unpleasant for others. When he went to Ireland as governor for his brother Richard I, he laughed at the old-fashioned appearance of the Irish lords and amused himself by pulling their long beards. The Irish were deeply offended by such behaviour, and no wonder.

Just as foolishly, John angered the English barons. They were already discontented as a result of the heavy taxes they had

*The medieval baron was a powerful ruler in his own lands.*

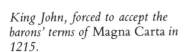

The terms of Magna Carta were quoted regularly by opponents of royal authority, especially by the enemies of Charles I in the 17th century.

King John, forced to accept the barons' terms of Magna Carta in 1215.

to pay for the Crusading campaigns of Richard I. John demanded yet more taxes for his French wars and, what was far worse, John's wars were unsuccessful. The barons resented the king's cruel and unpredictable behaviour towards individuals; they suspected him of having his nephew, Prince Arthur, secretly murdered. They were annoyed by John's refusal to seek advice from the men who, according to tradition, should have been his chief counsellors – themselves.

By 1215 John was faced with opposition from practically all his subjects – at least, from all his subjects whose opinions counted for anything. He was forced to give in to their demands and accept the terms of the document we know as *Magna Carta*, 'the Great Charter'.

What makes *Magna Carta* so important in history is not what it actually says, but what people came to believe it meant. It was not really a statement of the liberties of the people, as later ages interpreted it. It did not say in so many words that trial by jury was the right of every accused person, or that taxes should only be imposed with the agreement of the taxpayers, although these principles were read into it later – for example, by the opponents of Charles I in the

17th century and by the rebellious American colonists in the 18th. *Magna Carta* was a bit of a hodge-podge of a document. Apart from grave matters of law and liberty, it also dealt with the correct standards of measurement, and with fish-traps in the Thames.

All the same, *Magna Carta* was something more than the victory of the small class of barons, intent on making sure of their traditional rights, over the king. Its most important effect was to proclaim the rule of law. The sense of the whole charter, as well as the meaning of many of its clauses, made clear that the law was supreme, and that the king, no less than his subjects, was governed by the law.

The charter did not say how the law was to be enforced. The king might be 'under the law', but what was going to keep him there? No sooner had John got away from the barons at Runnymede, where the charter was signed, than he declared that his signature had been forced from him, and therefore did not count. He drummed up some support, mainly from France, and civil war began. Fortunately John died in 1216, leaving the crown to his son Henry III, who was only nine years old. However, the problem of how royal government could be prevented from becoming a tyranny had not been solved. It cropped up again at various times during the next four centuries and, in 1649, it caused the execution of a king.

When Henry III became old enough to rule, he turned out not much better than his father. He was equally untrustworthy and equally unsuccessful in war; he kept the barons out of government by using officials of the royal household, many of them Frenchmen. It was partly the fault of his father and uncle that the Crown was so short of money, but partly his own, for he was a big spender. It was infuriating to pay heavy taxes to the king and then see him spending the money on luxuries.

To be fair to Henry, some of his extravagance had magnificent and long-lasting results. He was an admirer of the arts, especially church building, which he supported generously. He rebuilt Westminster Abbey – another example of French influence, as anyone can see by comparing it with French cathedrals – and parts of many other great churches. Salisbury Cathedral was begun and almost finished in his reign.

When the barons were in conflict with the king, they were always divided among themselves and usually without a leader. For their natural leader was the king. When a leader of real character, Simon de Montfort, appeared in Henry III's reign, the result was civil war. The struggle dragged on for some time: at one stage the king was Simon's prisoner and Simon ran the government. But Henry, however bad his government, could always attract supporters simply because he was the king, and Simon's chief supporters were knights from the shires and townspeople rather than great noblemen. In 1265 he was defeated and killed at the battle of Evesham.

The man who restored royal authority was not Henry III but his son, a far more capable character, who succeeded him in 1272 as Edward I. Edward was a big man with a drooping eyelid that made him look as though he were giving a sinister wink. His legal reforms, like those of Henry II, were really conservative, and were designed to strengthen royal justice. They were not 'modern improvements'. When Edward ordered a careful inquiry into legal rights and land-ownership throughout the kingdom (rather like William I's Domesday inquiry), his reason was to make sure that the Crown was receiving all the taxes of various kinds that were due to it. Edward needed every penny he could get for his wars.

Like nearly all medieval kings, Edward thought of himself as, first and foremost, a war leader. He was determined to strengthen his kingdom, and to leave it greater than he found it. To do that, he had to demonstrate his authority in Scotland and in Wales.

# Scotland keeps its Independence

After 1189, when William the Lion bought the independence of Scotland for a sum of 10,000 gold marks, there was peace with England for over a hundred years. William's successor Alexander II and his son Alexander III concentrated on opponents nearer home, like the Lords of Lorne and the Lords of the Isles, who recognized the king of Norway, not Scotland, as their overlord.

These efforts by the Scottish kings roused old King Haakon of Norway, and in 1263 a large Norwegian force appeared in the Clyde. Bad weather scattered the ships, but the Norwegians managed to force their way ashore in Ayrshire. There Alexander met them and soundly beat them in the battle of Largs. As a result, Norway gave up the Hebrides to the king of Scots. However, the Lord of the Isles, caring little for overlords, whether Norwegian or Scots, continued to behave as an independent prince.

In 1286 Alexander III died after a fall from his horse. His sons had died before him, and the heir to the kingdom was a baby girl, Margaret, daughter of the king of Norway and Alexander's granddaughter. Scotland

was left again without a strong head to wear the crown, at a time, unfortunately for the Scots, when the English crown was resting on a very strong head indeed, that of Edward I.

Edward suggested that the 'Maid of Norway' should marry his son. He sent a ship, with boxes of sweets, to fetch her, but she died on the way from Norway. Who was to reign now? Several nobles had claims of a kind, and the strongest candidates were Robert Bruce and John Balliol. Edward hastened to Scotland, declaring that he would help to judge who had the better claim. Under his menacing eye, the Scottish nobles selected Balliol, Edward's choice.

It was obvious that Edward's real aim was to gain control of Scotland himself. His chief reason for preferring Balliol to Bruce was that he believed Balliol would do what he was told. He knew both men, for both had fought with him in France and both held lands in England, which made them Edward's vassals.

Neither the Scots nor the English were yet a *nation* in our sense of the word. Edward I could count on support from the many Scottish nobles with English estates if he interfered in Scotland. When Balliol rebelled against his control, Edward

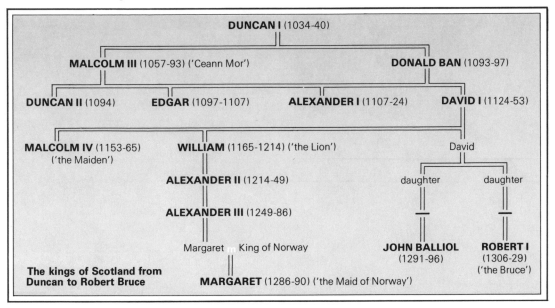

The kings of Scotland from Duncan to Robert Bruce

invaded Scotland and defeated him with the aid of many Scots, including Bruce.

Balliol fled to France. Edward stormed through Scotland and forced the Scots to recognize him as king. When he returned to England, he left Scotland under English rule and carried away with him the Stone of Scone – the symbol of Scottish kingship brought from Ireland by the Scots of Dalriada 700 years earlier.

Trouble soon broke out. The leader of Scottish resistance was Sir William Wallace, who defeated an English army near Stirling (1297) by delaying his attack until the English were halfway across a bridge. This brought Edward, the 'Hammer of the Scots', to the scene once more. Wallace was defeated and, after seven years of guerilla fighting, captured and executed as a traitor in London.

A more powerful leader then arose. In 1307 Robert Bruce (son of Balliol's rival) had himself crowned king of Scots at Scone. He was swiftly defeated by the English and had to flee to the Highlands for safety, but the flame of independence was not put out. Like the spider which, an old legend says, Bruce watched trying to climb its web while he was hiding in a cave, Bruce never gave up. The Black Douglas, his friend and ally, boldly drove the English out of his own castle. The ancestors of great clans like Campbell and Donald gave their support to

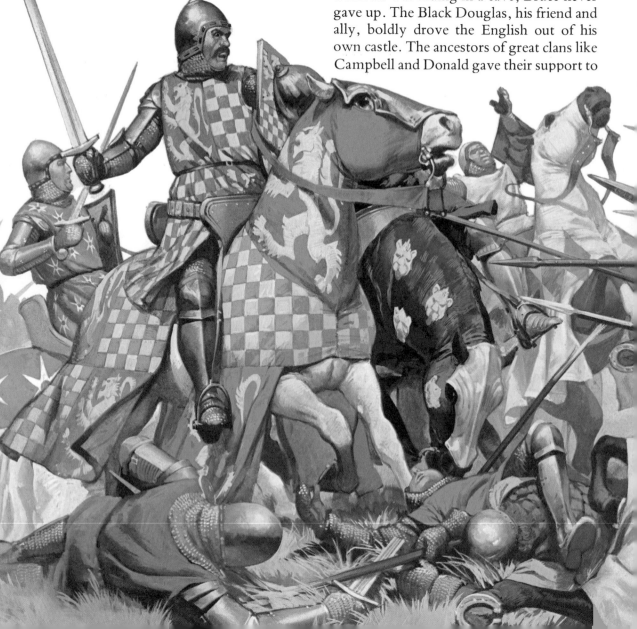

*The Stone of Scone, the symbol of Scottish royalty, was carried away from Scone Palace by Edward I in 1296. It was taken to Westminster Abbey to form part of Edward the Confessor's Chair, since when almost every ruler of England has been crowned on it.*

Bruce. The English, in their captured fortresses, hung on grimly.

In 1307 Edward I, now old and failing, marched north yet again. But the Hammer of the Scots had struck his last blow. In Cumbria, his steps faltered, and at Burgh Sands, north of Carlisle, he died. His son, Edward II, who was no warrior, broke off the campaign.

One by one the English strongpoints in Scotland fell to Bruce and his men. By 1314, only Stirling was left. Pulling himself together, Edward II marched to the relief of Stirling castle. By the Bannock burn (stream), in sight of the castle, Bruce met him and routed him.

The battle of Bannockburn was the greatest victory the Scots ever won against the English. Although it marked the beginning, not the end, of a long war, it ensured the independence of Scotland from the English for 400 years.

*Bannockburn: the English were out-generalled and out-fought; after the battle a man could cross the burn on a bridge of English corpses.*

# Wales and the English Conquest

From Saxon times the English kings had tried to make Wales part of their kingdom. Some had been more successful than others, and the power struggle between England and Wales had swung to and fro like a seesaw: for a time Wales would be subdued, then a new outbreak would drive the English out, then a new English campaign would restore the balance.

In 1196 the Lord Rhys, justiciar of South Wales under Henry II and organizer of the greatest *eisteddfod* ever seen, died. After him, the royal house of Gwynedd, North Wales, provided the chief leaders of the Welsh. Llewellyn ap Iorwerth, 'the Great', who reigned for nearly half a century, almost succeeded in establishing a single united kingdom. He acknowledged the king of England as his personal overlord, but ruled most of Wales entirely in his own right.

Llewellyn was succeeded by his son David II, who died in 1246 without a direct heir. His brother Gruffydd, who had been killed by the English, left three sons, Owen, Llewellyn and David, to divide the inheritance between them.

The most famous of the three is Llewellyn ap Gruffydd. He is a great Welsh hero for his resistance to the English. Yet in the end Llewellyn, because he refused to give up, ensured that Wales would be brought permanently under the direct rule of the English government.

For about ten years Llewellyn ap Gruffydd ruled nearly all Wales without serious opposition. But he failed to pay agreed taxes to England, he avoided making his oath of loyalty to the English king, and he plotted with the French, and with rebellious English barons, against the king. These were risky tactics, even if Llewellyn's position in Wales were secure. It was not: he had quarrelled with his brother David, and in 1274 David fled to England.

Three years later Llewellyn's power suddenly crumbled. As the English armies advanced on Wales, his support withered away in Powys and South Wales. Within a few months he found himself no more than Prince of Gwynedd and humble vassal of Edward I.

In those days there were great differences between the Welsh and the English. They were different races with different customs and, more important, different laws. Having subdued the Welsh, Edward said they should keep their old customs, though

*Harlech Castle is a rectangular fortress, built by Edward I between 1285 and 1290. It stands on a steep, rocky hill.*

*The crossbow which had to be cranked, and the longbow, probably a Welsh invention, which proved a better weapon. The secret of good bowmanship was to press the weight forward into the bow, not to pull back on the string. A skilful longbow man was able to fire up to twelve arrows per minute.*

whether he was sincere or not, arguments over laws and language broke out frequently between Welsh and English.

In 1282 the Welsh rose in revolt. This time Llewellyn was in alliance with his brother David and the princes of the south. It was almost the first, and the last, truly national revolt.

The powerful forces of Edward I approached – knights from Gascony, mercenaries from Flanders, the great Marcher lords, and fighting men from all over England. There could be only one result. Llewellyn ap Gruffydd was killed while attacking an English castle. Edward had his head stuck on a spike at Conway Castle, with a wreath of ivy as a crown: an old Welsh story said that a Welsh prince would one day be crowned by the English. David, after being driven across North Wales, was betrayed to the English, who executed him as a traitor. All resistance ceased.

Welsh independence was lost for ever.

Edward built great new castles at Conway, Caernarvon, Harlech and other places to guard against a revival in North Wales. The government was reorganized on the English pattern: the country was divided into shires with a sheriff ('shire reeve') for each shire (these shires disappeared in 1974 under a new local government act). The towns, inhabited mostly by Englishmen and pro-English Welsh, were strengthened and given charters of rights and liberties. But not even Edward I cared to challenge the Marcher lords: they remained supreme.

While Edward was at Caernarvon in 1284 his eldest son was born, and the king declared that, since Llewellyn's line was extinct, he would present the Welsh with a new prince who 'could not speak a word of English'. It was a conqueror's joke.

But not only a joke. Seven years later, the young prince was created Prince of Wales and the eldest son of the English monarch has been given that title ever since.

*Salisbury Cathedral, unlike most English cathedrals, was built quickly and not constantly altered in later ages. It is therefore all in one style (except the steeple) and is a perfect piece of early English Gothic.*

# The Church in the Middle Ages

In the Middle Ages the largest building in every town and village was the local church. In a continent without factories, motors or radios, the loudest noise to be heard was the clanging of church bells. Except for a few Jews (expelled by Edward I in 1190), everyone was a Christian, and there was only one Christian Church: the Church of Rome. All Christians were the subjects of the pope.

Below the pope were the cardinals, whom he used as legates (ambassadors), figures of great influence who could overrule bishops and sometimes kings. Below them were archbishops, governing provinces, and bishops, governing cities; they also controlled the Church courts. Then came the parish priests, paid out of parish taxes called tithes. There were about 20,000 priests in England in the 13th century (far more than the number of parishes), and even more clergy in lower orders, called clerks. They often did office work for great households, which explains how the word clerk has changed its meaning. Nearly every educated man was a priest or a clerk, and in the whole population, about one man in every thirty was in holy orders.

This organization was more efficient than any other form of government. Education and social welfare, so far as they existed at all, were the business of the Church. Bishops were royal officials; clerks worked in government and the courts. Great conflicts, like the quarrel between Henry II and Becket, did arise, but on the whole the Church and the State worked together. Neither could have existed without the other. King William I had treated the pope politely but kept him at a distance; his great archbishop, Lanfranc, was the king's man more than the pope's man. A weaker king, like John when he quarrelled with Pope Innocent III, was forced to grovel, acknowledging the pope as his overlord and paying him a large tribute, or tax. In Edward I's reign Pope Boniface VIII tried to free the clergy from taxes, but the king refused to allow such a thing. From that time there was a growing feeling that the pope was too much like a foreign prince rather than a religious leader, that he interfered too much in English affairs, and demanded far more in tributes than he was entitled to.

Criticism of the clergy altogether was increasing. There were too many of them: the Church was overstaffed just as (we are told) the Civil Service is now. Though some were good men, many were idle and dishonest, and a few behaved more like drunken cowboys than priests. There were probably many who were ignorant and unqualified, such as the priest whose parishioners complained that he kept confusing Jesus with Judas.

The best jobs in the Church went to young men with influence. The same man might hold several parishes, or even several bishoprics, which he treated as sources of income. Reforming popes like Innocent III tried to stop this, but without much effect. 'Our bishop', someone said, 'is like the strawberries. He comes but once a year and stays not long'.

Besides the parish clergy and clerks, the 'regular' clergy – monks – came in for their share of criticism. By about 1200 the monasteries had reached their peak and seemed ready to decline. A new stimulus came with the arrival of the friars in the 13th century. The Dominicans, or 'black' friars, and Franciscans, or 'grey' friars, worked mainly in the fast-growing towns. Many were townspeople themselves. Unlike the monks, they travelled from place to place among the people, preaching, visiting the sick, hearing confessions – and teaching. The universities of Oxford and Cambridge (founded in 1167 and 1209) welcomed the friars, who soon became the chief teachers there. For about 200 years religious leadership in England came mainly from friars. But some of them, like some monks, grew fat and lazy on charity, and so invited the same contempt that many intelligent people felt for other clergy.

Hostility towards clergymen did not mean that people were not religious. It is difficult for us to realize how deeply religion penetrated into everyday life. We do not easily understand the kind of feeling that made an old woman hauling firewood remember Jesus carrying his cross, or made a monk cut his apple into three in memory of the Holy Trinity of Father, Son and Holy Ghost. Perhaps we cannot even imagine the feelings that drove the great men of the Middle Ages to build their churches and cathedrals – the most beautiful objects that Europeans have ever produced – with their leaping vaults and columns, and their noble spires pointing sternly but hopefully towards Heaven, where man should fix his thoughts.

*The friars, unlike monks, mixed with ordinary people, especially in towns. They were preachers and teachers.*

# The Hundred Years' War

Events in history often have names which are convenient but not accurate. The Hundred Years' War against France is an example. It began in 1337 and ended in 1453, which is more than a hundred years and anyway included long periods of peace. The English had often fought the French before 1337 and often fought them after 1453 – and with greater bitterness, for one sad effect of the Hundred Years' War was to make the English hate the French, in spite of the fact that educated Englishmen spoke French and often *were* part-French.

The Hundred Years' War was fought over one basic question: who should rule France?

The trouble really began with Henry II's empire, which had included more than half of France. By the time Edward III came to the throne in 1327, most of that empire had been lost. The English held only a small region in the north and in the south, in Gascony, the country where claret comes from. In the same year King Charles IV of France died without an heir. He had two nephews, one of whom, Philip VI, became king. The other nephew was Edward III of England.

Philip annoyed the English by trying to regain Gascony and by supplying weapons to the Scots. Civil war had broken out in Scotland after the death of Bruce and Edward III had taken the chance to seize Berwick and overrun the Lowlands. With French help, Robert Stewart, ancestor of the dynasty which was to gain the English throne as well, drove out the English who, by that time, were involved in the Hundred Years' War.

In 1337 Edward III declared himself the rightful king of France (a title kept by English kings until 1801). The following year he invaded France.

From our point of view six and a half centuries later, Edward's policy seems crazy, even when we take into account all the reasons for declaring war, such as guarding the precious Flemish wool trade, which the French were trying to break up. Edward III, who was fond of jousting and tournaments, was certainly a warrior king like his grandfather Edward I (though more likeable) and not at all like his father Edward II. But the Hundred Years' War was a miserable business, worse for the French than the English because it was fought in France. Even during years of truce, bands of unemployed mercenaries wandered through the country, robbing and raping. The English suffered less, but in England too the beginning of the Hundred Years' War was the start of a rather grim time.

Yet for English people the reign of Edward III seemed a glorious one, with banners flying, trumpets braying, and the French fleeing. Off the harbour of Sluys in 1340 the English won a great naval victory, in spite of a wounded Edward and the presence of a large number of court ladies on their ships. The victory gave the English command of the Channel, which made the invasion of France easier.

Still, Edward did not find things simple. He was very short of money, his allies on the continent were unreliable, the Scots were raiding the north, and the pope's messengers were clamouring for a truce. After much summer skirmishing, the French army caught up with Edward at Crécy in 1346. Though Edward had fewer men, his tactics, already successful against the Scots, were more up-to-date. Fast-firing archers and foot soldiers proved superior to the heavily armoured and clumsy French cavalry and they were miserably defeated.

At Poitiers in 1356 Edward's warlike son, known by the colour of his armour as the Black Prince, used the same tactics to win another crushing victory and to capture the French king, John.

In a treaty signed a few years later, the French were forced to give up much land, but from then on Edward found events running against him. The Black Prince, after some years of fighting and feasting in southern France, returned to England in 1371 a dying man, and the gains in the south were lost. Edward himself was growing old and senile. The French avoided major battles and sat tight in their fortresses, which were almost impossible to capture. By the time Edward died in 1377 nearly all his conquests had vanished. The war slowly petered out, and in the reign of Richard II a truce was patched up.

Edward III had been a very good general. Not only were his tactics skilful, he knew how to keep the loyalty and respect of his officers and (so far as we know) of ordinary soldiers also. The morale of the English

*Even before the invention of gunpowder, armies had powerful machines of war for battering walls or hurling missiles over the top.*

army was much higher than that of any other army of the time.

In Edward's great-grandson, Henry V (1413–22), these qualities of generalship were magnified. To us, Henry V is a slightly frightening figure – the nearest thing to an Alexander the Great or a Napoleon that England ever produced. Henry was not a bad man and not even a cruel man by the standards of his age. When the old men, women and children were pushed out of the city of Rouen, which Henry was besieging, because they were 'useless mouths', Henry left them helpless in the hard Normandy winter. But what of the city leaders who pushed them out?

Henry V was a great war leader who believed his own propaganda. He once called his army 'people of God' and spoke of knocking on the gates of Jerusalem, though no English king had taken Crusading seriously since Edward I.

Henry's conquest of the French was made easier by trouble inside France. He might have got what he wanted without fighting, but his demands for land were so greedy that the French could only refuse. Amid the cheers of the people, Henry's army – English nobles and yeomen, wild Irish fighters, skilled Welsh archers, German artillery experts, Flemish sappers, Dutch and Portuguese – set out from Southampton to conquer France.

Harfleur was soon captured, but then disease and desertion began whittling down the army. Winter approached, and the royal counsellors advised retreat. Henry, with less than 6,000 men, decided to march overland to Calais. On the way his tired, sickly and hungry men were intercepted by a French army five times as large at a place called Agincourt.

Next day the English won an extraordinary victory. It was made possible by foolish French tactics – they had forgotten the lesson of Crécy – and by the inspiring leadership of Henry. When the battle ended, half the great nobles of France lay dead on the marshy field.

France was in a desperate state. Henry swept through Normandy, capturing Rouen, and ravaged the Ile de France – the French heartland. The French surrendered. It was agreed that Henry should marry the French king's daughter and should succeed him, in due course, as king of France.

Soon afterwards, Henry himself died –

*Joan of Arc inspired the French people with patriotism and helped to drive the English out of France.*

*Heavily armoured knights on horseback were the cream of any army, but good bowmen protected by pointed stakes were a match for the French knights, caught in muddy ground, at Agincourt.*

which was perhaps just as well. The Agincourt campaign had given the English hopeless dreams of glory: the French would never have accepted an English monarch.

After Henry's death, the English were slowly forced on to the defensive. The French learned better tactics, and the disasters they had suffered made them more determined not to give in. The greatest figure of the later stages of the Hundred Years' War was no great king or general, but a French peasant girl, Joan of Arc. Inspired by religious visions, she rallied French patriotism. The spirit that she represented was worth more than a whole army of noble knights. Meanwhile, England under Henry VI was breaking apart with aristocratic feuds and civil war. By the formal end of the Hundred Years' War in 1453, all the English possessions in France had been lost except Calais.

# The Horror of the Black Death

The disease called plague has been unknown in Europe since the late 17th century, but for centuries before that it was a frequent and terrifying visitor. The worst outbreak occurred in 1347–49. It is known as the Black Death.

There are three varieties of plague. Bubonic plague is the most common, but there are two others which are even more deadly. The Black Death probably included at least one of these as well as the bubonic variety. The plague germ is carried by the fleas of rats, but 14th-century people did not know that. Even if they had known, they could not have done much to help themselves. For most of them, the Black Death was simply a sign of God's anger.

Sometimes it began with a sore throat. The patient's temperature rose, he became feverish and dizzy, and was violently sick. Large swellings appeared, or dark inflamed patches on the skin, with intense pain and raving delirium. Death came in a day or two.

The Black Death reached Europe from Asia in an Italian merchantship. It swept through Italy and France, reaching England in 1348 and Scotland in 1349. Graveyards filled up, and trenches were dug for more bodies. Farm animals wandered about untended and the corn stood unharvested in the fields. Grass grew in the streets of Bristol and the Oxford colleges closed. Prices slumped: a good horse could be bought for six shillings which in normal times would have cost forty. Some places escaped but in others everyone died and whole villages disappeared for ever. In East Anglia a woman named Matilda Wyninge watched three husbands die of plague in two months. Then she caught it. In Derbyshire, Sir William de Wakebridge lost father, wife, three brothers and two sisters – in two months.

No one can say exactly how many people died; probably about one-third of the total population, perhaps more. It was the greatest disaster the English people ever suffered, and what made a horrible situation worse was that the Black Death was not the end of it. Every ten years or so, plague returned, not as fiercely as in 1348, but killing thousands more. In the years between 1348 and 1400 about half the population of England and Wales must have died of plague.

As a breed, human beings, like other animals, are tough: they bounce back from the worst catastrophes. Historians used to believe that the Black Death was responsible for the changes that were happening, sometimes violently, in the late 14th century. But they have now discovered that many of those changes were already underway before the Black Death. Consider population, for example: it had been rising slowly for centuries; but in the 14th century it dropped. Hardly surprising, if

*Victims of the Black Death: no wonder people believed that God was angry with them.*

one in three people died of plague in 1348-49. Yet we now know that the population had stopped growing *before* 1348. Plague reduced it further, of course, and helped to prevent it growing again for over a hundred years. (The population of England in 1500 was probably no higher than it was in 1300.)

The Black Death caused no permanent changes. What it did was to speed up certain developments that were taking place in any case. There was a great shortage of farm workers and, as a result, wages went up (in spite of the government's attempts to enforce a wage freeze). Also, landowners who had previously farmed their own land with the labour of their tenants now found it easier to lease their land to a farmer who paid rent in cash. But the rise in wage rates, and the new policy of landowners, had both begun before the Black Death.

Trade and business suffered, though recovered very quickly. The wool trade was back to its pre-plague level as soon as 1351. The men who 'farmed' the customs (this meant that they paid the king a fixed sum in return for collecting customs duties themselves) went bankrupt in 1349, but they were in difficulties already for various reasons.

The plague certainly caused a lot of disturbance. Law and order collapsed completely in some places. Religious life was badly affected because so many clergy died. Some monasteries lost nearly all their monks, and half the parishes lost their priests. People were unsettled and moved about more, because their village had been destroyed, or they were in search of higher wages, or they were trying to escape from serfdom. All this increased the troubles and discontent of the country which were to explode suddenly in 1381 in the Peasants' Revolt.

# The Rebellion of the Peasants

The outbreak of 1381 known as the Peasants' Revolt was not a general rebellion of all the peasants in England. Some counties remained peaceful, and others besides peasants were involved in the revolt. Its immediate cause was the government's attempt to levy a poll tax – a tax on every adult person. It was the third poll tax in four years and, as rich and poor were taxed the same amount, it was very unfair. People were already fed up with the downright incompetence of the government, which was run by a group of quarrelling nobles as the king, Richard II, was under age. Paying taxes felt like pouring money down a drain: the government could not even defend the country properly. The French were having a fine time raiding the English coasts.

In the general disturbance, many old grievances were paid off. In Oxford and Cambridge there was fighting between 'town' (the local people) and 'gown' (university people). In the towns the craftsmen seized the opportunity of striking at their old enemies, the local governments, which were dominated by the richer merchants. In Norfolk and some other counties, landowners, disgusted with the government, took the side of the rebels.

But most of all the revolt was a demonstration of discontent by the people who made up much the largest part of the population – the peasants. They had come to resent the laws and customs which restricted them to their manor, compelling them to work for and obey the local landlord. Their discontent grew sharper when they saw that the old system was in any case breaking down – especially since the Black Death.

Disturbances increased in the years before 1381. The records of one manor, at Harmsworth in Middlesex, between 1377 and 1380, show men being fined for working on their own land instead of the lord's and for failing to give their labour at harvest time. We hear of trouble in the manor court: juries refusing to give a proper verdict and workers speaking out against the lord. In 1378 someone opened a sluicegate and flooded the hay field. In 1379 two men were fined for beating up the lord's servants and next year one of them, for some new

*Rebelling peasants destroyed the manor records, which contained the evidence of their serfdom.*

*The young Richard II confronts Wat Tyler and his men.*

offence, had his land confiscated. The same sort of behaviour was going on in many other places.

Labourers were annoyed by the government's efforts to keep wages down, unsuccessful though those efforts were. Some labourers made very extravagant demands. Two Essex ploughmen were receiving twenty-eight shillings a year when the official rate for such work was ten shillings. They demanded a rise to forty shillings a year plus fringe benefits – free clothing and corn. When that was refused, they unhitched their ploughs and left.

Some revolutionary characters soon appeared on the scene and a priest named John Ball began to preach a kind of communism. He asked:

*When Adam delved and Eve span*
*Who was then the gentleman?*

This was class warfare, and although John Ball himself was a doubtful character who encouraged useless violence, others were saying much the same thing.

The 'establishment' in Church and State was being challenged. The lower clergy were often sympathetic to the peasants and shared some of their complaints, but otherwise there was strong hostility to the Church – that is to clergymen, not to Christianity. Friars, who had mostly forgotten their vows of poverty, were especially disliked. The pope too came under heavy fire. The status of the popes was severely weakened at this time because they had fled from Rome and set up their court at Avignon in southern France. To many English people, the pope had become merely the puppet of the king of France, their ancient enemy.

A much more serious reformer than John Ball was the Yorkshire-born priest, John Wyclif. Though a narrow, rather dry man, he became a great hero with the people for his attacks on the Church establishment. We might almost call him a 'Protestant', for he attacked not only the practices of the Roman Church but also some of its treasured beliefs. He translated the Bible from Latin (which only priests could read) into English, so that people could judge for themselves whether the Church was teaching true Christianity.

Wyclif's disciples, some of whom were not so intelligent as he, were called Lollards (the name came from a word meaning 'sing softly'). They were persecuted by the government not only because they were heretics (a heresy is a belief contrary to the official doctrine of the Church), but also because they attacked the whole organization of society. But they survived, in spite of excommunication and execution, mainly among the poorer people in the towns.

Some of the tax-collectors responsible for collecting the poll tax in 1380–81 went about their jobs in a highly tactless manner, and it was their behaviour in Essex and Kent that set off the first explosion. A judge was kidnapped and manor houses were smashed up. The Kentishmen, with some from Essex, gathered at Maidstone and chose Wat Tyler as their leader. They invaded Canterbury Cathedral during Mass and released John Ball from the local jail. Two days later they were at Blackheath, outside London. (Such fast progress shows they were no wild rabble.) North of the river, Essex men camped at Mile End.

The government was taken by surprise and made no attempt to confront the rebels with force. Yet their demands were frightening. They had come, they said, to save the young king from bad ministers and the first thing they wanted was the head of John of Gaunt, his uncle. Wat Tyler crossed the river at London Bridge, and the rebels surged through the city, burning legal records and killing lawyers, opening the prisons, and destroying John of Gaunt's palace of the Savoy, the finest house in England. In spite of the savagery, Wat Tyler stopped all looting.

The panic-stricken court sheltered in the Tower. As his advisers had no useful advice in the emergency, King Richard II, fourteen years old, announced he would meet the rebels in the open at Mile End. There he promised to grant their demands, but meanwhile the Kentishmen had captured the Tower and lynched the Archbishop of Canterbury and several others. Richard confronted the Kentishmen at Smithfield. Tyler, carried away with his new importance, addressed him with deliberate rudeness. He demanded a charter of liberties; the ending of all lordship except the king's; Church lands to be given to the people; serfdom to be ended, and various other drastic reforms. Richard kept cool and promised that all this would be done, but a scuffle started involving the mayor of London and Wat Tyler. Someone drew a knife and Tyler fell.

The mob rushed forward with shouts of rage, but Richard, thinking fast, rode to meet them. 'Sirs, will you shoot your king?' he cried. 'I am your captain, follow me'. Like sheep, they followed.

The young king's quick (and brave) action ended the rising in London, but not in other parts of the country. It spread quickly, like a forest fire that throws sparks out to set distant trees alight. The most serious trouble was in East Anglia, where manors and monasteries were ruined, abbots and landlords killed, and priceless documents burned.

The revolt was violent while it lasted, but it was not an organized rebellion and it did not last long – no more than one weekend in many places. With peace restored and the government back in control, Richard II's promises at Smithfield were conveniently forgotten. Villeins remained villeins, lords remained lords. The leaders of the revolt were executed, but otherwise, by 14th-century standards, the government was merciful: although there were acts of bloody revenge.

# The Stuarts in Scotland

David II, the son of Robert Bruce, was not the man his father was. Robert had grown from an Anglo-Norman noble into a great Scottish patriot; but David seemed to care little for Scotland. He took over the government in 1341 after Robert Stewart had cleared out the English. (Although Robert Stewart was David's nephew, he was seven years older.)

When the French were defeated by the English at Crécy in 1346, they called on their Scottish allies for help. David reluctantly marched south, but was easily defeated and captured by the English. He spent the next eleven years at the English court. In those days of chivalry, prisoners were usually treated according to their rank, and David found Edward III's court more pleasant than his own. He was only too glad to be rid of the cares of governing Scotland.

But he was still the king, and eventually the Scots bought him back for a huge ransom – 100,000 marks (a mark was one-third of a pound). Scotland was a poor country, and such a payment was a severe handicap, especially as the country had hardly recovered from the Black Death and a series of ruinous floods.

David II soon proceeded to make a bargain with Edward III, by which a son of the English king would become heir to the Scottish throne (David had no children). The Scots angrily rejected this idea, and when David died in 1371, he was succeeded by his Stewart nephew, Robert.

Robert II had been a good regent while David II was in England, but he was not a successful king. The hardest task of the king of Scots, then and for many generations afterwards, was to keep the great nobles in check. They were powerful, violent, proud and bad-tempered. The king could not rely on their loyalty and they fought constantly among themselves. The border lords were always invading England – or being invaded. The Douglases carried on a feud with their rivals, the Percys of Northumbria, as if they were rival kings.

Robert II could not control these feuds and nor could Robert III, an invalid who admitted quite honestly that the job of governing the Scots was too much for him. His son, the future James I, was sent to France for safety's sake as a small child, but by bad luck he was captured by the English and did not return to Scotland until he was a mature man.

As so often happened in the troubled Scotland of the late Middle Ages, the government was headed by a regent – Robert III's brother, the duke of Albany. Albany made no serious effort to get the young

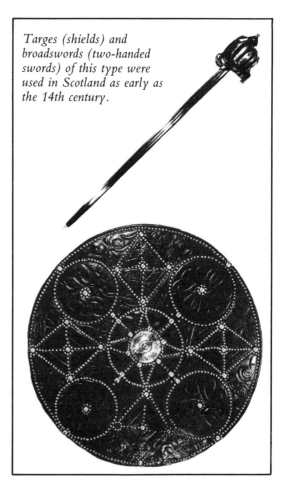

*Targes (shields) and broadswords (two-handed swords) of this type were used in Scotland as early as the 14th century.*

*Caerlaverock Castle, Dumfriesshire, was destroyed during the Border Wars of the 14th century, but was later rebuilt.*

Scottish foreign policy was always simple: alliance with France in order to damage the English. A Scots army went to France in 1421 to help resist the victorious Henry V. The French were impressed by the amount of wine the Scots drank and the amount of mutton they ate. Henry was also impressed, but in a different way. As he said of the Scots on his deathbed, ' . . . a cursed nation. Wherever I go I find them in my beard'.

Peace came at last in 1424, and with the peace came James I, now aged thirty, intelligent, well-educated, and very quick both in mind and body. For the first time since the death of Robert I, a strong and capable monarch reigned in Scotland. The new king did not hesitate to assert himself.

Almost his first move was to execute the male members of the family of Albany (the duke himself was dead). Three years later he arrested forty Highland chiefs, and though most were soon released, one or two were executed. This kind of justice was a little too rough. Not surprisingly, the Highlands

King James back from England, and he did nothing to prevent the nobles building larger castles, grabbing more lands, and becoming harder to control.

Apart from the powerful Douglas clan, the greatest prince in Scotland was the Lord of the Isles, chief of the MacDonalds. He was treated by the English as an independent ruler, and in the late 14th century he became an ally of England by formal treaty.

Fortunately for Scotland, the English did not give their ally much help in 1411, when he became involved in a dispute with the son of the regent Albany. The MacDonalds advanced across Scotland towards Aberdeen. With them marched their allies, the Macleans, under their formidable leader, Red Hector of the Battles. A bloody battle was fought at Harlaw, and though it was the kind of battle in which neither side can honestly claim a victory, its result was the withdrawal of the Islesmen – with the Macleans grieving over the death of Red Hector in the battle. Future Lords of the Isles were to prove no less troublesome than Donald; but if the MacDonalds had won at Harlaw, the Stewart monarchy might have fallen.

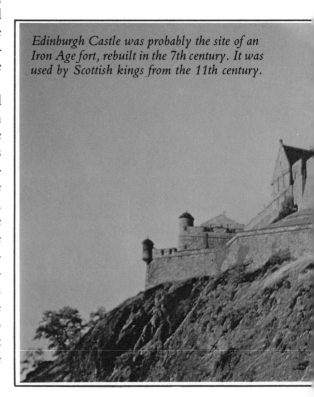

*Edinburgh Castle was probably the site of an Iron Age fort, rebuilt in the 7th century. It was used by Scottish kings from the 11th century.*

rose in fury; the Lord of the Isles sacked Inverness, and James was forced to take to the field himself before they were driven off.

James was equally tough in the Lowlands, imprisoning the Earl of Douglas and driving the Earl of Mar into exile. In various ways, mostly legal, James gained the estates of several great nobles and thus righted the balance of power between the Crown and its great subjects.

Energetic and intelligent, James reorganized the system of law and government. He crossed swords with the pope over his efforts to make the Scottish Church less dependent on Rome; he renewed the policy of helping the French against the English; and he tried hard to make Scotland a less savage, more cultured place. James himself was a part-time poet, and his court at Linlithgow palace was a splendid place of fine music and elegantly dressed, intelligent people.

James made many enemies, and in 1437 he was assassinated in Perth. His son, James

II, was only six months old, and until 1449 Scotland was again ruled by regents. One of them, Sir William Crichton, pursued the Stewart policy of subduing the Douglases by simple and savage means: he invited the fourteen-year-old earl and his brother to dinner and when they arrived, had them killed.

Murder as a political weapon was becoming all too common. James II got rid of another earl of Douglas in the same way, stabbing him to death over the dinner table at Stirling Castle. In a short civil war, the power of the Black Douglases was crushed for ever.

James II inherited most of his father's ability and determination. He successfully resisted a formidable combination of enemies and restored peace in most of Scotland. The Wars of the Roses in England gave him a tempting chance to interfere in English affairs, but while he was laying siege to an English castle, one of his own siege cannon exploded and killed him in 1460.

# Chapter 5

## The Growth of Parliament

Kings of England were never absolute rulers, not even in the days of a mighty monarch like William the Conqueror. Their power was great, but there were always other powers which the king had to consider. He could never ignore completely the wishes of his subjects.

The word parliament means roughly the same as 'parley' – a meeting at which some kind of discussion takes place (a 14th-century poem, by Geoffrey Chaucer, is called 'A Parliament of Fowls'). The name was first used to describe meetings of the king's great council in the reign of Henry III (1207–72).

Parliament as we know it today is an ancient institution, but it is an institution which has always been changing (and still is). The modern British Parliament has developed from a great number of laws and customs, some of them very old but some quite recent. It is a different kind of institution from the Parliament of even two or three hundred years ago. Although we can trace its growth farther back than that, we have to remember that the modern Parliament would hardly be recognized by the people of the Middle Ages. Many of its most important characteristics were at that time unknown and unthought-of.

Oaks grow from acorns, but an acorn is nothing like an oak tree. Nor is the modern Parliament like the Anglo-Saxon witan. But if we are looking for the most distant beginnings of Parliament, we may find them in the witan, an assembly of wise men, like the elders of a tribe, who advised the king on questions of law and government.

When England was conquered by the Normans in 1066, the Anglo-Saxon witan disappeared. William the Conqueror had his council, made up of officials of the royal household, bishops and abbots, barons and knights – anyone the king wished to consult. In the great council, the king also met regularly with his chief tenants, the men who held the greatest estates in the country – barons and earls.

*Magna Carta* had something to say about this council which shows that it was something more than an instrument for the king's use. The Charter said that no extra taxes should be imposed by the king without the agreement of the 'common council of the realm' – in other words, the barons. Although it was called the 'common' council, it did not contain the 'commons' (representatives of ordinary people) at that time. In fact, *Magna Carta* itself had little to do with the growth of Parliament. Yet within a few years changes were taking place – quite small changes they seemed at the time – and as a result an institution appeared in which the ancestor of the modern Parliament can be recognized.

What happened was that it became the custom for the council, or Parliament, to be attended by knights from the shires (country gentlemen) and by burgesses (important citizens) from the towns.

Although knights, and perhaps townsmen too, had come to earlier Parliaments, the three classes – barons, knights and townsmen – were first summoned as regular representatives (two knights from each shire, two citizens from each town) in the Parliament of Simon de Montfort in 1265. During the late 1250s many of Henry IIIs subjects had been rebelling at the king's incompetence and extravagance. By this time Simon was on top in his struggle with the government. Much of his strength came, not from his fellow-barons, but from what might be called the 'middle classes' – the kind of people whom he called to Parliament. No doubt he hoped to talk to them as a class and make sure of their support. However, in the next reign, the custom of summoning the representatives of the shires and towns was continued by Edward I (though he did not call them to every Parliament).

What was Parliament in the 13th century, and what was it supposed to do? Its most important business was not the business of the modern Parliament. It was not chiefly a place where laws were made or where taxes were voted. It was not an assembly of representatives in the sense that modern MPs are the representatives of the people of their constituencies. Nor were the members elected by vote of the people in each consti-

tuency. The knights were originally elected in the shire courts, probably by a jury like the jury in a trial. Parliament itself was little more than an enlarged royal court, where political matters could be discussed, petitions could be presented asking for some right to be granted or some nuisance to be abolished, and where state trials could be held. (Nowadays, the royal court means something different from a court of law, but originally the word meant the same in each case.)

No one invented Parliament. It developed gradually, with stops and starts, as a way of exchanging information and reaching agreement about future action. It was a way of keeping in touch – the king with his subjects, subjects with their king. Edward I summoned the representatives of county and town because he wanted to know what people up and down the country were thinking. But he did not expect them to tell him what to do, nor did they do so. He wanted them to listen to his plans, so that they would carry the news to each part

*The Exchequer: the department of government which deals with national income is still called the Exchequer, but the present Chancellor no longer needs a 'chequered' table to calculate tax returns.*

*The seal of Simon de Montfort. Simon is remembered for his part in the early development of Parliament. He hoped to attract support from knights and townsmen, so summoned them to meet him.*

of the country and take what action was required in each community.

Those who went to Parliament from the shires and the towns felt they were performing a public duty, a necessary but annoying duty. They felt much as people feel nowadays when they have to sit on a jury. They certainly did not think they were receiving some valuable new privilege. Some towns tried to get out of their parliamentary duty. In the reign of Edward III the borough of Torrington in Devon presented a petition asking to be excused from sending members to Parliament: it was a long way and, as the borough had to pay the expenses of the members (five pence a day), it was costly.

By summoning a Parliament which represented all classes (except peasants), Edward I hoped to make the royal government stronger and more efficient. Tax-collecting was made easier, as the representatives of each community – the 'commons' as they came to be called – could present exact information about local conditions, giving the government a better idea of how – and how much – taxation could be raised. The commons could also explain the meaning of government policy to their people.

It was an ancient custom for people to present petitions to the king and his council. The more important petitions were discussed in Parliament, and in the 15th century they began to take the form of bills, presented by the commons and passed into law by the whole Parliament. That was how the commons' right of originating laws or acts of Parliament began.

By that time Parliament was divided into two 'houses'. In Edward I's time the lords and commons had met as one body, together with the king and officials of the government. The commons were very much the junior members. They probably did not speak unless the king asked them a question. Laws, in the form of statutes (not quite the same as a modern act of Parliament) could be passed without the commons' agreement. In fact, some of the great statutes of Edward I were passed by Parliaments at which the commons were not present.

Sometimes the commons (knights and burgesses) would discuss among themselves what reply they should make on a

*Parliament in the 13th century: no one knows exactly what the seating arrangement was, but we can be sure that the king had the chief position and the Commons a humble one.*

difficult question. They appointed one man to speak for them in Parliament, who was called the Speaker. In time it became the regular custom for the commons to meet separately. In the reign of Edward III they had a regular meeting place too – at Westminster, where Parliament has met ever since.

By the beginning of the 16th century the House of Commons had become much more important than it was in the reign of Edward I. The king was still the greatest power in the kingdom, followed by the barons. The Church was still a mighty – and partly independent – power (bishops sat in the House of Lords, but the lower clergy, by their own choice, were not represented in the House of Commons; they met in an assembly called a Convocation). But the power of the Commons had grown and was soon to grow greater. Statutes were passed only with their consent, and no special taxes could be imposed unless they voted in favour. In the course of the next two hundred years, all three of the major powers of the kingdom – barons, Church and king – were to be severely reduced in one way or another, leaving the House of Commons supreme.

# Merchants and the Wool Trade

Medieval Britain had no towns to compare with the great cities of Italy and Flanders. Edinburgh was still a small place with few stone buildings. Neither York nor Norwich, nor even fast-growing Bristol, was as large or as grand as the cities of north Italy. The one exception was London, and even London was probably no larger than Florence. Yet London was a great city. It had, for instance, no less than fifty-two goldsmiths' shops. They were grouped together, like all the crafts in a medieval town, as the names of old city streets –

*Merchants travelling with their goods on packhorses.*

Bread Street, Milk Street, Fish Street – remind us. When towns were small, it was not necessary to have a butcher or a baker in each neighbourhood.

Large towns, if they were not actually on the sea, were nearly always close to a port. For the wealth of towns was built on trade, and goods, including many for internal trade, were carried by ships.

In some ways, commerce was a simpler business in the Middle Ages than it is today. But although there were not so many rules and regulations, the merchant had other problems to deal with. For one thing, the merchant himself was rather an odd figure in medieval society. The Church, as a rule, regarded him with deep suspicion. It taught that making large profits from business was sinful, and many merchants, if judged by that standard, were quite wickedly rich. Lords did not much like merchants either. Who were they, and where did they come from? They were not serfs, but they were not nobles either. They were often rich, and they gained their riches in a way that most lords did not understand.

A worse problem was the difficulty of moving goods about. Most roads were just tracks, too rough for carts. Sea voyages were risky, for ships were easily wrecked and sometimes captured by pirates. War was another danger, or at least a nuisance, as it cut the merchants off from their markets. However, most of the 12th and 13th centuries were fairly peaceful, and it was then that trade and towns grew fastest.

Like some new states in Africa and Asia today, England, and still more Scotland, were 'under-developed'. Their main exports were food and raw materials – things that they grew or mined, not things that they made.

To this day, the Lord Chancellor in the House of Lords sits on a 'woolsack'. It is a symbol of the product on which the prosperity of England was built, for wool was far the largest export. English wool was better than any other country's, and fetched top prices in Europe (as it still does). England was not alone in depending on English wool: the cities of Flanders grew rich on the cloth trade, and the best Flemish cloth was made from English wool.

Sheep farming was the biggest business of medieval Britain. The chief sheep-rearing districts were East Anglia, the West Country and Yorkshire, where the Cistercian monks had turned the dales into huge sheep pastures. Prosperous places usually spent their profits on church building, and that is why so many splendid parish churches can be seen in the old sheep-rearing districts.

Other products were also exported: iron from Cleveland and the Forest of Dean, tin from Cornwall and coal from Newcastle. Derbyshire lead reached the heart of Europe by a slow journey across the Midlands, over the North Sea and up the German Rivers. Hides and salt fish, especially from Scotland, went to Scandinavia and the Low Countries.

For its wool and other products, England bought goods that could not be produced at home. Wine came from Gascony, long ruled by English kings. Furs and timber came from the Baltic, cloth from Flanders, oil and leather from Spain, which also sent rare luxuries like oranges and lemons. Other luxury goods were imported from the Italian cities, which controlled trade with the Middle East and Asia. Eastern spices were the most desirable of these goods: pepper concealed the taste of bad meat; cloves stopped a toothache; ginger, people believed, improved a man's sex life. These things were very expensive. Together with cottons and silks, dyes, precious stones and other luxuries, spices

*Trademarks of medieval wool merchants.*

travelled overland across Europe from the Mediterranean; but in the 13th century, the Italians began to trade directly by sea with northern Europe. The rise of Southampton, which was a convenient port of call, dates from that time.

In all these commercial dealings, English merchants played a big part. Like successful businessmen today, they were often engaged in several different kinds of business. William of Doncaster, who was three times mayor of Chester, was a government official and supplier to the army as well as a merchant and ship-owner. He was an importer of Gascon wine and an exporter of wool and other goods, which he sent to Ireland and Flanders. Besides all that, he managed the Welsh lead mine which supplied the lead for the roof of Chester castle.

Although there were other great English merchants like William of Doncaster, most of England's trade was run by foreigners. Kings looked kindly on foreign merchants, who paid handsomely for the privilege of trading in England and would lend money

*Paycocke's House, Coggeshall, Essex. A merchant's house dating from about 1500, showing unusually rich panelling and wood-carving. Wool merchants were the richest of the English tradesmen (cloth was the most valuable item of trade in the Middle Ages).*

to the government. The greatest of these foreigners were the merchants of the North German Hanse ('trading company'). Their headquarters at the Steelyard in London – a prime site on the river – was like a city within a city, and they also had little colonies in ports like Ipswich, Yarmouth, Boston and Hull. There were many other foreign merchants in London. Gascons, Dutch, Flemings and – the wealthiest of all – Italians, could be seen busily working in the warehouses, offices and shipyards.

In the 14th and 15th centuries, English trading patterns changed. The most important change was a switch in exports from wool to cloth – the finished product instead of the raw material. The English realized that if the Flemings could grow rich making cloth from English wool, then they could grow richer by making the cloth themselves. And that is what they did. Gradually, English cloth exports increased, until Flanders was left behind. In the wool-growing regions, villages like Bradford and Halifax became little industrial towns, where workers in barns and cottages sat spinning and weaving.

The change from wool exports to cloth was the result of government policy. Trade altogether was coming under more government controls. All wool had to be sold at the same place – the 'staple' at Calais, where merchants were given the exclusive rights to buy goods for export. Heavy duties were placed on the export of wool, and some-

*A merchantship attacked by pirates in the English Channel. Bad weather and raids of this kind made sea voyages particularly hazardous.*

times it was forbidden entirely, to help the new cloth-making industry.

Putting restrictions like customs duties on trade usually results in smuggling, and one of the first professional smugglers we know of was caught taking wool out of the country in 'empty' wine barrels in the 1290s. Wool smuggling later became a profitable occupation in parts of the southeast, where the smugglers were known as 'owlers' – perhaps because they worked at night.

England in the 15th century was on its way to becoming a country that lives by trade. Kings like Edward IV and Henry VII helped merchants as much as possible, and both of them took part in trade themselves as private merchants. Companies of merchants, called Venturers, pushed into new regions. The men of Bristol took the lead in advancing trade, men like Robert Sturmy, who sent a ship into the Mediterranean in 1446 to sell tin and wool to the people of Florence. His ship was wrecked coming home, but a few years later he tried again. This time he had two ships, well-armed, for they were going to try to break the monopoly claimed by Genoa to trade in the eastern Mediterranean. Sturmy himself sailed on the voyage, but he was caught by the Genoese and his ships were sunk or captured. When the news reached Bristol, the angry mayor of the city successfully sued the Genoese merchants in England for £6,000.

Robert Sturmy's venture failed, and over a hundred years were to pass before the English gained a foothold in the Mediterranean trade. But it was the spirit of merchants like him – brave, determined, ambitious men not much bothered by old rules – that made England rich.

# Town Life in the Middle Ages

Towns in the Middle Ages looked like overgrown villages, and that is what most of them were. Except in London, the only place that could be called a city by modern standards, there was no sharp difference between life in a village and life in a town. The townspeople often had to work for their lord just as villagers did. Most of them grew vegetables and kept cattle in the common pasture.

Many people today regret that towns have lost their countrified character. It must have been pleasant for a man like the poet Chaucer (*c*. 1345–1400), living in the heart of London, to take a stroll in the fields only a

*A physician ordering his drugs and potions at the apothecary's shop. Medicine was a mixture of common sense and superstition.*

minute or two from his door. And how convenient to walk to any part of the town in half the time people nowadays may spend waiting for a bus. But although medieval towns had many attractive qualities, they had others that were very unattractive.

They were dirty and unhealthy. Towns would have grown faster than they did but for the killing diseases, like the plague, which carried off far more townsfolk than country people. There were no drains or dustbins, and no one to clear the piles of filth that lay about the streets, As there were so many animals about, the stink was rich. Pigs wandered in the streets, snuffling for food among the litter that was thrown out of houses. Only in London was this forbidden: there, a man who came across a wandering pig had the right to cut its throat and treat his family to roast pork. Most people did not mind the dirt much, not realizing how dangerous it was to health, but rich citizens carried sweet-smelling herbs in a ball or, like King Henry VIII, an orange stuffed with sponge soaked in vinegar.

The houses were as bad as the streets. The floor of ordinary houses was hard mud, strewn with rushes. The Dutch philosopher, Erasmus, advised the English to give up this practice of covering the floor with rushes which, he wrote, were 'so carelessly renewed that the foundation sometimes remains for twenty years, harbouring spittle and vomit and urine of dogs and men, beer that has been spilt and remains of fish and other filth unmentionable'.

Towns had no refuse collectors, no health inspectors, and they had no police. The wise citizen did not go out after sunset in the unlighted streets. In some towns a man could be severely punished for walking about at night: it was almost certain he was up to no good. The evidence of crime stood in the town square: the whipping post, the stocks and the gallows.

Yet English and Welsh towns were less violent than the towns of most other countries in Europe. In Germany or France, no town of any size could exist without a great stone wall to protect it. English towns often had walls too, but sometimes the walls were incomplete, and some had no walls at all. People had less reason to fear marauding soldiers or large bands of well-armed bandits. Although England suffered several civil wars, the fighting often passed by the towns, and town life carried on much as usual. And in England, although there was

*The blacksmith at work in his forge; his apprentice works the bellows to fan the furnace.*

jealous rivalry among towns, there were no ferocious feuds like those between Ghent and Bruges in Flanders, or between Florence and Pisa in Italy.

In a country where nearly everyone had some connection with farming, we must ask why and how towns developed. The question is important because it is in the towns that we see the most obvious signs of progress towards a more modern society in the late Middle Ages. Political changes usually come from the rowdy towns, rather than quiet villages.

A modern map of England gives a clue to the growth of towns. They are often located at an important crossroads of some kind, especially at a place where a bridge crossed a river. London grew up at the spot nearest the coast where the Thames could be crossed. Ships were the only means of bulk transport, and cities like Norwich or Cam-

bridge were sea ports in the Middle Ages: they could be reached by sea-going ships.

Other towns grew in the shelter of castles or monasteries, which provided a refuge in troubled times. Towns meant money, and many landlords planned and built towns as an investment. Stratford-on-Avon, for example, was the result of an investment by the Bishop of Worcester.

As these settlements grew larger, the craftsmen and merchants (a merchant was simply a man who bought and sold goods – often a craftsman-shopkeeper) began to seek some control over their own affairs, or at least to regain the rights they had possessed in Anglo-Saxon times, when the towns were more privileged. Landlords were not always willing to grant privileges to the

*Most clothes were made at home, but they could also be bought at shops and country fairs.*

towns, but often did so because the townsfolk were prepared to pay for them – and landlords were usually in need of cash. The granting of a royal charter, which gave a town some self-government, was one way in which the king could raise money. Once a town had gained its charter, it attracted more and more people from the country roundabout.

Towns often had to struggle hard for their privileges. In the Middle Ages the town of King's Lynn – one of the richest towns in the country – was known as Bishop's Lynn. Its lord was the bishop of Norwich, and the citizens of Lynn had to struggle for generations to throw off the control of the bishop.

The chief citizens of a town would band together to form a guild (or gild) merchant. This was an organization of the chief tradesmen – all those who enjoyed full rights of citizenship. We only have to look at the guildhalls that still stand in many old cities to realize how important the guild was to the medieval town.

It is easy to think of the guilds as the ancestors of trade unions. They had some

characteristics in common: like the unions, they were concerned with protecting the interests of their members. But the society of a medieval town was vastly different from the type of society we live in. The differences between a medieval guild and a modern trade union were greater than the similarities.

The guild merchant controlled all trade in the town. It also looked after matters of justice and welfare – the tasks of local government nowadays. It governed prices, and prevented anyone who was not a member from carrying on business in the town: no 'foreigners' (and that meant anyone from outside the town) were allowed to trade; or if they were, they had to pay a hefty tax. However, the guild tried to be fair. Profits were controlled, and anyone who sold

*Among all their other purposes, guilds held regular feasts, where the members sometimes ate and drank a little too much.*

poor-quality goods would be punished by the guild court.

Within their narrow limits, some guilds were democratic. Officials were often elected (to hold office in a guild was unpopular as it was unpaid). But in practice, and in spite of the fact that no one was supposed to make larger profits than another, guilds were sometimes dominated by the richest members.

Guilds were not only concerned with business affairs. A member of the guild was expected to be a good man as well as an honest tradesman. As in every institution in the Middle Ages, religion played an important part. When the guild put on its annual entertainment, as many did, the subject of the play was usually religious. Some guilds had their own altar in the church, and some put up stained-glass windows which have lasted to this day.

The merchants obviously benefited by forming a guild. But others benefited too. Buyers were not cheated, and the lord, whether he were a local baron or bishop or, as he often was, the king himself, found it easier to deal with the citizens of a town as a single body. So he sometimes encouraged them to form a guild. The merchant guild often was, or became, the town government.

In the 13th century, when towns were growing fast, craft guilds appeared. They had the same purposes as the merchant guilds, except that membership was restricted to a single craft – weavers, butchers, shoemakers, etc. In time, the craft guilds, in spite of frequent quarrels among themselves, replaced the merchant guilds, and the heads of each craft guild often formed the town council.

# Country Life in the Middle Ages

Although towns were growing fast, both in size and importance, in medieval England, most people lived in the country. There were almost as many villages then as there are now, and as the population was about fifty times smaller, it is obvious that the villages must have been very small. A village of five hundred people – about a hundred households – was larger than average.

If the villages were small, so were the houses of the villagers, which were usually just one room. A cottage built in 1325 for a man named Whitring, who had a wife and child, measured about 7 metres by 3.5 metres. Ten houses like that would fit on a tennis court. The Whitrings were poor people, and another cottage, built for the widow of a tenant farmer, was larger. It had three doors and two windows, which were covered by wooden shutters, not glass.

These cottages of the poorer people were ramshackle little buildings. Not one of them has survived the centuries, so we cannot be certain what they were like. Some were built of timber, but many had mud walls and a mud floor. Probably they were little different from the poorer homes of Saxon and Norman times, or from the shacks found in the wilder parts of the country up to the 18th and 19th centuries. One advantage of such miserable homes was that, as they were so small and simple, with no floor or foundations, moving house was easy. The whole thing could be hoisted on to a cart and shifted to a new position.

The poorer people of the countryside – labourers and serfs – had few possessions. Some farm tools – axe, hoe, bill-hook and spade – and a few pieces of furniture –

stools, a chest and a table, perhaps a bed in which the whole family slept – these were all they had.

Their food was simple too. Bread and beer were the usual diet, but both depended on a good harvest. One or two bad harvests in a row, and the country was in the grip of famine. It would be hard to say how many people actually starved to death in England, but certainly many died as a result of a poor or skimpy diet. Meat was a luxury, though there was some mutton and beef and there was often a pig in the yard, so bacon could be had now and then. With the pig were some hens, which provided eggs until the day when the hens took their place in the pot.

Vegetables – peas and beans and some simple root vegetables which have since been replaced by better types – were grown by the villagers and cheese was made locally too. People ate a good deal of fish, not only fish like trout and herring, but also fresh-water fish which we seldom eat nowadays, such as pike and bream. Every manor and monastery had its fishpond where carp grew fat; and fish, like meat, was salted for the winter months. Salmon ran up the Thames in those days, and some people must have eaten very well at times.

The trouble was that food supplies were unreliable. Nowadays we get upset when a spell of dry weather forces up the price of potatoes, but in the Middle Ages, problems of that kind were a hundred times worse.

Human slavery had disappeared, but people were still slaves to the weather. An extra-cold winter could kill the seed in the ground. Storms could destroy the harvest. The price of corn varied enormously from year to year, and after several bad harvests bread might cost ten times as much as it did in good times. Poor people then were forced to scrabble for bark and berries.

There was another source of food besides the fields and the fishponds – the forests. There were far more deer than people in the British Isles and swarms of other animals, large and small. Rabbits were a menace to crops in some parts: they often ended their lives in a peasant's snare. Game was strictly protected, as it always was in England from Norman times to the 19th century, but that did not stop people taking it. Poaching was the most common crime in the countryside. Even clergymen took part, and efforts to prevent it were useless. With dogs and nets, with crossbow and trap, with hawk or hounds, the Englishman eagerly pursued the birds and beasts of the forest – for sport if not for food. Neither laws nor gamekeepers stopped him.

Law enforcement was no better in the country than in the town. Life was short and violent, and the records of the old manor courts tell many a nasty tale of muggings and murders. Most men carried a weapon, and people who carry weapons usually end by using them. A man named John Smith was fined 3s 4d (16½pence) for drawing a

*A 15th-century yeoman's house built in the 'half-timbered' style. A large hall was still the main room.*

knife to stab a curate. So small a fine (though money was worth a hundred times more) must mean that the crime was not really considered too serious.

Was the lack of police such a bad thing for ordinary people? The poor and the weak, especially women, must have suffered most from lack of protection. But if all the laws had been enforced, then in many ways people would have been worse off. If the laws against poaching had worked, for example, many a peasant's family would have eaten less well. If the laws of Edward III against rises in wages had been obeyed, workers would have been poorer. Tougher law enforcement might have made life for ordinary people more oppressive than it was anyway, or it might have caused more and fiercer outbreaks like the Peasants' Revolt of 1381 (*see page 74*).

One of the demands of Wat Tyler and other leaders of the peasants was the ending of serfdom. We know that serfdom was already disappearing, and that the old duties of tenants to their lord, such as working in his fields, were being replaced by simple cash payments: instead of paying their rent with labour and crops, more and more tenants paid in cash. Serfdom did not disappear in a moment, and many curious old rights and duties survived in places for hundreds of years. But this general development – the increasing independence of peasants from their lord – continued. (Perhaps the Peasants' Revolt speeded it up, perhaps it slowed it down – that is one of the questions historians enjoy arguing about.)

From the old class of peasants tied by numberless duties to their lord, two types of people emerged. The first was the ordinary farm worker. He was a man who owned no land, except perhaps a vegetable plot, and worked for a weekly wage. His place in life had not changed very much, except that he was no longer under the weighty protection of a lord. He could move more easily to another district, or perhaps (especially if he were skilled in some craft) to the nearest

town. Norwich, one of the three largest towns after London, contained people from some 400 Norfolk manors Not all of them were free men; some were runaway serfs, who gained their freedom automatically after an absence of a year and a day.

The second type emerging from the peasants was the yeoman. This rather vague word usually means a small, independent farmer. But a 'yeoman' could also be the steward of a castle, a miller, a dealer in corn, or any countryman who had risen above the class of peasant though not to the rank of knight. (The original Robin Hood was a yeoman, not the nobleman of later versions of the story.)

The English yeoman holds a rather heroic place in history. It was he, we are told, who won the battle of Agincourt, and he was the subject of any number of patriotic ballads. This is partly romance. The English showed the same kind of affectionate respect for sailors – 'jolly tars' – in the 19th century, although most sailors would rather have been anywhere else than in the navy.

Yet the yeoman must not be dismissed. He was, in a sense, the 'backbone of England', energetic, clever, rough and successful. He produced more of the country's wealth than any other class, and he was soon to gain a powerful voice in the way the country was run. Looking far ahead, we can see Oliver Cromwell emerging from old yeoman-farmer stock.

History books have to discuss people as classes, groups and categories. Of course this is not true to life. Only think of the people living in any one street or block of flats: how would you put an Irish building worker, a bank clerk's widow, a West Indian window cleaner, a director of a catering firm and a writer of books all in one class or category? Life was simpler in the Middle Ages but, then as now, people were individuals. Historians have to remind themselves of that whenever they make grand statements about 'peasants' or 'yeomen' or 'the middle classes'.

*Fairs were held at certain places once or twice a year, and lasted several days. The most successful became international markets, attended by dealers from Spain, Holland, Scandinavia and other countries.*

# Sports, Games and Entertainment

Medieval people did not have much time for entertainment. Except for the small upper class, they spent all the daylight hours working, except on Sundays, and then no noisy games and shows were supposed to take place. In spite of this, there was almost as great a variety of games and entertainment in the Middle Ages as there is now. Man is an inventive creature, never more than when he is thinking of ways to keep himself amused.

Most entertainment was amateur – the kind of thing still sometimes seen in village halls. There were no printed books, so story-telling, often in verse, was a popular amusement, as it had been in Anglo-Saxon times. However, professional performers did exist: travelling musicians, actors, jugglers and clowns. Though they were popular, the authorities, especially the Church, frowned on them. Certainly, some of their performances were crude: stripteasers were

*Boys playing club ball, the ancestor of rounders and possibly of cricket too.*

not unknown, and plays and songs were often very coarse, more so than they are today. The Church might disapprove of all rough entertainments, but the clergy enjoyed them too. At the annual 'Feast of

Fools', a choirboy dressed up as a bishop and preached the sermon. This type of fun, when everyone behaved like an idiot for a few hours, was popular with all kinds of people.

The better type of entertainer, such as the professional musician who held regular jobs in noble households, helped to improve the reputation of his profession. A respectable guild of musicians existed in London and other towns.

*Football, played with a pig's bladder, was a tough game with no rules.*

The rich also kept zoos for their amusement. King Henry II sometimes travelled around with his tame bear, and Henry III kept an elephant in the Tower of London. Performing bears were popular attractions at the fairs, and large animals like bears and bulls were 'baited' with dogs – a nasty sport, like cock fighting, which was also popular.

For anyone who could afford it, hunting was the finest sport, though a medieval huntsman would have laughed at the idea of chasing so miserable an animal as a fox. The kingly stag was his quarry. Hawking – setting tame hawks after game birds – was equally popular. It was more strictly a sport than hunting, as it did not bring in much food for the pot and it was expensive: the professional falconer was a skilled man.

Indoor games could be played during the long winter evenings. Gambling with dice was one of the oldest games; playing cards did not appear until the 14th century. Various board games, something like ludo or checkers, were played, sometimes on 'boards' scratched on stone benches which have lasted to this day. Of games still played now, the commonest were backgammon and, among the upper classes, chess, a 'war game' invented in ancient Persia. The British Museum has a set of chessmen from Scotland which were made from walrus tusks in the 12th century.

Children had more time for games than adults. The ancestors of many of the ball games we know today were played by young people in the Middle Ages. But we would not recognize them. There were no set rules, no pitches or courts, and any number could play. Medieval football, played with a pig's bladder, was more like a

*A cruel but popular entertainment was to set two cocks fighting. Special 'cockpits' were built.*

riot than a game. It might go on all day, and cover several kilometres of country.

With no police, the authorities were afraid of all occasions when large mobs of people gathered together. Laws were passed against football and other games declaring – in vain – that they should not be played. The government wanted young men to practise

archery instead. Not only was it less likely to end in a riot, it was good training for future soldiers. But even kings played football. In the accounts of the Lord Treasurer of Scotland in 1497 there is a charge for buying 'fut ballis' for the king. Henry VIII of England was a keen tennis player, and his

*Duelling with staves was an old English sport.*

tennis court at Hampton Court Palace is still in use, though it has been rebuilt. This was 'real' tennis: lawn tennis is a recent invention. The strange shape of a real tennis court, and of fives and squash courts, is a reminder that such games were first played in the courtyards of castles and monasteries.

The national summer game of Scotland is golf, and it was popular enough in the 15th century to be forbidden – always a sure sign that a game was growing. As usual, the ban was disobeyed; no player was more keen than King James IV himself. Golf did not catch on in England, but judging by the illustrations on old manuscripts, games that look vaguely like hockey and cricket (or baseball) were being played in England in the late Middle Ages.

In medieval London boys and young men – apprentices, labourers and craftsmen – played games in the fields on Sunday after-

*Experts believe that this chess set dates from the 11th or 12th century. Known as the Lewis set, the pieces were found on the west coast of the Isle of Lewis and are attributed to Scandinavian craftsmen working in Scotland.*

gallant to ladies. A knight was expected to be not only a man of war but a man of honour, in all his dealings with other people, including enemies. The word chivalry originally meant the knightly class, as in the phrase, 'the chivalry of England'. It came to mean also the behaviour or way of life of the good knight: chivalry had its own set of rules for correct behaviour.

Like many fine ideas, chivalry unfortunately remained little more than that – a fine idea. Knights all too often behaved in a way that no one could call chivalrous. People spoke of 'chivalry' in the same way as many 'religious' people have fought for their 'beliefs'. In both cases, the idea is far from the facts.

Still, there were some truly chivalrous knights about, men who tried to live up to the ideal of chivalry that is expressed in the

noons. Older citizens used to ride out to watch. Although they played rough types of ball games, the more common sports were physical contests of some sort, like wrestling or quintain. The object in this game was to strike a target with a lance, sometimes from a wooden horse on wheels, or from a boat. It was a simple form of the favourite 'game' of the ruling class – the tournament, in which knights jousted on horseback.

Like other, less spectacular, medieval games, the tournament was really a war exercise. One reason for encouraging tournaments was that the French knights were better fighters than the English, probably because they had practised this form of jousting: tournaments began in France.

The tournament was also a display of chivalry, that important ideal of how knights – we could say 'gentlemen' – should behave, which is portrayed in so much of the art and literature of the Middle Ages. Chivalry was more than a matter of being romance of King Arthur and his Knights of the Round Table – a popular story throughout Europe.

The earliest tournaments in England were held in the 12th century. They were knockabout affairs, with many people taking part and quite a few getting badly injured or killed. Edward I, who was himself a fine performer in the joust, tidied things up. Proper rules were made, and arenas set aside especially for jousting.

Those taking part paid an entrance fee, and used blunted weapons. Helped by the development of stouter armour, serious injuries became less common. The tournament grew into more of a social occasion, like the Royal Ascot race meeting, where more attention is paid to ladies' hats than to race horses. But it also had a practical purpose. A young knight without fame or fortune might, by his success in the tournament, win himself a reputation and the hand in marriage of a rich – perhaps even beautiful – wife.

*In the tournament, knights charged full-tilt with lances. The marshal, or umpire, ensured chivalrous behaviour.*

# The Wars of the Roses

For much of the 15th century England was troubled by disorder and civil war. The original cause of the trouble began in the 14th century, with the large family of Edward III, which resulted in rivalry and conflict among his descendants.

Edward III was succeeded by his grandson Richard II, son of the Black Prince. Richard was a gifted but unreliable man. He made the mistake which King John had made before him and Charles I was to make after him: he thought of himself – the king – as the fount of all law. The king could do no wrong. He confiscated the estates of his powerful cousin, Henry of Lancaster (son of John of Gaunt), while Henry was abroad, but was taken by surprise when Henry returned with an army and threw him off the throne.

Henry IV (1367–1413) wore the crown that he had won uneasily, and he was handicapped by the debts he owed to the great nobles who had helped him overthrow Richard. His son, Henry V (1387–1422), was strong and popular, but he died young, leaving the crown to his nine-months-old son. Henry VI (1421–71) grew up to be a gentle, likeable man, though not always quite sane. He was not the man to keep his father's French conquests; nor to deal with the Kentish rebels led by Jack Cade, who forced him to flee from London in 1450; least of all could he control the bickering nobles, whose quarrels soon developed into civil war.

The Wars of the Roses have a romantic name, but it is a false one. It is a label invented later, and refers to the emblem of a red rose sometimes worn by supporters of the House of Lancaster and the white rose of the House of York. The conflict was hardly a war at all, more of a family feud fought out by the servants and tenants of the leading families. The armies were small, few big battles were fought, and no expensive sieges were undertaken. The numbers killed were small, as the idea was to kill or capture only the nobles. When Edward IV

*An early siege gun which fired stone balls at the enemy. Gunpowder was used in the 14th century, but for a long time guns were weak and unreliable.*

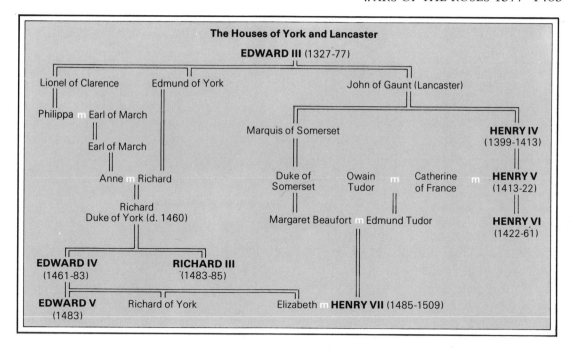

The Houses of York and Lancaster

EDWARD III (1327-77)

Lionel of Clarence     Edmund of York                John of Gaunt (Lancaster)

Philippa m Earl of March          Marquis of Somerset                    HENRY IV
                                                                         (1399-1413)
Earl of March

Anne m Richard          Duke of          Owain   m   Catherine   m   HENRY V
                        Somerset         Tudor        of France      (1413-22)
Richard
Duke of York (d. 1460)   Margaret Beaufort m Edmund Tudor           HENRY VI
                                                                     (1422-61)

EDWARD IV          RICHARD III
(1461-83)          (1483-85)

EDWARD V    Richard of York         Elizabeth m HENRY VII (1485-1509)
(1483)

(1442–83) prepared to chase the fleeing Lancastrians at Towton, he called to his men, 'Spare the commons! Kill the lords!'

The effect on the economy was not too serious either. There were some slumps in the cloth trade, but they did not last long.

Looking back, we can see that England in the 15th century was on the verge of a speedy growth in prosperity. The country had great potential, and all it needed was the security of a strong government. Some people, merchants especially, recognized this at the time, and one reason for the eventual victory of the Yorkists was that people were fed up with danger and uncertainty and were ready to back the power that looked like restoring order soonest. But the accession of the Yorkist leader as Edward IV and the defeat of the Lancastrians at Towton, fought in falling snow in 1461, did not end the wars. Edward lost the throne in 1470–71, when his powerful cousin, the Earl of Warwick, known as 'the King-Maker', changed sides. Poor bewildered Henry VI was briefly restored to the throne and Edward fled. But he soon returned, defeated Warwick at the battle of Barnet in 1471, and made his throne secure.

Edward died in 1483 leaving two small sons, Edward V and Richard, in the care of his brother, Richard, Duke of Gloucester (1452–85). On the excuse that his brother's marriage had been unlawful and his children therefore illegitimate, Richard had himself crowned king as Richard III. The young princes were at that time living in the Tower of London, which was a palace as well as a prison; soon they disappeared and were never seen again.

Who did away with the princes in the Tower? It is the most famous question in English history. In the 16th century, no one doubted that the villain was their uncle, Richard. But that may have been the result of the propaganda of the Tudor dynasty, whose founder, Henry VII, had gained the throne by defeating and killing Richard III at Bosworth (1485). In recent times, many ingenious explanations have been made of the fate of the princes, which attempt to prove someone else – maybe agents of Henry VII – was guilty. But although no one thinks Richard murdered the boys with his own hands, many people find it hard to believe that he had nothing to do with their convenient deaths.

# Chapter 6

## Art and Music in the Middle Ages

Most art in the Middle Ages was religious. The finest examples are still to be seen in the cathedrals and churches of the country. However, religion was not sharply separated from ordinary life. In early stained-glass windows, like those in Canterbury Cathedral, we can see everyday activities – a monk teaching schoolboys, a farmer sowing seed, etc. These scenes appear in richly glowing colours. The blues of the 13th century glass are mysteriously strong and deep; no one was able to reproduce this effect until the 20th century.

Unfortunately, not much early stained glass has survived in England (there is more in France). Still less has survived of the wall paintings and embroidered altar cloths and

*At Canterbury Cathedral, Kent, English medieval glass of the finest quality can be seen.*

robes which also decorated churches. In the middle ages, churches were more colourful and less severe than they usually look now.

Making colours was a difficult process without modern chemicals, and that is probably one reason why people were so fond of vivid colours. Religious books – all made by hand – were ornaments as well as things to read. Every margin and spare corner was crowded with figures of people and animals, often against a background of twining leaves and flowers.

There was little sculpture before the 14th century, and not many painted pictures, though we have a few painted on wooden panels. There are some portraits and tomb carvings of kings, though they are not what we would call lifelike. When a medieval sculptor carved a figure for a tomb he did not try to make it look like the dead man he was commemorating. He simply made a standard, handsome, medieval face. That is why portraits of early English kings all look alike: it was not just family resemblance.

Other paintings were treated in this way too. The medieval artist did not try to be realistic. When he painted a tree, he painted a symbol of a tree, as young children often do. It was a perfectly recognizable tree, but it was not any particular tree. If there was a forest, all the trees were the same.

By the reign of Richard II (1377–99), which was a splendid period for the arts and literature, realistic portraits were appearing. We have, for example, several portraits of the king himself. (The most famous is the Wilton Diptych in the National Gallery, London.) By comparing them, we can tell what Richard looked like: a foxy-faced man with a sharp nose and small chin. Even the painting in Westminster Abbey, which was in the 'old-fashioned' style – showing a typical medieval kingly figure sitting stiffly on a throne – has the same face as the Wilton portrait.

Medieval church music was simple but beautiful. Harmony had already been developed in the monasteries by the 12th century. Gradually, more complicated forms of harmony were devised, leading in 16th-century Italy to the music of Palestrina, which some people would say is the most beautiful church music ever written.

Secular ('non-church') music was also growing in the Middle Ages. It was mostly ballads and love songs, often performed by travelling musicians. We hear a lot about 'troubadors' in France and 'master singers' in Germany (the latter are the heroes of two operas by Wagner). There is the story too of how King Richard I's place of imprisonment was discovered by his faithful minstrel, Blondel, singing outside the prison walls.

Travelling minstrels accompanied themselves on simple stringed instruments. There were as many different musical instruments then as in a modern orchestra; but we would not easily recognize most of them, perhaps not even the cathedral organs. There was a great organ at Winchester in the 12th century which was said to need seventy people at the bellows to keep it going. Two organists played the notes by smiting the keys with their fists.

*A contemporary painting of medieval musicians; one man playing a portable organ, another an early violin, while the third sings.*

*The Wilton Diptych is dated about 1380 and shows Richard II and his patron saint (left) and the Virgin Mother and Child (right).*

*An exquisitely embroidered ecclesiastical robe, made in 1350.*

# Literature in the Middle Ages

Educated people in the Middle Ages usually read and wrote Latin or French. But poems and songs had been composed in English since Anglo-Saxon times. Besides religious poetry, there were many ballads and songs which have been lost with the passing centuries. Of those that have survived, we seldom know the names of the authors, who were often wandering entertainers, or 'gleemen'. The idea of chivalry inspired many writers, including Thomas Malory, whose *Morte d'Arthur*, written in the 15th century, is the first great story in English prose. It tells of King Arthur and his Knights – a story well-known in earlier versions.

Poetry often did not rhyme; it was based on rhythm and alliteration (starting syllables sounding similar – a good example), as in the famous *Vision Concerning Piers the Plowman*. Written by William Langland about 1375, the poem attacked the evils of the time and celebrated the good and simple life of the ploughman.

At this time there was no such language as 'standard' English. People spoke the dialect of their district, and a man from Sussex could hardly understand a man from Northumbria.

The dialect that became the accepted form of English was the East Midlands dialect, partly because it was the dialect of Geoffrey Chaucer (1340–1400). For that, and for his use of a form of verse called the heroic couplet (two rhyming lines of ten syllables each), Chaucer deserves his honorary title of father of English literature.

Like Shakespeare or Dickens, Chaucer understood people of all sorts, the mighty and the humble. Though he wrote in verse, his greatest gift was for straightforward story-telling. In a later age he would have been a playwright or novelist. He was not greatly interested in general ideas, more in the oddities of ordinary people. He is England's greatest comic poet, and although he is difficult to read because the language has changed so much (modern 'translations' can be found), we still find him entertaining.

Chaucer's most famous work is *The Canterbury Tales,* a series of stories told by each member of a party of pilgrims travelling from London to St Thomas's shrine at Canterbury. Some are very funny, like the Wife of Bath, some moving, like the Knight's

*Three characters from Chaucer's Canterbury Tales: the Miller, the Cook, and the Wife of Bath.*

*'Mystery' plays were for the 'man in the street' — and that was where they were performed.*

Tale, and some richly earthy, like the Miller's Tale. They are all extremely English: for the first time, in Chaucer, we get a vivied picture of real English characters, a portrait of life as it was for ordinary people in the England of the late 14th century.

The great achievements of this period which included John Wyclif's English Bible as well as Chaucer's work, were not equalled in the 15th century. Chaucer had imitators in England, but the best poets writing in English came from Scotland. William Dunbar (born about 1460) is the most famous – a kind of 15th century Rabbie Burns, though he was a Franciscan friar. He wrote crisp, punchy verse, using rhyme and alliteration, and his insults were as savage as any in later literature.

The earliest plays in England were in Latin, and they were really lessons in religion. By 1300 they were also being performed in English, and the actors were ordinary people, though the subjects of the plays were still religious. Several series, or cycles, of 'mystery' plays were written in the 14th century to be performed by the guilds ('mystery' was another word for 'craft'), especially in the north of England. The stage was a cart, which could be moved from one part of town to another. On the feast day when the plays were performed, the audience could see the whole cycle, each play performed by a different guild. All parts were played by men, as they still were in Shakespeare's time, and although the purpose was serious and educational, there was plenty of rough humour too. The composer Benjamin Britten (1913–1976) based his opera *Noah's Flood* on one of these old mystery or 'miracle' plays.

A later development was the 'morality' play, in which the characters are not individuals, like Noah, but ideas personified, like Idleness, Death, or Everyman. This was a fashion that did not last long.

# The Building of Churches and Castles

The greatest creations of the Middle Ages were churches. Nowadays, a town council with money to spare builds new houses or a new pool. In the Middle Ages, it rebuilt its church. People strove to create larger and grander churches; if one town erected a tall spire, the next town built one taller.

We know little about the actual building of churches. There were no professional architects in the Middle Ages, and only occasionally do we find a man like Alan of Walsingham, designer of the Octagon tower of Ely cathedral. As a rule, the most important person involved was the master mason, who was a craftsman, though a craftsman of a very superior kind who talked on equal terms with bishops, even kings, about the work in progress. The masons had one of the strongest of medieval guilds. They moved about from one building site to another, in wild and lonely places if they were building a border castle. At each place they erected their 'lodge', a lean-to shed which was their home from home.

Few stone buildings were built in Britain before 1066, but the Normans were great builders of castles, and cathedrals. They introduced the style known as Norman, or Romanesque – 'like the Romans'. Durham Cathedral (*see page 41*) is mainly a Norman building. The Norman style lasted until the late 12th century, when it was replaced by Gothic, which many people still think of as the best possible style for churches.

It would be hard to describe the Gothic style in a few words, but the breakaway from Norman is easily seen in the use of pointed, instead of rounded, arches. This allowed greater height, thinner walls (supported by buttresses) and larger windows. It was a great technical advance, and the insides of churches became much lighter and more open.

All medieval art and architecture is called Gothic, but of course styles did not remain unchanged between 1200 and 1500. The first great phase of Gothic in England is known as Early English: its most famous example is Salisbury Cathedral (*see page 66*). By about 1300 a new phase had appeared, which is known as Decorated. As the name suggests, it was more ornamental: the vaults (curved stone ceilings) of churches sprouted a pattern of intersecting ribs, making a web-like pattern, and elaborate stone canopies were built over tombs.

So far, English architecture had remained close to continental, especially French, styles; but the Hundred Years' War created anti-French feeling which helped the growth not only of English literature but also a more national style of architecture. This final phase of Gothic, beginning about 1340, is called Perpendicular. The word means 'straight up', and it is another good description, as any visitor to Cambridge can see in the chapel of King's College. Slim, attached columns ascend dizzily to delicate sprays of 'fan vaulting' high overhead, and the sides of the building are filled with great shimmering windows of stained and painted glass. The Gothic style could go no further.

Castles changed less than churches in style, as their purpose was defence, not beauty. It is possible to see how the new ideas of the Decorated period affected the Welsh castles of Edward I when they are compared with earlier, Norman castles; but more important was the lie of the land and the danger of attack. The development from a square building to one based on the plan of circles within circles was caused by military thinking rather than changing fashion. When gunpowder and artillery became really effective, castles became lower and walls thicker – as in the squat, coastal castles built at Deal and other places by Henry VIII, the last genuine castles to be built in England.

*The spectacular vault and stained-glass windows of King's College Chapel, Cambridge.*

# The Birth of New Ideas

In the last half of the 15th century, many old customs and ways of thinking were dying, and people were learning to look at the world in a new light. This change of ideas, which marks the beginning of modern times, is called the Renaissance ('rebirth').

One important influence in the Renaissance was a revival of interest in the ancient Greeks and Romans, whose ideas, art and standard of living were in some ways superior to those of the Middle Ages. The ancient Greeks and Romans were 'pagans': they had lived before the age of Christianity. Although they had religions of their own, they took them less seriously than medieval people took Christianity, and were much more interested in ordinary people, as individuals. This interest in man – his mind and body and all his works – was another aspect of the Renaissance.

Gothic artists had painted the human figure as though it had no bones – the fingers curving smoothly with no apparent joints. A Renaissance artist like Leonardo da Vinci cut up dead bodies to see how they were made, and when he drew a human figure he saw in his mind's eye the skeleton beneath the skin. Others dissected bodies for practical reasons: the Italian physician Vesalius founded the science of anatomy with his book *On the Fabric of the Human Body* (1543). Copernicus studied the anatomy of the universe. He founded modern astronomy with his work proving that the earth revolved around the sun.

Scholars began to ask questions about things they had long taken for granted, including the Christian Church. They rediscovered the wisdom of ancient writers, which led them to make discoveries of their own.

The Renaissance began in Italy and spread all through Europe. It was not an event with a sharp beginning and end, but a slow transformation spread over many years. In Italy the Renaissance was underway by the beginning of the 14th century. But if we had to pick out twenty years in English history when the Renaissance, measured by the output of writers and artists, was at its height, we would probably pick the last twenty years of the 16th century.

*Caxton's printing mark. Of about a hundred books printed by Caxton, over a third exist today.*

*William Caxton set up his wooden press at Westminster in 1476*

*This illustration was one of the first printed by Caxton.*

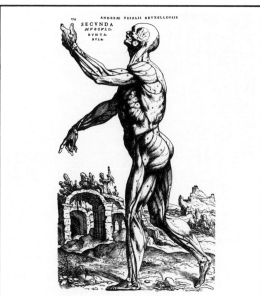

*The Italian physician, Vesalius, founded the science of anatomy with his book* On the Fabric of the Human Body.

The spread of the new learning would have been impossible without an invention of the 15th century which was to have effects on the future so great that they cannot be calculated even now. This was the invention of printing. Before, all books were manuscripts. Extra copies had to be written out by hand. But printed books could be quickly reproduced in hundreds. Not only was this vastly less expensive, it meant that a book written in Paris could be read a few months later in London, Hamburg, Rome and Madrid.

The first English printer was William Caxton, who set up his press in Westminster in 1476. Caxton and his successor, Wynkin de Worde (a good name for a printer), produced over 200 books by the end of the century, including Malory's *Morte d'Arthur* and Chaucer's *Canterbury Tales*. Printers, unlike the makers of manuscripts, were not clergymen: they printed in English as well as Latin and they were interested in a variety of non-religious subjects. Besides stories and poems, Caxton printed books on chess, hunting and fishing.

The new spirit of curiosity affected everything. Ships, which had for centuries clung to well-known coasts, began to push out into undiscovered seas. Columbus discovered the West Indies, and in 1497 John Cabot, an Italian in the service of King Henry VII, discovered North America. These voyages were made possible by improvements in ship-building and in methods of navigation, themselves the result of the new spirit of scientific inquiry.

A more practical reason for the voyages of discovery was the desire to find new trade routes to the East, since the old overland routes were falling under the control of hostile Muslim peoples. In 1453 the Ottoman Turks captured the city of Constantinople, centre of a Christian empire in the Near East for a thousand years. Refugees from Constantinople fled to Western Europe, bringing with them old Greek and Roman books which had been lost in the west. Another important source of knowledge was the Muslim society of North Africa and Arabia, which was more advanced than Christian Europe in the Middle Ages. There, the works of Greek scholars had been preserved in Arabic translations, which were now re-translated into Latin.

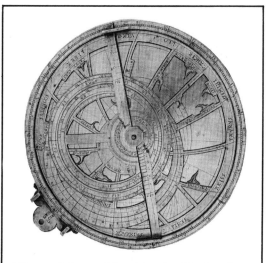

*The astrolabe, used for taking the altitudes of stars, was the predecessor of the sextant.*

# Chapter 7

## Scotland in the Age of James IV

In 1488 King James III was stabbed to death by a man disguised as a priest during a rebellion in favour of his son. The father had been an unpopular and incapable king, but the son, James IV (1473–1513), was the best king of Scots since Bruce. He was a man of many talents, a dashing general, an energetic governor, a pious Christian; intelligent and well-educated, generous, friendly and a great lover of women.

The character of the king reflected the times. The Renaissance was in full flower in Scotland, with poets like Dunbar and Robert Henryson, with splendid stone buildings and gorgeous feasts where musicians played and court ladies displayed their brilliant clothes.

The Highlands had never been, except in a remote way, a part of the Scottish realm. Among the clans, the chief ruled like the father of an old-fashioned family. His men were all related to him by blood; their possessions, which were few enough, were his; he was their protector, governor and judge. It cannot be denied that life in the Highlands was rather savage. The people were poor,

*James IV, most gifted of Scottish monarchs, always had time to admire a bold falcon or a beautiful woman.*

*The Highlanders were poor: their tough little black cattle were their most precious possessions.*

depending on their skinny black cattle for a livelihood. Their quarrels were frequent and bloody.

All this had its good side too. The old Celtic clan spirit was based on loyalty in exchange for kindness, and every Highlander was as proud of his own clan as the Macleans who cried: 'Thank God I am a Maclean!'

James IV's efforts to control the clans were more diplomatic but no more successful than earlier efforts. A revolt by the powerful Macdonalds and Macleans seemed to have ended in 1490 when Angus Og, the Lord of the Isles, was murdered. Yet it flared up again in 1501 under his son, Donald Dubh ('Black Donald').

As always, the threat from England was the greater danger. James IV, who dreamed of a new crusade to recapture Constantinople, tried to act as mediator between his old enemy, England, and his old ally, France. He signed a treaty of friendship with England and married Henry VII's daughter. But in 1512, when England joined an international alliance against France, he felt bound to help the French. Invading England with a large army in 1513, he suffered a terrible defeat at the hands of the Earl of Surrey in the battle of Flodden, and his splendid reign ended in horrible, bloody destruction. With him lying dead on Flodden field was the cream of Scottish chivalry – the great lords and earls, Highland chiefs like Campbell of Argyll, and their bravest followers.

Scotland was left in a desperate position. The ambitious English king, Henry VIII, sought to control the kingdom, and a pro-English party struggled for power in Edinburgh with a pro-French party. When the young James V became old enough to rule, and escaped from the control of plotting nobles, he reasserted Scottish independence, but was defeated at Solway Moss in 1542. He died a bitter death soon afterwards, after learning that the child his French queen was expecting had been born a girl.

This child Henry VIII was determined to marry to his sickly son, Edward VI. To enforce the match he invaded Scotland, causing frightful destruction. It was, as the Scots said, a 'rough wooing', and the infant Mary Queen of Scots was packed off to France, to marry a French prince.

# Strong Government in England

In the last thirty years of the 15th century, Edward IV died young; his heir was murdered; Richard III was killed in battle; his successor, Henry VII, resisted a dozen plots or revolts. Yet in those thirty years, a strong, secure monarchy was created.

The long, wasting Hundred Years' War with France was ended, although a firm peace was impossible and both Edward IV and Henry VII made wars against the French. But they quickly agreed to a truce in exchange for French gold. As Parliament had voted extra taxes for the campaigns, they made good profits.

The extra income was useful, as lack of money was a big problem for the royal government. In peacetime the king was expected to manage on the revenue from royal estates, customs duties, fines in the courts, and from certain ancient rights which the king held as a kind of national landlord (including, for example, the right to manage an estate when the owner was under age).

Government revenue could be increased by more efficient administration – improving the royal estates and making sure that the king actually received everything due to him. Edward IV and his successors made use of their household officials to bypass clumsy old government departments, like the Exchequer. Some of these officials came from modest backgrounds: the father of Cardinal Wolsey, chief minister of Henry VIII, was a butcher and grazier. They were professional administrators, and they were 'king's men', owing loyalty to no one else.

It was a risky profession. Henry VII employed Empson and Dudley to squeeze the last penny in taxation out of his subjects, but when Henry VIII came to the throne, he had this wolf-like couple executed for 'treason', to the great delight of the taxpayers.

The king could also increase revenue by confiscating the property of traitors. Edward IV gained the huge estates of defeated Lancastrians, and Henry VII was never short of traitors.

Far from it! Henry had won the crown by force. Several others had a better claim to it and no one could pretend that Henry was king by right. Anyone feeling annoyed with the government could support one of the pretenders who popped up claiming that they were one of the missing princes in the Tower or the Earl of Warwick (who had the best claim to the throne but really *was* in the Tower).

Yorkist pretenders found support in Ireland. Lambert Simnel, who claimed to be Earl of Warwick, was actually crowned in Dublin. In 1494 Henry VII sent out one of his household officials, Sir Edward Poynings, as governor, and he pushed a law through the Irish Parliament stating that all acts of the English Parliament should apply to Ireland also. But Poynings was recalled soon afterwards; the only part of Ireland securely under English control was the Pale (meaning 'a fenced-in area') around Dublin.

Poynings did succeed in preventing Perkin Warbeck, a more dangerous pretender than Simnel, from landing in Ireland in 1495. Warbeck eventually surrendered and was executed, as was the unlucky Warwick.

A century of foreign and civil wars had left too many men with nothing better to do than make trouble. Disorder had become a habit. Every noble had his army of 'retainers', in spite of laws against private armies. The laws had little effect until the Court of Star Chamber began to enforce them in the reign of Henry VII. This court was simply the royal council, sitting as a court of law (it took its name from the star-painted ceiling where it met). In the country, judges and juries, with the armed servants of the local lord breathing down their necks, could be easily frightened. But no one bullied the royal council.

An institution like the Court of Star Chamber smells a little of secret, political trials. But if law and order were to be restored, it was essential to cut the proud and disorderly lords and squires down to size. That was what the tough measures of Henry VII were meant to do. And they succeeded. When Henry died in 1509, he left a kingdom in which the royal government was in control, perhaps more securely than ever before.

Henry VIII (1491–1547) nearly spoiled the good work of his father. He was handsome, talented, every inch a king – but also mean and cruel. It is easy to think of him as a cruel man: he had six wives and executed two of them. But he was married to his first wife, Catherine of Aragon, for twenty years, and would never have divorced her if she had managed to bear him a son that lived.

The young Henry could not resist the glamour of war. But his men fought poorly and the French noticed that some of his cannon were made of wood. He did build up the navy, and England survived his escapades fairly well, thanks to the skilful minister, Thomas Wolsey (1475–1530).

'The Cardinal rules the king and the entire kingdom', the Venetian ambassador reported. Wolsey was certainly a magnificent figure. He improved justice, especially for the poor, but he was less successful at raising government revenue, partly because he could not handle Parliament. The Commons sometimes refused to vote for the taxes he requested.

In the end, even Wolsey's foreign policy failed. England was a small country, and Wolsey tried to gain more influence in Europe by a tricky balancing act between Francis I of France and the Emperor Charles V, who ruled most of Europe between them. But when they reached agreement at the treaty of Cambrai (1529), England was shut out. Weeks later, Wolsey fell from power.

*When dealing with the king's tax collectors, men pretended they were poor and could not afford to pay. Anyway, they thought taxes were unnecessary.*

# England becomes a Protestant State

The power and magnificence of Cardinal Wolsey caused fierce dislike, not only of him, but of the Church in general. The clergy and the pope had not grown more popular over the years. The English had become aware that they were a nation, and they resented the power of the pope in England. The pope looked more and more like a political prince and less like a religious leader. The Papal States covered a large part of Italy; the pope engaged in wars and alliances like any other ruler. He raised money by doubtful methods. It was the protest of a German monk, Martin Luther, against 'indulgencies' – bits of paper promising forgiveness of sins to anyone who bought them – that marked the beginning of the Protestant revolt against the Roman Church.

Many of Luther's ideas had been held by John Wyclif in the 14th century. But he added his important belief in 'justification by faith'. This meant that it was only necessary for a person to have faith in Jesus Christ to be saved. Salvation could not be 'bought' by good deeds; nor could the saints or the pope have any effect.

Luther's views spread quickly in Germany. In England, the Lollards had never died out, and the ideas of Luther and other reformers, like the Swiss, Zwingli, found a welcome.

The Protestant Reformation in England, which ended the power of the pope, was a political, not religious, reformation. King Henry VIII did not share Luther's beliefs and wrote a book attacking Luther, which so pleased the pope that he granted Henry the title *Fidei defensor*, 'defender of the Faith'. (English monarchs have kept the title: look for the letter F. D. on any coin.) However it was this religious background – with most people disgusted by some Church practices and a good many ready to become Protestants – that made the political reformation possible.

English kings had been struggling off and on against the power of the pope for centuries. But Henry VIII had a particular quarrel with Rome, which was to end in a complete break. Henry wished to divorce his wife, Catherine of Aragon. She was past the age of child-bearing and had only a daughter (Mary). Henry wanted a male heir, and he had fallen for a young woman of the court, Anne Boleyn. He had some reason for thinking that his marriage to Catherine had been illegal, as she was the widow of his brother, who had died young. In the ordinary way, the pope would probably have granted the divorce, but in 1527 he had fallen into the power of the Emperor Charles V, who was Catherine's nephew. There was no chance of him allowing the divorce.

The matter dragged on a long time. Wolsey failed to win the pope round, and fell from power. He was replaced in the king's confidence by Archbishop Cranmer (1489–1556), who was secretly favourable

*Anne Boleyn, Henry VIII's second wife, beheaded in 1536.*

*Not all rebellions are revolutionary: the Pilgrimage of Grace was conservative: the rebels disliked the recent changes brought about by Thomas Cromwell.*

to Protestantism, and by Thomas Cromwell (1485–1540), who cared little for religion but was a brilliant politician and administrator.

The Reformation was largely the work of Cromwell. He really created the modern nation-state, which was defined in the most important act of the Reformation, the Act in Restraint of Appeals (1533), drafted by Cromwell. 'This realm of England is an empire', the act declared, meaning a state where there is no authority above the king. The king no longer needed a divorce from the pope: he got one from Archbishop Cranmer and married Anne Boleyn, who was already expecting the baby Elizabeth.

The importance of the political Reformation was that it was carried out by acts of Parliament. This seemed the most convenient way to go about it; but what no one, not even Cromwell, realized at the time was that it gave Parliament a more powerful position in the government. The conflict between king and Parliament lay far in the future, and no one would say that the Reformation directly caused the Civil War, over one hundred years later. But it did give Parliament a generous push up the ladder of political power.

The next step was to destroy those ancient – and rich – institutions, the monasteries. Cromwell organized an inspection which reported that the monks were corrupt and dishonest – true in some cases. The smaller monasteries were dissolved in 1536 and the larger ones in 1539. The king thereby got his hands on vast riches (the Church owned a quarter of the land in England). Yet it would be hard to say what happened to all the money, as Henry was soon short again. Most of the lands were given away or sold. Many a landed family owed its estates to the dissolution of the monasteries.

Dislike of Cromwell's actions was one of the causes of the Pilgrimage of Grace, a rebellion in the north of England in 1536. The government made vague promises to persuade the rebels to go home, but a second outbreak gave Henry's representatives the excuse they needed to hang the leaders.

# Religious Changes

Henry VIII had destroyed the power of the pope and made himself 'Supreme Head' of the English Church. But he had not changed religious belief. In his last years, Protestants were burned as heretics, although Catholics also died for refusing to accept the king as head of the Church. But Henry did appoint Protestants as guardians of the young Edward VI (1537–53), his only son, by his third wife, Jane Seymour. (Henry had three more wives but no more children.)

Under the two Lord Protectors, the dukes of Somerset and Northumberland, a religious reformation was carried out to match the political reformation. Somerset's new Prayer Book (1549) still included a form of the Roman Catholic Mass, but Northumberland's Prayer Book (1552) attacked all the customs of Rome. It even banished words like 'priest' and 'altar' as smelling of superstitious, popish practices.

Edward's death at sixteen brought to the throne Mary (1516–58), daughter of Catherine of Aragon and a devout Roman Catholic. She was determined to put the clock back, restoring not only the old religion but also the pope. But she angered many people by marrying Philip II of Spain and by burning about 300 people as Protestant heretics, earning the name 'Bloody Mary'.

Mary's sister Elizabeth (1533–1603) was the daughter of Henry VIII and Anne Boleyn and therefore, as she liked to boast, totally English. She was also a brilliant politician.

It was the task of Elizabeth and her able ministers to settle the problem of religion. There had been too many sharp changes in the previous thirty years. Elizabeth herself would have chosen the religion of Henry VIII – Catholicism without Rome. But she was pushed towards a more Protestant settlement by people influenced by John Cal-

*'Thou shalt not worship graven images,' says the Second Commandment. Protestant mobs took this literally, smashing statues in churches*

vin in Geneva, the most extreme among the great Protestant reformers.

The Elizabethan settlement was therefore Protestant, although it left some questions vague, in the hope of satisfying people of different opinions. In the 16th century religion and politics could not be separated and, although Elizabeth would have liked to be more tolerant, those who rejected the established Church were, simply, traitors. Unfortunately, that included not only Catholics who plotted against Elizabeth but also ordinary people who were loyal to the old religion.

The Scottish Church was in as bad a state as the English Church in the early 16th century, with teenage bishops, priests who could not read, and parish churches in ruins. But the Reformation came later.

An important figure in Scotland from 1542 to 1560 was the French queen-mother, Mary of Guise. She represented Scotland's past – Catholic and pro-French. But another group, growing in numbers, represented Scotland's future – Protestant and pro-English. In 1557 some Scottish lords launched the First Covenant, signed by thousands, which demanded a national, Protestant Church.

The accession of the Protestant Elizabeth in England and the death of Mary of Guise (1560) turned the tide in favour of the Protestant, English party. The Treaty of Edinburgh was the first treaty between Scotland and England sincerely based on common interests. It was a victory for Protestantism in Scotland, and it pointed towards the union of Scotland and England.

John Knox, the fiery leader of the religious reformation, began work on the foundation of a national Church. He was disciple of Calvin, and the Protestantism of Knox's Kirk ('Church') was stricter, more severe, than the Church of England. There were no bishops, for instance, no pictures or musical instruments in churches, and ministers were appointed by local 'presbyteries'.

The Kirk soon became even stricter: even the festival of Christmas was abolished. It was a rather grim country to which Mary Queen of Scots returned in 1561 after the death of her husband, the king of France. Mary was young, sexy, adventurous – and Catholic. She did not fit in Knox's Scotland, and she made things worse for herself by two quick marriages – the second husband having probably murdered the first. Eventually, she was forced to seek the protection of Queen Elizabeth in England, where she was kept under house arrest.

But in that time of plots and counterplots, Mary became involved with Catholic opponents of Elizabeth, who hoped to make her queen of England. Elizabeth hesitated to strike down a queen who was also her cousin, but in the end she signed the death warrant, and the executioner's axe ended Mary's doomed career.

*The religious settlement which established the Church of England was supported by Elizabeth I and tough bishops, like Archbishop Whitgift.*

# The Growth of England

Henry VIII's attack on the Church and the monasteries was a blow to education, especially university education. Oxford and Cambridge were themselves religious institutions of a kind: the teachers were all clergymen and the students were all training for the Church.

In the long run, the shake-up under Henry VIII improved them, making them less narrow. They admitted bright young men (no girls) who were going to be lawyers, justices, even merchants, as well as clergymen. Discipline was better since the universities had become divided into colleges. In college, teacher and pupil lived like master and apprentice: the pupil, whose age was sixteen or less, often slept in his teacher's room.

Many grammar schools were founded in the 16th century. Some grew out of old monastery schools; others were new foundations like Rugby and Harrow. They admitted clever boys as well as rich ones, and could rightly be called 'public' schools.

Life never stands still, but in the Middle Ages changes had taken place slowly. In the 16th century, everything began to happen faster.

It was a time of growth. More babies were being born and people were living longer; so population was increasing. Trade was growing: cloth exports shot up in Henry VIII's reign, and though they slumped around 1550, they were soon rising again. Industry was growing: John Winchcombe had 200 weavers working for him at Newbury (so it was said), and the first deep mines were being dug. Business was growing: the Royal Exchange was founded in 1571 and London was becoming an international centre of finance. Building was growing: nearly every decent-sized house in England was 'modernized' between 1560 and 1640, and many new houses were built.

Economic growth is always exciting. It means that someone must be getting rich.

*Children learned to read from a 'hornbook', a piece of wood with a handle. The ABC on a sheet of paper was covered with a thin layer of transparent horn.*

*In 1549 rebels led by Robert Kett protested against enclosure of fields for sheep. They camped near Norwich, living off the sheep they so detested.*

But in the 16th century it did not mean that everyone's standard of living was going up, nor that the country had no serious economic difficulties. England had very severe problems, the names of which may sound familiar: inflation and unemployment.

Beginning in the late 15th century, prices began to go up, and they went on rising, sometimes slowly, sometimes more quickly, until long after 1600. By the death of Elizabeth (1603), prices were about five times what they were when her father Henry VIII became king (1509). It was the worst inflation England ever had until this century.

No one is quite certain what caused inflation then any more than they are now, but the large amount of silver pouring into Europe from Spain's new empire in America was certainly one reason. When the *amount* of money increases, its *value* goes down. Henry VIII made things worse by issuing new coins with less silver in them. That made them less valuable and sent prices up. Later, Elizabeth called in the poor coins and reissued a better coinage, but that only slowed down the price rise.

As we know, inflation hits some people harder than others. Today, most wage-earners are protected, but in the 16th century they were not. Although wages were going up as well as prices, they were not going up nearly as fast. A man who earned five shillings a week in 1500 would have earned six or seven shillings by 1600. But the amount of bread that he could buy for one shilling in 1500 would have cost five shillings in 1600.

Inflation also caused difficulties for landlords and tenants. Some tenants were protected against an increase in rent by the terms of their lease. But when the lease ended, the landlord, who had been chewing his nails watching prices shoot up while his income remained the same, seized the

119

*People were frightened by the great number of beggars roaming the country.*

chance to raise the rent sky-high, often far above what the tenant could pay. Probably the landlord wanted to get rid of the tenant because, when the price of food was rising fast while farm workers' wages were rising slowly, it was more profitable to be a farmer, growing crops for sale, than to rent the land to a tenant.

Farming became more efficient. Landlords got rid of the old system of strip farming when they could, and made the land into regular fields enclosed by fences. 'Enclosure' had been going on since the 14th century and it continued into the 19th; but it was in the 16th century that it caused the loudest complaints. Some landlords enclosed old common land, ignoring the right of the peasants to graze their animals there. But others enclosed marshland and, by good drains, made the barren marshes fertile.

Where land was enclosed for ordinary crop farming, few people complained because it led to better farming and did not deprive people of work. It was the other kind of enclosure – for sheep pasture – that caused the fuss, because that did put people out of work. As one expert explained, 'where both corn of all sorts and cattle of all kind were reared afore time, now is there nothing but only sheep. And instead of some 100 to 200 persons that had their livings thereon, now be there but three or four shepherds and the master only that hath a living thereof'. Yet historians tell us that the amount of land enclosed in the 16th century was quite small, much less than in the 18th. Enclosure certainly caused some misery, and Parliament tried to stop it, but it seems also to have been a scapegoat for all difficulties, just as today's troubles are sometimes blamed on 'trade unions'.

Unemployment in 16th century England was very high. One man in four or five was without a proper job. Some were unlucky people who for one reason or another – perhaps because they were blind or crippled – could not work. Others could not get work, and some did not want it. They included ex-soldiers, the men who had once made up the private armies of the nobles; monks who no longer had a monastery; as well as tenant farmers and farm workers who had lost their jobs to sheep enclosures.

Someone who earned no wages and owned no property could only stay alive by begging – or by stealing. Bands of these 'sturdy beggars' roamed about the country, often causing trouble.

Some roaming vagabonds lived by various kinds of crime. There were the 'hookers', for instance, who used to slink along the hedges looking for washing hung out to dry, or open bedroom windows from which they could snatch the linen with long, hooked sticks.

All governments in the 16th century tried to do something to stop the problem of roving beggars and thieves. At first, they simply announced severe punishments, but they came to recognize that not every beggar was a vagabond and that some kind of help would have to be given to those who could not earn a living. The final statement of this policy was the Elizabethan Poor Law of 1601. It aimed to put an end to beggars of all kinds, including the 'legal' beggars who had a license from the justices of the peace. The poor were put into workhouses or almshouses in each parish and local taxes – rates – were raised to pay for poor relief, including apprenticeships for the children of the poor. Roaming vagabonds were whipped and sent back to their parishes.

The main purpose of the Poor Law was to stop lawlessness and disorder in the countryside; it was not passed out of kindness. Still, in other European countries, the poor were ignored, or treated much more cruelly. The Elizabethan law was ahead of its time and lasted until 1834 almost unchanged.

The Poor Law was one example of the way in which the national government was taking control of local affairs. Wage rates, prices, trade regulations – matters that had once been managed by the guilds in each town – were controlled through acts of Parliament and enforced by local justices. Control by the government was less rigid than control by the guilds.

The government wanted to encourage foreign craftsmen, but it also wanted to keep as tight a grip on affairs as the guilds had done. The Act of Apprentices said that a boy had to serve an apprenticeship of seven years – longer than in most other countries. One advantage of so long an apprenticeship was that it kept young men out of mischief. But we should not be too cynical; the act also tried to protect workmen and apprentices by fixing wage rates.

*A shoemaker's apprentice at work.*

# Traders'Voyages and Sailors' Fights

In the 15th century, the world of 'Christendom' (Christian Europe) was a small place. Europeans knew little of other continents. A few travellers had been to Africa and Asia, but a large part of the world was undiscovered. No one knew, for example, that North and South America existed.

Ships never sailed far out of sight of land, if they could help it. Even the Portuguese, who were steadily exploring the western coasts of Africa, found it hard to break old habits and cut across the open sea. In the end they did, and discovered the route to India via the Cape of Good Hope. Meanwhile, an Italian navigator called Christopher Columbus, had boldly struck out from Spain across the Atlantic and discovered the West Indies in 1492.

The reason behind these voyages was the need to find new trade routes. Many of Europe's most valued imports came along ancient overland routes from Asia. The old

*The Italian navigator, John Cabot, sailed from Bristol under the English flag. In 1497 he sighted Newfoundland.*

routes had been taken over by a hostile Muslim people, the Ottoman Turks, who in the early 16th century advanced deep into eastern Europe. This pressure in the east forced Europe to expand to the west.

The discovery of America had proved a sad disappointment. Columbus believed that the islands he had discovered were near Japan. He expected that by advancing a little farther he would find the rich states of Cipangu and Cathay (China) where, legend said, the houses were roofed with gold. But as more ships sailed across the Atlantic and more of the New World was discovered, it became clear that Columbus was mistaken.

A few years later, Spain found riches enough in the New World. By conquering the peoples of Mexico and Peru, the Spaniards gained an American empire which brought them huge loads of silver.

*The Spaniards called their Armada 'invincible'; and it was true that English guns actually sank few Spanish ships. But they won the battle.*

As for Newfoundland, it was half-forgotten. Bristol fishermen sailed there to catch cod, but the mainland did not look attractive.

By the time of Elizabeth, everyone knew that America was a new continent. Some still hoped to find a sea passage through the continent, to Asia. Martin Frobisher, a very tough captain, sailed into a narrow inlet in northern Canada in the 1570s and, seeing Eskimos, who looked 'Asian', on the northern bank, he thought he was sailing through a strait which divided America from Asia.

But Frobisher did not find the passage to Asia, and spent most of his time collecting a worthless mineral which he thought contained gold. Later captains, like John Davis and Henry Hudson, had no better luck; yet the attempt to find an eastern passage, north of Norway, did lead to the beginnings of new trade with Russia and the Near East.

America was not just an obstruction in the way to Asia, and many Elizabethans thought that some use could be made of the place. Sir Humphrey Gilbert tried to start a colony in Newfoundland, and his half-brother, Sir Walter Raleigh, one of the ablest men at Elizabeth's court, founded a colony on an island off North Carolina. The colonists disappeared without a trace, but another attempt was made in 1607, at

Jamestown, Virginia. This time the settlement took root. The colonists survived hunger, disease, quarrels among themselves, and an Indian attack. Jamestown became the first permanent English colony in North America.

One reason why the English took such a long time to become interested in North America was that Spain claimed ownership of both continents, North and South, and refused to allow foreigners to settle or even trade there. Spain and England were joined by a friendly treaty of Henry VII's time; Henry VIII had married a Spanish princess and Mary Tudor had married the Spanish king, Philip II. It was only in the reign of Elizabeth that Spain slowly changed from a friend to an enemy.

Philip II of Spain was the greatest Catholic monarch in Europe and leader of the Counter-Reformation – the attack on Protestantism. Elizabeth represented the greatest Protestant power in Europe – a very small power compared with mighty Spain, but fast growing stronger.

Another cause of disagreement was the situation in the Netherlands, where the Dutch rebelled against the rule of Spain. The English were closely interested in what happened in the Netherlands, a close neighbour, an important trading partner, and a Protestant nation.

The clash of interests between Spain and England was sharpest in the New World. The English had never agreed to the Spanish monopoly of two continents, and in the 1560s John Hawkins sailed to the West Indies to sell slaves, whom he had seized·in West Africa, to the Spanish colonists. The Spaniards were ready to buy, although the trade was illegal. On his third voyage, Hawkins was ambushed by a Spanish fleet and lost most of his ships. One which escaped was commanded by Francis Drake,

*A 16th-century fighting ship, cut away to show the arrangement of decks and holds.*

*A 16th-century ship's compass.*

At the same time Drake, his red beard jutting fiercely, attacked Spanish harbours, then crossed the Atlantic and captured the big colonial cities of San Domingo and Cartagena. Philip II declared that England must be crushed.

Philip's armada ('war fleet') was supposed to set out in 1587, but Drake made a daring raid on Cadiz ('singeing the king of Spain's beard', as he described it) to damage the ships and force a year's delay. Next year Elizabeth was again hoping to avoid war; she kept Drake at home and the armada sailed.

The 'invincible' armada, as Spanish propaganda called it, had about 150 ships. Its plan was to pick up the Spanish army in the Netherlands and transport it across the Channel. But the whole expedition was clumsy and badly planned. All the way up the Channel, the Spanish ships were chivvied by the smaller English. They were so strongly built that the English shot bounced off them, and more harm was done by fireships than by gunnery. (Fireships were old empty vessels, filled with explosive and burnables, which were set alight and drifted with the current on to the enemy ships at anchor.) The battle lasted nine days, and it proved that English ships and sailors were superior. No Spanish troops were landed, and the fleet was forced to sail on northward, around the British Isles, back to Spain. Less than half the ships reached a Spanish port.

The defeat of the armada was the beginning of a war which lasted until 1604. England, with no regular army, stayed on the defensive, except in the West Indies. There Drake tried to repeat his successes, but found the Spanish fortifications much stronger. The Spaniards tried again to invade England, and a few troops succeeded in landing in Cornwall, giving some fishermen a surprise. Meanwhile, in the Netherlands, the Dutch made certain of their independence.

and the incident made Drake, like many of his Protestant countrymen, a ferocious hater of the Spaniards. In the 1570s he and other English 'sea-dogs' constantly raided Spanish ships and colonies. On one famous occasion, Drake sailed through Magellan's Strait at the tip of South America to attack the Spanish colonies on the Pacific coast. He sailed as far as northern California before turning to the west, across the Pacific, and so right around the world. Drake's ship, the *Golden Hind*, was the second to make this voyage, after Magellan's *Vittoria* fifty-eight years before.

Spain naturally protested violently at the raids of Drake and others like him. Elizabeth was unwilling to get involved in a war with Spain, especially without a strong ally (she was trying to lure the French into an alliance by flirting with the Duke of Anjou). She told the Spaniards that Drake had acted without the authority of the English government, though anyone could guess that she encouraged him in private.

Events came to a head in 1585. The Dutch revolt, after the murder of its leader, William the Silent, seemed to be failing. The French, under a feeble king, promised no help. Spanish troops landed in Ireland, and Spanish plots against Elizabeth were being unearthed almost every month by Sir Francis Walsingham, secretary of state and head of a large English intelligence network. The queen plucked up her nerve and made the decision to send an army to help the Dutch.

# The Golden Age of Elizabeth I

*A performance of Shakespeare's* Titus Andronicus *at the Globe Theatre, Southwark.*

Many people feel that the reign of Elizabeth I is the most glamorous, the most exciting period in English history. The English had found themselves as a nation: they had terrific pride and confidence, and a dashing sense of style. It does not matter whether Sir Walter Raleigh really threw his costly fur cloak in a puddle to save the queen getting her feet wet; it was a very Elizabethan thing to do – a mixture of gallantry, showing-off and humour.

The last twenty years of the 16th century saw the Renaissance come to full flower in England. Thanks to printing, an interest in art and literature spread far beyond the court. There was a wonderful harvest of art, of music, of poetry, and most important, of theatre. In William Shakespeare (1564–1616) England produced its greatest genius. But he was only the best in a gallery of gifted playwrights. There was Christopher Marlowe, whose *Tamburlaine* (1587) showed Shakespeare the way to write dramatic blank verse; Thomas Kyd, whose *Spanish Tragedy* (1594) led to Shakespeare's heroic tragedies; George Peel, whose style Shakespeare cruelly mimicked (though he also stole a plot from him); and the great humourist Ben Jonson, who mocked the fashions and foolishness of Elizabethan London.

English as a language of literature was still young in the age of Shakespeare. The Elizabethans took great delight in it, and they were not afraid to make it grow and change by using it in new ways. Shakespeare's enormous store of words included several he invented himself. It was great good luck that he happened to live at a time when the English language was molten gold, not yet cold and rigid. From it, glorious shapes could be formed – not only great poetry, but great prose, as in the King James version of the Bible (1611), and even great political speeches. Winston Churchill himself never made a greater war speech than Elizabeth's speech to her soldiers at Tilbury when the Spanish invasion was expected.

*This beautiful miniature by Nicholas Hilliard was thought to have been of the Earl of Essex.*

*The recently restored manor house, Mapledurham, is a fine example of Elizabethan building. Set in woodlands, its grounds run down to the banks of the Thames.*

Shakespeare was a professional actor. He acted in Ben Jonson's comedies and in his own plays (tradition says he played the ghost in the first production of *Hamlet*). The plays were performed in the first public theatres built in England since Roman times – tall, round buildings which unfortunately caught fire all too easily. The Globe, where many of Shakespeare's plays were first seen, burned down twice in a few years.

Poets and artists liked to feel they were inspired by the queen herself, and Edmund Spenser's famous poem *The Faerie Queen* (1590) was really about Elizabeth. Roman Catholics worshipped the Virgin Mary; the Protestant English came near to worshipping the 'Virgin Queen'. For Elizabeth never married: she encouraged several foreign princes, whose help she needed, to think she might make them king of England, but in the end she disappointed every one of them.

By staying unmarried she inspired greater devotion – also rivalry – among her courtiers. She was a demanding mistress (Raleigh fell right out of favour when he married one of her ladies) and entertaining her was expensive. She often travelled about the southern counties where Tudor gentlemen, instead of building shrines to the Virgin Mary, built great houses in which they might welcome the Virgin Queen.

This was the first great age of the English country house. The days of the castle were over, killed by gunpowder; but the English nobleman and squire liked to live in the country. Some of these Elizabethan houses, like Longleat in Wiltshire, were large and expensive, almost palaces. The builders borrowed ideas on style and decoration from Italy, France, Flanders and ancient Rome, while not forgetting their Gothic traditions. Yet the results of this mixture were usually handsome, and somehow remained thoroughly English.

In the gracious galleries of a great house, the evening air would be filled with music. This was the age of secular ('non-religious') music, especially the madrigal – a song for voices in harmony, unaccompanied – which reached its finest form in the sweet and sour songs of Thomas Morley and John Dowland. The queen herself, we are told, played beautifully on the virginal (a distant forerunner of the piano) while elegant young men would play the stringed lute or viol. Plenty of religious music was still composed, especially by Thomas Tallis, William Byrd (the finest composer before Purcell) and Orlando Gibbons.

The Tudor squire, as he sat listening to the music of his daughters, might have rested his eyes on his pictures. Tapestries were still preferred for decorating walls: they also kept in the warmth. Most painted pictures were portraits, as the rich of the 16th century were more interested in themselves than in art, and there was still very little sculpture outside churches. The best

*A contemporary drawing of Elizabethan court dancers.*

artists were often foreigners, like the great German Holbein, Henry VIII's court painter. But Elizabethan England produced one really extraordinary artist in Nicholas Hilliard, who painted miniatures, in the tradition of the illuminated manuscripts of the monks. It is no surprise that Hilliard was trained as a goldsmith: his art is as close to jewellery as to painting.

Although they produced so little painting, the Elizabethans loved colour. Fashion in clothes, especially men's clothes, was rich and exotic. Some flashy young gentlemen exaggerated their natural height with dizzy, plumed hats and high-heeled shoes. Women's dress was not quite so extravagant, but uncomfortable and clumsy, with wide skirts braced by metal hoops. Large lace ruffs (fancy collars) were coming into fashion for both sexes.

The queen owned 2,000 dresses. Perhaps some of them were less elaborate than the gorgeous garments shown in her portraits; otherwise, it is hard to see how she managed to dance or hunt. Nor does she look capable, in those stiff, restricting clothes, of spitting on the floor, thumping the table, or swearing at the Polish ambassador in Latin.

In spite of such behaviour, the queen was an exalted figure. No one spoke to her unless kneeling, and the complicated ceremony that went on at meal times meant that she never had her food hot.

Except for the poor, the English ate well, better than people of other countries, travellers said. Meat, including chicken and bacon, and bread were still the chief foods, but one or two new vegetables, like the potato, were appearing on the table. The rich ate white bread, made from wheat. The bread of poorer people was made from rye or barley; in bad times from beans, oats, even acorns.

A balloon trip across Elizabethan England would have revealed some parts of the country looking much as they do today, but others still looking quite different. There were fewer buildings (the population was less than five million) and more woodland, although timber was becoming scarce enough for houses to be built of brick (like Hampton Court). In the farming areas, there were still plenty of open fields. But the fens were not yet drained: the fenmen walked about on stilts, setting tunnel-like traps for wild geese and paying their rent in eels.

On the other side of the country, Wales was more peaceful than it had been for centuries. The people happily remembered that the Tudors were a Welsh dynasty; the power of the Marcher lords had finally been broken during the Wars of the Roses (*see page 100*); and in everyday matters of government and economy, the Welsh were becoming 'English'.

The north of England, though much disturbed by Henry VIII's agressions against the Scots, was growing more accustomed to law and order. The great northern lords rose against the government in 1570, but their revolt failed, and their power was lost.

Ireland was a special problem. Rebellion against England was aided by the Spaniards, in revenge for England's support of the Dutch. Ireland was still a primitive, medieval country, and its people were Catholics, not Protestants. The English tried to subdue the Irish by force, but caused only hardship and hatred. There were at least four rebellions in Elizabeth's reign, mostly led by great Ulster chiefs like the O'Neills. In 1598 the English were defeated at the battle of Yellow Ford, losing 1,300 men. Elizabeth sent out her young favourite, the Earl of Essex, but he was a failure and returned in pique to lead a half-hearted revolt himself, which cost him his head. Finally, the Irish revolt was crushed and the able Earl of Tyrone surrendered (1603). The government then tried a new policy. It 'planted' Ulster with Scottish, Protestant colonists. That was the origin of the Protestant majority in Ulster.

# The King of Scots reigns in England

The exile of Mary Queen of Scots brought no peace to the turbulent affairs of Scotland. Civil war flickered, and regents came and went. Over Mary's infant son, King James VI (1566–1625), the Catholic and Protestant parties quarrelled fiercely. For a while James was held prisoner, but in 1583, aged seventeen, he escaped, and declared that henceforth he would be king in fact as well as name.

Considering the state of things, James managed well. He did not make an impressive monarch – he dribbled when he talked and relied too much on court favourites – but he was clever by nature, well educated, and a sharp politician. Though he was more sympathetic to the Catholic party, and tried to stop the drift towards a more extreme form of Presbyterianism, James remained a Protestant. He had good political reasons for this choice. Elizabeth of England had no direct heir, and James was in line for the English throne. He was careful to keep on good terms with Elizabeth's ministers, especially Robert Cecil, who planned to make sure of his own position by preparing the way for James to succeed. Even the execution of James's mother (whom he could not remember) hardly disturbed the peaceful relations between Scotland and England.

In March 1603 Elizabeth died. At the end, when she could no longer speak, she made a sign agreeing that James should succeed her. As she breathed her last, Cecil signalled to Sir Robert Carey, who leapt on to his horse and galloped north. In less than three days he was in Edinburgh. He would have been even quicker, he said, but he fell on the way and his horse kicked him in the head. James, now James I of England, had gone to bed, but he willingly got up when he heard the news.

A contemporary drawing of Guy Fawkes and the 'Gunpowder Plotters'.

James's progress to London was a stately procession of triumph. He was immensely pleased to be king of England, which he expected to be an easier country to govern than Scotland. He did not know England, however. Government was not going to be as smooth and easy as he supposed.

One of the things James admired most

A group of Roman Catholics plotted to blow up Parliament in 1605, but Guy Fawkes was caught on November 5th.

about England was the Church. Here was a great institution closely linked to the State, with elaborate customs and rituals and ruled – not by disagreeable local presbyteries – but by bishops, appointed by the Crown.

But not all English people liked the Church of England. The Puritans, like the Scottish Presbyterians, wanted to abolish bishops, which James recognized as a dangerous idea when he made the comment, 'No bishop, no king!' The Puritans wanted other reforms in the Church. Some wanted a Presbyterian system, while others wanted a looser organization of independent local congregations. One small group was so disgusted with the Church of England that its members emigrated, first to Holland, then to North America, where they founded the colony of New Plymouth (Massachusetts) in 1620.

The Puritans were well represented in the House of Commons, and they were not afraid to criticize the government. So strong was the opposition that Elizabeth had tried to ban all discussion of religion in Parliament. But this had only caused another row, over the rights of members.

The royal government, living largely on rents from royal estates, had suffered badly from inflation. It needed extra subsidies – taxes – from Parliament. But Parliament was not always ready to vote taxes for the government if it disliked government policy. Elizabeth more than once had to retreat when she found her policy opposed in Parliament. As far as possible, she lived without subsidies, to avoid having to deal with Parliament. James, who was never loved or respected like Elizabeth, found Parliament even more difficult.

# Chapter 8

## Critics of the King's Government

In the middle of the 17th century, England suffered its greatest upheaval ever. Yet between 1600 and 1640 the way of life of ordinary people changed very little. Prices were still going up, land was changing hands, industry was growing. Trade was increasing too, though the East India Company, soon to become the biggest merchant company in the world, found Dutch competition in the East Indies too strong, and shifted its activities to India.

Scotland and England, though they shared a king, remained separate countries. The fens were being drained, to the fury of the fenmen, and the Poor Laws had removed most of the roving beggars. Many old ideas lingered on. People still believed in witches; James I did, and several people were executed for witchcraft in his reign.

No obvious changes appeared on the surface. Yet the whole atmosphere of 17th century England was different. In Elizabeth's later years, which people looked back on as a golden time, many writers expressed a growing sense of dissatisfaction with life. This comes out in Shakespeare's later plays (written in James I's reign), and the whole subject was discussed in Robert Burton's *The Anatomy of Melancholy*, published in 1621.

Some historians of art and literature say that artistic taste was worse under James I – himself a rather vulgar man. In the theatre, for example, Jacobean plays tended to be full of blood and horror, and lacked the character and poetry of Shakespearian tragedy. Even the furniture of the time was dark, heavy and deeply carved.

Between 1600 and 1640 a serious political conflict was growing – a struggle for power between the king and Parliament, which was to end in civil war.

Parliament in the 17th century represented the landowners, especially the lesser landowners, the 'gentry'. The typical MP was a rich squire, whose family estates had probably been built up in the past hundred years. He was only a little more representative of the people as a whole than one of the barons who forced King John to sign *Magna Carta* in 1215. Like the barons, 17th-century MPs were concerned with their own interests, not with abstract ideas like 'liberty' or 'democracy'.

On legal, or constitutional, grounds, the king's position in the conflict with Parliament was the stronger. The privileges that Parliament often claimed by ancient right had sometimes been invented, consciously or not, very recently. James I and still more his son, Charles I (1600–49), were tactless in claiming that kings ruled by 'divine right'. No doubt Elizabeth or earlier monarchs would have heartily agreed, but under Charles I 'divine right' began to look like dictatorship.

However, these questions of legal 'rights' and 'wrongs' do not matter very much. Great arguments are decided by other means. The king was to lose the power struggle for one vital reason: Parliament controlled revenue. The king was still expected to 'live of his own'; but the old sources of income were simply not enough.

*The Duke of Buckingham with his family, favourite of both James I and Charles I.*

Elizabeth, who was careful with money, had been forced to sell royal lands to pay government expenses. The king had to have more money, which could only come from taxation. But taxes could only be raised by the vote of Parliament.

James annoyed Parliament by his foreign policy – the warlike squires did not want peace with Spain, and they wanted to help the Protestant side in the Thirty Years' War, which broke out in Europe in 1618. James, though, was for peace all round. Parliament did not like the government's economic policy either, especially the granting of monopolies (exclusive rights in some business, such as selling soap, making pins, etc.). This brought in money, for a man who wanted a monopoly had to pay for it, but Parliament suspected bribery and corruption. On such charges, it impeached Francis Bacon and Lionel Cranfield, James's best ministers. (Impeachment was a legal process in which a man was accused by the Commons and tried by the Lords: it was the only way Parliament could get rid of an unpopular minister.)

In the 1620s, the most unpopular person in England was the last of James's glamorous young favourites, the Duke of Buckingham. He was responsible for marrying Prince Charles to a French princess, Henrietta Maria, a Catholic. The French insisted that, as part of the marriage bargain, Catholics should be allowed freedom of worship in England. Parliament was furious and refused to vote even the usual customs duties to Charles I when he became king. He collected them anyway, and raised more cash by a 'forced loan'. Many who refused to pay were imprisoned.

When Parliament met again in 1628 it presented Charles with a Petition of Right, a list of what it regarded as illegal government actions. They included the collection of taxes without Parliament's consent and the imprisonment of people without cause.

One of their chief objections to Charles's government was removed when the Duke of Buckingham was assassinated by a half-mad soldier in 1628. The murder of his friend made Charles bitter and suspicious.

Unable to agree with Parliament, Charles dissolved it in 1629 and decided to rule without it. For eleven years he succeeded. During that period, known as the 'Eleven Years' Tyranny' thanks to parliamentary propaganda, Charles's chief ministers were Thomas Wentworth, Earl of Strafford, and Thomas Laud, Archbishop of Canterbury.

Strafford had been a critic of the king in Parliament, but changed sides in 1628. Charles never fully trusted him, and Strafford was unwise to trust Charles, who allowed him to be executed in 1641 by a vengeful Parliament.

Laud was an equally hateful figure to Charles's Puritan critics. Not only was he head of the State Church, which Puritans wanted to abolish, but his form of Protestantism seemed very close to Roman Catholicism. There was a Roman Catholic party at court gathered around the queen, and Laud was blamed for encouraging that. He was also held responsible for the government's refusal to assist the Protestants in the Thirty Years' War.

There was no question of Charles's government embarking on foreign adventures, as it was desperately short of money. In order to keep the government running at all, Charles had to use some doubtful methods to raise cash. In 1635 a tax known as Ship Money, which had normally been paid by coastal towns as their contribution to the navy, was levied on inland towns also. The same thing was done the following two years, and John Hampden, a leader of the opposition to Charles's government, brought a case against Ship Money as an illegal tax. The judges, king's men anyway, decided in Charles's favour – but by a narrow margin. The Hampden case concentrated opposition to personal government by the king.

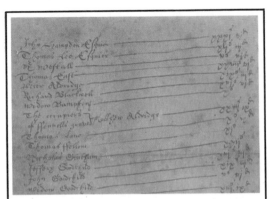

*A record of the unpopular tax, Ship Money. John Hampden, a leader of the opposition to Charles I, claimed that Ship Money was an illegal tax.*

During the years when Parliament was advancing towards its claim to be the defender of religion, liberty and property against the tyranny of Charles I, the mass of the people were silent. One result of the Civil War, soon to break out, was that ordinary people owning no property made themselves heard for the first time.

In James I's reign, the gap between prices and wages reached its widest point. The ordinary farm worker, depending on his wages, could not afford to buy anything except bare necessities. Unemployment tended to increase because it was not worth a man working, and the Poor Laws, harsh though they were, prevented people actually starving. In many places, the wage rates fixed by local justices of the peace were so low that even those in work needed supplementary benefit – poor relief provided from the rates.

Life was much shorter, harder and more risky than today. A poor man was middle-aged at thirty and, on average, dead before forty. When the justices in Devonshire fixed the wage rates for women, they only allowed for women up to thirty. Beyond that age, women, if not dead, were past working. Children went to work as soon as they were able. They did not go to school: what use was education to them?

The poor had no organizations like trade unions to protect their rights. They had few rights to protect. In 1618 about a hundred young people found half-starving in London streets were packed off to Virginia.

Yet not all landowners and employers were selfish or cruel. The rich in general gave more of their money to charity in the 17th century than they do now. But acts of charity cannot solve such a vast problem.

There were a few cases of attacks on property-owners by the poor in the early 17th century, though nothing serious enough to call a rebellion. When rebellion did come, it was not the poor but the property-owners themselves who rebelled.

# The Scots, the English and Civil War

*Riots against the new prayer book in St Giles's, Edinburgh.*

James I had restored bishops to the Church of Scotland, to the anger of Presbyterians, and Charles I caused further annoyance by trying to regain the Church lands which had been seized by Scottish nobles. Charles came to Scotland himself in 1633 to be crowned king in St Giles's, Edinburgh, with all the rites and ceremony – candles, crucifixes, priests in surplices – of the Anglican Church. His Presbyterian subjects were disgusted, frowned blackly and murmured 'Popery!'

The worst was to come. In an attempt to bring the Kirk into line with the Church of England, a new Prayer Book was introduced for use in Scotland. Presbyterians disliked set prayers, even those written by John Knox, and they certainly did not like them from Archbishop Laud. The first time the new Prayer Book was used in St Giles's, a riot broke out and the congregation hurled stools and bibles at the Dean. At Brechin the bishop conducted the service with a couple of loaded pistols by his hand.

Charles's government was slow to recognize that a national revolt was brewing in Scotland. A fresh covenant, known as the National Covenant, was signed by thousands of people all over the Lowlands in protest against the new religious practices. At a General Assembly in Glasgow, the covenanters abolished all bishops and threw out the new Prayer Book. Royal authority in Scotland had vanished. Arms were being shipped in from abroad, and Alexander Leslie, an experienced general, was selecting his officers. Charles raised men to meet him but could not pay their wages. A truce was signed, but Charles insisted that bishops should remain in charge of the Scottish Church, and a second 'Bishops' War' broke out.

*When the Speaker tried to end a session of Parliament because of criticism of the king, angry members held him in his chair so the meeting could continue.*

Again there was no serious fighting, but in 1640 Charles was forced to call Parliament. His opponents, who had been muzzled for eleven years, now had their chance. Charles listened to the uproar for a while, then hastily dissolved the 'Short' Parliament.

But the Scots still had to be dealt with and the king still had no money to fight them. After casting about without success for some other way to raise money, Charles reluctantly called another Parliament. The Short Parliament had lasted three weeks. The 'Long' Parliament was not officially dissolved for twenty years.

The Long Parliament quickly set about the destruction of Charles's personal government and made sure that no king would ever be able to behave in such a way again. Laud and Strafford were impeached, and other ministers smartly left the country. New acts of Parliament declared that Parliament should be summoned every three years at least, and that it should not be dissolved without the members' agreement.

The judgment in Hampden's case against Ship Money was reversed, the court of Star ·Chamber was abolished, and the right of the king to raise any kind of tax, including customs duties, without Parliament's consent was ended.

In 1641 Parliament produced a document called the Grand Remonstance. It was really a piece of propaganda, to be printed and distributed around the country, and it listed all Parliament's complaints against Charles.

So far, the king had surrendered to all Parliament's demands, however unpleasant he found them. He really had no other choice, for he had very few supporters inside Parliament or out of it. But when the Grand Remonstrance was put to a vote in the House of Commons, it passed by only eleven votes. The king had gained a party, and now he felt he was in a position to resist. With a group of soldiers, he went down to the House of Commons and tried to arrest five leading members of the opposition. But someone had tipped off the five, and they had slipped away before Charles arrived. 'I see the birds have flown', said the king angrily.

Realizing that his capital city was no longer in his control, Charles left London and, after dithering about for some time, went to Nottingham. There he set up the royal standard, an act signifying the beginning of war. No one wanted war, and a few weeks earlier it had seemed most unlikely, for Parliament had gained almost everything it wanted peacefully.

One question had not been settled. In 1641 rebellion had broken out in Ireland; hundreds of English people had been killed. Parliamentary leaders suspected, or said they suspected, that the king was behind the whole business. They were unwilling to allow Charles command of an army which might be used against them instead of the Irish rebels. But Charles was not willing to let Parliament control the army.

Looking back at the Civil War from our point in time over 300 years later, it seems that Parliament was bound to win. That did not seem obvious in 1642. In fact few people could imagine the king losing. Hardly anyone believed in the idea of a republic, with no king and no aristocracy. Among those who did, none was a man of influence.

When the war began, the king had one enormous advantage: he was the king. Men's ancestors had fought for their king since the beginning of England's history. Rebellions, however well justified, always seemed unnatural. In 1642 men without strong political opinions on one side or the other were more likely to take the king's side than Parliament's.

The king had other advantages. At the start he was better supplied with soldiers, especially cavalry, and he had an excellent cavalry commander in his nephew, Prince

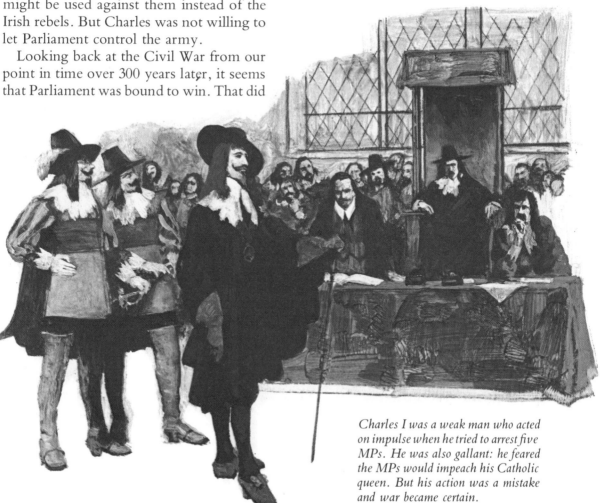

*Charles I was a weak man who acted on impulse when he tried to arrest five MPs. He was also gallant: he feared the MPs would impeach his Catholic queen. But his action was a mistake and war became certain.*

Rupert, who had fought in the Thirty Years' War. Charles also had sympathy and support from abroad, although some Frenchmen who came over to fight for him found themselves fighting for Parliament by mistake.

The advantages enjoyed by Parliament were far greater. The map (*page 140*) shows that the king controlled the north and west, Parliament the south and east. Of course this gives only a rough idea of the situation. Not everyone in the north supported Charles; not everyone in the south supported Parliament. In general, Parliament had the support of the towns, including London, which dominated the country even more in the 17th century than it does now. Parliament also controlled most of the ports – and the navy. Thus Charles was cut off from foreign aid and from the profits of trade and business which poured into London. In the end, his defeat in war was due to the same cause as his defeat in peace: shortage of cash.

Most (but not all) of the big landowners, the old noble families, supported the king. So did the poorest people. But the middling sorts of people – squires, bankers, merchants, lawyers, shopkeepers – supported Parliament. They were mostly people who had been growing more wealthy and more powerful for the previous hundred years or so, and they were hostile to the old-established powers of the kingdom – king, lords and bishops.

Charles could have won if he had won quickly. And he nearly did. The first battle of the Civil War, at Edgehill in October 1642, ended in a draw. Charles marched towards London, but at the village of Turnham Green he was checked by the London trained bands (part-time soldiers), who were dug in among the vegetables in the cottage gardens. Charles fell back to Oxford, which became his headquarters.

All the same, things did not look good for Parliament. After Edgehill, John Hampden

discussed the near-defeat with his cousin, Oliver Cromwell. 'Your troopers', Cromwell told him, 'are most of them old decayed serving men and tapsters, and such kind of fellows. Their troopers are gentlemen's sons and persons of quality. You must get men of a spirit that is likely to go on as far as gentlemen will go'. However, Charles did no better in 1643, for his advance on London was again halted, and another drawn battle was fought at Newbury in Berkshire.

At the end of the year the Scots joined in on Parliament's side. The aid of Alexander Leslie and his Covenanting army was bought by the 'Solemn League and Covenant' which promised, though in vague words, to make England Presbyterian. The Scots took part in the battle of Marston Moor, July 1644, which was the first large battle of the Civil War to end decisively. As

a result, Parliament gained control of the north, though it still did not press the king hard. The older parliamentary leaders did not really want to win. 'If we beat the king ninety-nine times', said the Earl of Manchester, commander of the Army of the Eastern Association, 'yet he is king still. But if the king beat us once, we shall all be hanged'. This kind of talk annoyed men like Cromwell, his second-in-command. 'My lord', said Cromwell, 'if this be so, why did we take up arms at first?'

After a second battle at Newbury (bravely held for the Royalists by an eighteen-year-old governor) Manchester allowed Charles to escape in the moonlight. An eager colonel suggested pursuit, but Manchester yawned and said it was too late.

Cromwell (1599–1658) and others like him insisted on a change of policy. The Self-Denying Ordinance took away army command from all politicians. It would have disqualified Cromwell also, as he was an MP, but a way was found to make an exception for the general who was about to win the war.

For Cromwell had created a new force, the New Model Army, which was the first professional English army of modern times. The men were properly trained and equipped, and they believed in the cause they were fighting for.

Meanwhile, the Royalist cause was flourishing in Scotland, thanks to a brilliant general who used guerrilla tactics, the Earl

*Parliamentary soldiers arresting a Royalist.*

of Montrose. He had been a supporter of the National Covenant, and shared command of the army with Leslie in the Second Bishops' War. For all that, he considered himself a loyal subject of the king. When the Civil War began, Montrose had no difficulty choosing between the king and the Covenanters, whose ambitious leader, the cross-eyed Earl of Argyll, he disliked and distrusted.

In 1644 Montrose was at Oxford. Later that summer he appeared in the Highlands. He had two companions and a commission signed and sealed by the king. Just two weeks later he routed a Covenanting army of 6,000 near Perth and captured the city for Charles. The legend of Montrose had begun.

After Perth, he turned north to Aberdeen. Argyll pursued him, but was smartly defeated and retreated to the west as winter fell. To Argyll's horror, Montrose came sweeping down from the wintry hills, forcing him to flee down Loch Fyne in a fishing boat. Montrose ravaged Argyll's country and withdrew towards Inverness. Reinforced with regular troops, Argyll followed him, only to be ambushed in the shadow of Ben Nevis.

Montrose's victorious progress continued. He captured Glasgow in August 1645 and seemed master of Scotland. But the mass of the people had not risen in the Royalist cause, and the main Covenanters' army was away in England. Two months earlier, Cromwell's New Model Army had smashed the forces of Charles I at the battle of Naseby, the last real battle of the war. Leslie, with 4,000 Scottish veterans, returned to Scotland. At Philiphaugh, he took Montrose by surprise and soundly defeated him. It was the end of the legend.

After Naseby, Charles was finished, though another year passed before Oxford surrendered. Long before that, Charles surrendered to the Scots, who handed him over to Parliament – for a fee.

As often happens, the winners were quarrelling among themselves. The main conflict lay between Parliament and the Army, or between Presbyterians and Independents. When Parliament tried to disband the Army without paying its wages, there was mutiny. Cromwell and other officers took the side of their men. They set up an Army Council, which demanded reforms, including new elections. That did not please the members of the Long Parliament.

The Army strengthened its position by seizing the royal prisoner from Parliament, but some time later he escaped to the Isle of Wight. In 1648 the Scots invaded England, having signed a secret agreement to support

A map showing the principal battles of the Civil War

Charles. Cromwell marched north and defeated them, without much difficulty, at Preston, but Charles had also been plotting with conservative members of Parliament, and the Army leaders came to the decision that stronger measures were needed.

London was occupied by Cromwell's troopers. Colonel Pride, who commanded a brigade in Scotland, marched to Westminster and removed about a hundred MPs by force. The king was put on trial as a traitor in a court specially created for the purpose. The Chief Justice of Chester presided, as greater judges were unwilling. Charles was found guilty and was executed in Whitehall on January 30, 1649. When the brave Montrose heard the news of the death of his king, he collapsed in a faint.

As Charles himself said, there was no legal way in which a king could be tried by his subjects. In a strict sense, the trial was illegal and Charles's execution was murder. On the other hand, Charles had left his opponents little choice. In his eyes they were rebels and traitors, and he saw no need to act honourably with them. He had lied and deceived them and shown that he could never be trusted. The strange thing is that Cromwell and his associates gave the king a trial at all. It brought them no advantage and created sympathy for their enemies. In almost any other country, Charles would have been quietly murdered in some dark cell, as had happened to more than one English king in the past.

With Charles I dead, Royalists regarded his son, the future Charles II, as rightful king. In Scotland the young Charles was crowned at Scone. But before Cromwell could deal with the Scottish problem, he went to Ireland to crush the rebellion there. At Drogheda and Wexford he dealt savagely with the Irish, making his name hated there for evermore. Cromwell was not a cruel man and, compared with most others of his time, he was tolerant of various religious beliefs. But like other Englishmen who lived at different times, he behaved more cruelly in Ireland than anywhere else.

In 1650 Cromwell invaded Scotland and won the battle of Dunbar by good tactics, though as usual he gave the credit to God. The Scots were not convinced either by Cromwell's victory or by his attempts to reason with them ('I beseech you in the bowels of Christ', went his famous plea for tolerance to the Kirk, 'think it possible you may be mistaken'). The following year the Scots invaded England. Cromwell let them go as far as Worcester, and there he routed them. It was, he said, God's 'crowning mercy'; it was also the last battle of what is sometimes known as the Second Civil War.

*Charles I died on the scaffold in front of Whitehall. He faced his enemies bravely and with dignity.*

# Voices of the People

Revolutions grow more radical as they go on. The people who start them, however revolutionary their ideas may seem, are soon overtaken by others still more revolutionary. By the end of the Civil War, the Presbyterians who formed the majority in Parliament had become conservatives, anxious to reach agreement with the king.

The Independents, most strongly represented in the New Model Army, were also split into different groups, some more radical than others. The ideas of army commanders like Cromwell and his clever son-in-law, Henry Ireton, were more conservative than the ideas of the Levellers.

The Levellers believed in the 'sovereignty of the people'. Parliament's authority existed only because it represented the people who voted for it, said the Levellers, and therefore everyone ought to vote in parliamentary elections. These ideas seem natural to us, but they were very advanced for the 17th century. (In fact, the Levellers were not perfect democrats, as they did not think that women, servants or wage-labourers should vote.)

The Levellers had a large following among the ordinary soldiers of the Army. In 1647 they drew up a document called the Agreement of the People, a constitution or 'social contract' for England. It was debated in Putney Church by the Army Council, which included men of all ranks.

At Putney was heard, loud and clear, the voice of the ordinary man. 'The poorest he that is in England', said Colonel Rainborough, 'has a life to live as the greatest he'. Every freeborn Englishman who agreed to obey the government ought to have a say in it – through his vote.

Cromwell and Ireton were shocked by the demand for such great changes. Ireton defended the idea that power should go with property, because property gave a man 'a permanent fixed interest in this kingdom'. If men without property – men with no stake in the country – were allowed to vote, the Generals argued, they would vote for propertyless men like themselves, and the final result would be the end of all private property – 'communism' in fact.

This was not what the Levellers wanted, yet the Generals' insistence on traditional rights of property made them wonder what they had been fighting for. Said Edward Sexby, 'We have ventured our lives to recover our birthrights and privileges as Englishmen, but by your arguments they do not exist'.

The debate was polite and reasonable, but the argument could not be settled. Many of the reforms which the Levellers wanted, like the abolition of the House of Lords, were carried out by Cromwell after the Levellers themselves had been suppressed. Yet the traditional rights of property were not dethroned.

Cromwell once said that if the Grand Remonstrance had not been passed by Parliament in 1641 he would have sold his farm and emigrated to New England. Many other Puritans had already done so. Massachusetts Bay Colony, with its centre at Boston, had been founded in 1630, and in the following ten years about 20,000 people had emigrated from England. Although they were not all Puritans, most of the leading men were.

This great Puritan migration, far larger than earlier settlements, marks the beginning of the first British Empire. Harvard (the oldest university in the USA) was founded in 1636; a Boston printing press was working by 1639; other settlements, which were to develop into separate states, were begun by people moving away from Massachusetts Bay.

The first colonists aimed to create 'a City of God in the wilderness'. They were led by hard-headed men like John Winthrop, a Suffolk squire and trained lawyer, and they took with them the company charter of the Massachusetts Bay Company – their constitution. Together with the barrier of the Atlantic Ocean, this allowed the New England colony to develop without much interference from England. Later it would resent England's attempt to control it.

*Many Puritans were among emigrants to America in the early 17th century. They became the forefathers of a new nation.*

# The Government of Cromwell

Besides the Levellers, there were smaller groups of people farther to the 'left' (as we might say) who wanted more radical reforms. On St George's Hill, Weybridge, near London, Gerrard Winstanley and the Diggers tried to start a genuine commune, where land was owned and work done by everyone alike. Other left-wing groups were less attractive. The Clubmen also wanted a society without private property, but they were more interested in committing the violent acts by which, they liked to think, it could be brought about.

The collapse of royal government in 1641 and the war that followed allowed all kinds of cranks and criminals to creep into the daylight. The times were troubled. One sign was another nasty outbreak of witch-hunting, led by a sinister 'witch-finder', Matthew Hopkins.

Firmness was needed to restore order and enforce government of some kind. That firmness was provided by Cromwell. He realized that the Levellers were right in theory, but he was a practical man: apart from the fact that he represented the property-owners, Cromwell believed that the changes wanted by people like the Diggers were simply too great. He therefore checked the process of revolution. Some people say he 'betrayed' it, but that is a matter of personal opinion. Cromwell made certain the *political* revolution was safe: though monarchy was to be restored after his death, the king would never again overrule Parliament. That was a revolution certainly. But there was no *social* revolution. Private property remained sacred and the government of England remained in the hands of the owners of land.

The new leaders of England found Parliament no less troublesome than Charles I had done. Colonel Pride had thrown out a

*The Diggers believed in a humane, simple communism. 'True freedom,' said their leader Winstanley, 'lies where a man receives his nourishment and preservation, and that is in the use of the earth'.*

hundred members of the Long Parliament, leaving what was rather rudely called the 'Rump'. But in 1653 Cromwell lost patience with the Rump as well. The members were unwilling to be dissolved, and when they introduced a bill which would have given them control of new elections, Cromwell marched into the chamber with soldiers. He forced the Speaker out of the chair and removed the Mace – the symbol of Parliament's authority which always lies on the table during sessions.

A new Parliament was elected, known as the Barebones Parliament, a joke based on the name of one of its members, Barbon. His first name was much stranger as it happened, for his devout and Puritan parents had called him Praise-God.

The Barebones Parliament tried to bring in drastic reforms, and it was soon dissolved. A new constitution was proposed called the Instrument of Government, which gave Cromwell the title Lord Protector for life. But when Parliament met, the members objected to the new constitution and proposed one of their own.

The conflict between the government of the Protectorate and Parliament was as difficult to solve as the conflict between Charles I and Parliament. The members demanded control of finance and of the army, which meant controlling the government. But the government would not surrender these powers to Parliament.

Cromwell next tried the experiment of dividing the country into sections, each ruled by a Major-General. This was extremely unpopular – 'bayonet-rule' – and the country gentry (the type of people represented in Parliament) refused to cooperate. The rule of the Major-Generals was honest and efficient, but it stumbled on the old obstacle – lack of money. For that it depended on Parliament. When Parliament met it presented Cromwell with a 'Humble Petition and Advice' – a new constitution with a king and two Houses of Parliament.

*Milton, the greatest poet in English literature after Shakespeare, was a government official under Cromwell.*

Cromwell might have taken the crown he was offered but for fear of offending the Army.

In its early days, the government of the Protectorate had paid for itself partly through the sale of lands confiscated from Royalists. But that could not go on for ever. The money problem was worse because Cromwell, unlike Charles I, had set out an active, aggressive – and therefore expensive – foreign policy.

Fifty years earlier, the European nation whom the English liked best had been the Dutch – fellow-Protestants who had fought bravely and successfully against the hated power of Spain. By 1650, the English could no longer treat the Dutch as favourite nephews. They had become England's greatest rivals.

Like the English, the Dutch were a sea-going people. Dutch skill in ship-building was ahead of the English, and in the early 17th century the Dutch completely dominated the 'carrying trade' – sea transport. Most of the goods imported by England, never mind other countries, came in Dutch ships. Not only was this profitable, it also gave the Dutch a strong naval advantage: a strong merchant navy meant a strong fighting navy. The government of the Protectorate was determined to restore England's naval power and to regain the carrying trade. That was the reason for the Navigation Acts which, among other blows against the Dutch, said that trade should be carried on in English ships only.

The Navigation Acts led to the outbreak of war in 1652–54, the first of three naval wars against the Dutch during the next twenty years. (One result was that the Dutch colony of New Amsterdam became English, as New York.) Some stirring battles were fought – by Cromwell's great admiral, Robert Blake, and the heroic Dutch admirals, van Tromp and de Ruyter, but in the end the Dutch were bound to lose. The reason was simple: the English controlled the Channel.

It may have seemed strange that Cromwell, a Protestant hero, was so aggressive towards the Protestant Dutch. But even in the 17th century, economic rivalry was often stronger than religious fellow-feeling. And Cromwell did make war on a more accustomed enemy – Spain.

*Dutch captains discussing their plans during a fight against the English. They might win battles, but they could never win the war as England controlled the Channel.*

An ambitious target was chosen – Hispaniola, one of the largest West Indian islands and the oldest Spanish colony in the Caribbean. The expedition of 1655 was, however, a bit of a shambles. The English forces, many of them dragged from the London slums, landed on the coast. Hungry and badly led, they soon fled when attacked by Spanish cavalry

But there was another Spanish island nearby – Jamaica. As there were few soldiers there it was easily captured. Some Spanish treasure was captured too, though not enough to pay the cost of the war.

Although this expedition was not glorious, Cromwell, in a few years, had made England a country to be reckoned with, perhaps feared.

Cromwell was a leader in the tradition of Elizabeth, sensible, broad-minded and patriotic. He was not afraid of criticism – he allowed the Jews to settle in England for the first time since the 13th century though his associates all opposed it – but he did not try to push his plans too far, however good they were, when the opposition was too strong.

He never did find an answer to the problem of Parliament, perhaps because he did not have time. Though not yet sixty, his health began to fail in 1658, and the death of a beloved daughter was a terrible blow. Soon afterwards he developed pneumonia. On September 3, the anniversary of his victories at Dunbar and Worcester, he died, while a violent thunderstorm raged.

Oliver's son, Richard Cromwell, a pleasant country gentleman, succeeded as Lord Protector, but found the job too much for him. 'Tumble-down Dick' they called him, for he fell from power in eight months.

But what now? The old Rump Parliament was recalled, but quarrelled with the Army. The Army could not govern against the hostility of the taxpayers to military government. There was no money to pay the soldiers' wages, so there was soon not much of an army. One of the few reliable forces in the British Isles was General Monck's command in Scotland.

Late in 1659 Monck marched south. No one opposed him. In London he insisted on the final dissolution of the Rump and elections for a new Parliament. When it met, it had a majority of conservative Presbyterians, who favoured a monarchy. From Breda in the Netherlands, the son of Charles I had issued a declaration promising good behaviour, obedience to Parliament and no revenge against rebels. He was invited to take his father's crown.

# The Return of Royal Government

Some of the work of the Protectorate was undone by the government of Charles II (1630–85). Yet not all of the acts of the Long Parliament were repealed; nor could Charles forget that monarchy had been defeated, a king executed and himself driven into exile for fifteen years. He did not want to go on his travels again, he said, and he recognized that the power of the Crown had been permanently reduced. In foreign policy, religion and other important aspects of government, Parliament could no longer be ignored.

In some ways, Parliament under Charles II was more conservative than the king. Charles was in favour of religious toleration, chiefly because he wanted freedom for Roman Catholics. Parliament was hostile not only to Catholics but also to Presbyterians and Puritans who did not accept the Anglican Church. Over 1,000 priests were turned out of their parishes for their 'dissenting' opinions.

When Charles issued a Declaration of Indulgence, which would have removed some of the penalties against Roman Catholics and Dissenters, Parliament replied by passing the Test Act, which prevented Catholics holding any kind of public appointment.

Religion was still political. In the minds of most English people, Catholicism meant tyranny, and it was true that Catholic kings in Europe were absolute rulers, with few limits to their personal power. Louis XIV of France persecuted the French Protestants, who were called Huguenots, and drove thousands out of France. Many were skilled men who settled in Britain, to the great benefit of their adopted country.

Charles II himself was attractive, clever and witty. It is difficult to dislike a man who, when lying on his deathbed, could apologize for taking such a long time to die. But Charles was also dishonest and deceitful. He entered into a secret agreement with

*The Great Fire of London (1666) started in a baker's shop. Nine-tenths of the city inside the old city walls was completely destroyed.*

Louis XIV, by which the French king paid him money in exchange for Charles's promise that he would declare himself a Catholic and would use French troops to put down any revolt against Catholicism in England. Charles never intended to carry out his promise, but that did not make people less angry when his secret agreement became known many years later.

England had also agreed to help France against the Dutch. This was a doubtful policy, as France under Louis XIV was becoming a far greater menace than the Dutch could ever be. In spite of three Dutch wars, most Protestant Englishmen had never felt happy about fighting the Dutch, and Charles was forced to make peace with them in 1674. Against the might of France, the Dutch under the leadership of William of Orange narrowly managed to save their independence.

How serious was the political threat of Roman Catholicism? In 1678 a man called Titus Oates announced the existence of a high-level 'Popish Plot' to replace Charles II with his Catholic brother, James. Although Oates had the record of a born troublemaker, and his story was pure fiction, many people believed it. About thirty-five innocent people were executed.

The doubt and panic caused by Titus Oates was used by the opponents of the king to attack the monarchy. The Earl of Shaftesbury and his 'country' party (so called to distinguish it from the 'court' party) proposed that the king's brother should be excluded from the succession (Charles had no legitimate children, so James was his heir). Shaftesbury's choice was the young Duke of Monmouth, Charles's son by one of his many mistresses.

As he had done before, Charles adopted 'feather bed' policy in this crisis. A feather bed, as the Marquess of Halifax explained, gives way at the slightest blow but never actually breaks. Charles swayed with the blows. Had Shaftesbury's policy succeeded, then hereditary monarchy would have been finished. Therefore Charles was determined to pass his crown to James, though he felt none too confident that James would be able to keep it.

Francis Bacon (1561–1626), who had been Lord Chancellor under James I, was the first modern scientist, in our sense of the word. He lived in an age when people believed in astrology and alchemy, the medieval ancestors of astronomy and physics and chemistry. Alchemists searched for a mysterious essence that would bring back youth, or for a way of turning ordinary metals into gold. But Bacon worked by reasoning, inquiry and experiment. He died as a result of a chill he caught when he was conducting an experiment with a frozen chicken.

*St Paul's, one of England's finest Gothic buildings, was destroyed in the Great Fire of 1666. Sir Christopher Wren had to submit three designs before he was commissioned to rebuild it. The cathedral was completed in 1711.*

During the Civil War and the Protectorate, new ideas about politics and religion were being discussed with a freedom never known before. In that climate, science also flourished, for questions about religion often lead to questions about science and philosophy. The drunken trooper who asked why his beer mug should not be God was asking a question, not only about the nature of God, but also about the nature of a pewter pot.

William Harvey had published his evidence for the circulation of the blood (discovered independently by a French scientist) in 1628. In the 1650s a group of Baconian scientists gathered at Oxford. They were concerned with the advance of knowledge in every subject, and they quickly attracted other original minds, including Christopher Wren, best known as the rebuilder of London after the Great Fire (1666), John Locke, the political philosopher, and Robert Boyle, the father of the modern science of chemistry. These men were founders of the first great learned society in England, the Royal Society, whose patron was the king.

Among the glittering talents of the Royal Society, one name stands out above all others: Isaac Newton (1642–1721). In 1665 a serious attack of plague struck England (it was almost the last attack as it turned out). The young mathematician Newton left Cambridge for the healthier air of a Lincolnshire farm, where he spent the next two years. There he made his greatest discoveries, including the spectrum (the way light rays break into colours) and the basic law of the universe – the law of gravity. An old story says that he began thinking about gravity while sitting in an orchard and seeing an apple fall. Perhaps.

It is no exaggeration to talk about a 'scientific revolution' in the 17th century. At the same time, no sharp line can be drawn between the science of Bacon, Boyle and Newton and the older, foggier ideas of magic and witchcraft. Newton himself spent much of

*Newton using a prism while investigating the nature of light and colours.*

*In the Restoration theatres, actresses were seen on the stage for the first time. All Shakespeare's heroines had originally been played by boys.*

his long life studying obscure questions of religion and alchemy. Yet Newton was also a true scientist, with the great virtue of scholarly humility. 'I do not know what I may appear to the world', he wrote, 'but to myself I seem to have been only a boy playing on the seashore . . . now and then finding a smoother pebble or a prettier shell, whilst the great ocean of truth lay all undiscovered before me'.

King Charles II was the patron of other institutions less serious than the Royal Society, such as the theatre, which had been stopped by the Puritans since the Civil War. Restoration theatres were closed-in, with a curtained stage, artificial lighting (candles), and professional actresses instead of boys playing women's parts. The type of play being written was hard, cynical comedy, though John Dryden, a skilful poet, wrote tragedies which some considered better than Shakespeare. A greater poet, Milton, finished his *Paradise Lost* in 1665 though, as a Puritan, Milton hardly belonged to the age of Charles II. Nor did John Bunyan, who wrote *Pilgrim's Progress* while in prison as a Dissenter in 1675.

Milton had defended the freedom of the press, but Charles II's government slapped on strict censorship. Pamphlets, popular prints and newspapers had come pouring off the presses in the Civil War era, and some opponents of Church and State ignored the censorship laws after the Restoration. They suffered savage punishments, like the loss of a hand, if caught.

# The Glorious Revolution

Charles II had sensibly kept his own religious beliefs quiet. He died a Catholic. His brother James II (1633–1701), who succeeded him, was known to be a Catholic already. If more honest than Charles, he was less clever. Where Charles had rocked with the blows of opposition, James, stiff as a board, thought only of giving his opponents sore knuckles.

There is nothing like a revolt to make a government popular. A burst of affection for Charles and his brother had been set off by an unsuccessful plot to kill them as they returned from Newmarket Races in 1683. In the summer of 1685, James gained the extra benefit of a failed rebellion. The rebels came from Scotland, where they were led by the Earl of Argyll (son of Montrose's opponent), and from the Netherlands, where the leader was Monmouth.

Argyll was a poor conspirator and bungled things horribly. He was caught crossing the Clyde and swiftly executed. Meanwhile, Monmouth landed in Dorset with his band of political discontents. Though he gained some support from Puritan Dissenters among the cloth-workers, shepherds and miners of the south-west, he was quickly defeated. His uncle talked to him for a few minutes before sending him to his death.

James's blundering government wasted the goodwill that the rebellion had aroused among his more loyal subjects by the fierceness with which the rebels were punished. Chief Justice Jeffreys gained a nasty reputation for his 'Bloody Assize' in the West Country. He was really no worse than other judges, and cruel punishment of rebels was common enough. All the same, to burn an old woman to death just for helping some runaways seemed unnecessary even by 17th-century standards.

*Newspapers became popular in the 17th century.*

While the bodies still swung from the gallows in the West Country, James, like all his family, was quarrelling with Parliament. He wanted full toleration for Roman Catholics and meant to get it. He also wanted to keep a large army in existence. To many people, it looked as though Roman Catholicism was about to be restored to England by force.

Whether or not James intended that, he certainly did intend to regain some of the lost power of the Crown. In a law case of 1686, some carefully selected judges gave their opinion that the king could overrule Parliament. But James was steadily losing the support of those middling sort of people who, while they wanted peace and prosperity, regarded popery and personal government as too high a price to pay.

All the same, James, who was in his fifties, might have died with the crown still on his head but for the announcement of December 1687 that the queen was expecting a child (the future 'James III', the Old Pretender). This was a little unexpected, and when the baby was born some said that it was not the queen's, but had been smuggled into her bedroom in a warming pan – an object like a giant frying pan used for warming the sheets of a bed.

Hitherto, the next in line to the throne had been James's daughter Mary, a woman of twenty-five and a Protestant, married to a Protestant prince, William of Orange. But the new baby seemed to promise an unending line of Catholic monarchs.

A party of powerful men, including former ministers, got in touch with William in the Netherlands. William was the central figure of a European alliance against the powerful and ambitious king of France, from whom James was accepting money. If England were to be tied to the anti-French alliance in Europe, William saw that he would have to act quickly. He told the English messengers that if they could assure him of the support of the chief people in the kingdom, he would act.

That was in May 1688. In the same month James issued an 'Indulgence' which removed all handicaps from Roman Catholics (and Dissenters). Even for those pillars of royal government, the bishops, this was too much. Seven of them protested, insisting that the Indulgence was against the law. They were arrested and tried for treasonable libel, but to the consternation of the king, they were acquitted. Among wildly cheering crowds, the seven bishops passed to freedom. The situation was indeed desperate when Londoners cheered bishops!

A few days later an invitation was sent to William of Orange asking him to come and save the country from papist tyranny.

Almost the whole of England was united against James II. His only supporters were the tiny minority of Roman Catholics whom he had protected and appointed to important positions. At the last moment he realized the danger and started to reverse his

*Chief Justice Jeffreys bullying a witness during the trial of Dame Alice Lisle.*

policies. But it was too late. William landed at Torbay in November with 24,000 men. He had luckily avoided the English (and the French) ships thanks to an east wind – a 'Protestant wind' as people said – which kept the fleet in harbour.

For a week or two all was uncertain. James might still have saved the day, but in the end he slipped away to France. William took over the government, and a parliament was called, although there was no king to call it. The Commons, when they met, declared that James's flight amounted to abdication, and that 'the throne is thereby vacant'.

Were there any applicants for this interesting position? Mary II was the rightful heir (if James and his baby son were counted out) but, prompted by William, she said she would not reign without her husband. So it came about that for the only time in history England had joint monarchs. William III and Mary II reigned together until Mary's death from smallpox in 1694.

The revolution of 1688–89 deserves the name 'glorious' if only because, unlike most revolutions, it took place without bloodshed. It finished what the Long Parliament had started in 1640 and put a stop to the type of royal power that James had used to secure freedom for Catholics without confronting Parliament. There was no great overhaul of the English constitution. The Glorious Revolution confirmed that an English monarch could only rule with the consent of his subjects, and that he must be a Protestant.

James still had supporters – Jacobites, as they were called. He landed in Catholic Ireland with French troops, only to be defeated by William at the battle of the Boyne (1690). In Scotland William was generally accepted as king in the Lowlands, but the Highlands

*William of Orange landing in England: he brought 25,000 men with him but did not have to fight.*

*Massacre at Glencoe: it was far from being the first mass murder among the clans, but all Europe was shocked.*

rose in revolt (partly against the revived power of the House of Argyll). Under Graham of Claverhouse, Viscount Dundee, they smashed William's troops at Killiecrankie. But Dundee's death left them without a leader.

A large sum of money was spent to buy the loyalty of Highland chiefs, but as the Master of Stair (William's chief Scottish adviser) wrote to the Campbell Earl of Breadalbane, 'God knows whether it had been better employed to settle the Highlands or ravage them'. The government next insisted that all chiefs should swear an oath of loyalty to William III before January 1, 1692. They did so, but one or two were a few days late, among them MacIan MacDonald of Glencoe.

Soon after this, a company of Argyll troops were sent to Glencoe, where they were well received by the MacDonalds, whose chief was related by marriage to their commander, Robert Campbell of Glenlyon. After Campbell's men had stayed two weeks, secret orders came for the death of all the MacDonalds of Glencoe under seventy. On a black night, about thirty-six men, women and children were killed by their guests as they slept, and their houses set on fire. Others escaped to tell of the Massacre of Glencoe. 'This raised a mighty outcry', wrote Bishop Burnet in his history of his own times, 'and was published by the French in their gazettes, and by the Jacobites in their libels, to cast a reproach on the king's government as cruel and barbarous'.

# England and a Protestant Crown

William III was not fond of the English, but he needed England to strengthen resistance to France under Louis XIV. One hundred years after the Armada, England was again in danger of invasion by a great continental power, when the Anglo-Dutch fleet was defeated by the French off Beachy Head in 1690. But Louis missed his opportunity, and two years later the tables were turned when the French fleet was badly beaten at the battle of La Hogue. That battle, plus the defeat of James II's French troops in Ireland, made England safe from the danger of a French invasion.

'King William's War', as the English called it, continued until 1697, when the Treaty of Ryswick put an end to the fighting. The war had cost £40 million, but it had solved nothing. A larger quarrel was already looming up over the question of the Spanish succession.

William III's throne was secure by 1690. Yet he and Mary provided only a temporary answer to England's desire for a Protestant monarchy. As they had no children, the heir to the throne was Mary's younger sister, Anne, also a Protestant. Though Anne had many children, none of them lived past childhood (not so unusual in those days). When the eleven-year old Duke of Gloucester died in 1700, the end of the Protestant line was again in sight.

This time Parliament acted in plenty of time to preserve a peaceful succession. The Act of Succession (1701) declared that the crown should pass to Sophia, electress of Hanover, a granddaughter of James I and, of course, a Protestant. As it happened, the elderly electress died before Anne, in 1714, and therefore her son became the first Hanoverian king of England, as George I.

The act also tidied up a few matters that had not been settled by the Glorious Revolution. In future, it laid down, the reigning monarch should be a practising member of the Church of England (in James II's reign the Church had been in the peculiar position of having a non-member as its head). No monarch should wage war to defend other countries, or should leave the kingdom, without Parliament's consent. No foreigner should be a member of Parliament or of the privy council.

These rules were the direct result of Parliament's anger with William III. He had indeed left the country and made war to defend another country (Holland), and he had paid more attention to Dutch councillors than to English ministers. The act made

COFFEE HOUSE JESTS

*Printed for Henry Rodes near Bride lane in Fleet*

*The introduction of tea, coffee and cocoa from the East led to the opening of coffee houses where men could meet for a business chat and smoke their clay pipes.*

*This magnificent silver mirror belonged to William III. It is now at Windsor Castle.*

The system of government control of the economy had changed completely. Before 1640, the king had treated the national economy like a private business – granting monopolies, halting enclosures, raising or lowering customs duties, more or less as he pleased. The new economic system was controlled by Parliament, and its secret was that it was not a *system* at all. There was no tight regulation: business and industry were allowed to develop freely, with as few restrictions as possible. This allowed the growth of new economic institutions, like the Bank of England, founded in 1695. Trade, and the colonies which were formed in the wake of trade, were flourishing in 1700 where they had not existed in 1600. The East India Company was the greatest corporation in the country. Trade, in turn, encouraged shipping, as well as new businesses like insurance.

In James I's reign, anyone who was not a member of the State Church could be punished. Under Anne, there was religious freedom for all Protestants. Bishops no longer served as government ministers, and the Church courts, so powerful a weapon in enforcing obedience to the Elizabethan settlement, existed only as shadows of themselves. Religion has ceased to be a matter for wars and burnings.

In a thousand smaller ways life had changed for ordinary people. Food was better, or at least more varied. The growing of new root crops allowed more animals to be kept through the winter – hence more fresh meat. Tea and coffee had appeared and were growing popular. So was gin, introduced by the Dutch. Clothes were beginning to look more like the clothes of today, though enormous wigs for men, which had become fashionable with Charles II, had not yet disappeared. Forks had joined knives on the dinner table. China and glass had replaced wood and pewter. Plague had gone for good. England was prosperous, and about to become the greatest power in the world.

certain that a Hanoverian monarch should not do likewise.

People often say that rapid change is a characteristic of modern times; that the speed of change gets faster as history advances. That may be true as a general rule. Certainly Britain in the reign of Queen Anne would have seemed familiar in many ways to someone of Shakespeare's time. Yet in other ways, not always obvious on the surface, the changes that took place between 1600 and 1700 were greater than those of any other century.

The greatest change was in government. During the 17th century, England changed masters: by 1700 Parliament, not the king, was the supreme authority. The king was still head of the government; he still chose his ministers, but he could no longer choose those whom Parliament would not accept. He was no longer expected to 'live of his own': Parliament provided the revenue for government, most of it coming from a new tax on land. And he who controls the purse strings holds the power.

# Chapter 9

## The Union of England and Scotland

When James VI of Scotland had become also James I of England, he had tried to make the two kingdoms one. But the Scots, who did not want to be swallowed up by their old enemies in the south, would not agree. However, during the 17th century the two kingdoms were drawn closer together. The 'auld alliance' of Scotland and France was dead, though not quite buried.

There were disadvantages for the Scots in being treated as foreigners by the English. England was quickly becoming a great world power, but the Scots did not share its prosperity. The English Navigation Acts,

*Queen Anne receives the Act of Union, uniting Scotland with England and Wales.*

although they were aimed against the Dutch, were an equal handicap to the Scots. Scottish merchants were unable to trade into English ports.

In 1695 the Scots borrowed a leaf from England's book by founding a national trading company which they hoped might rival such giants as the English East India Company. The leader of this enterprise was William Paterson, one of the founders of the Bank of England. His idea was to start a colony on the Isthmus of Darien (Panama), which links North and South America. The colonists' job would be to shift goods across the isthmus, forming a link in a new route to

India and the Far East which would be much quicker than rounding Cape Horn. (Today, the link is made by the Panama Canal.)

Owing to the opposition of William III, no money for the Scottish company could be raised in London. By a great national effort, the Scots raised £400,000 themselves.

But the directors of the company were not worthy of the public's confidence. They botched up the arrangements thoroughly. Their worst mistake was to suppose that a colony could survive in Panama, which was Spanish territory anyway. When the Spaniards protested, William ordered the English colonies in America to give no help to the Scots in Darien.

No less than three expeditions set out for Darien in 1698–99, but all ended in disaster. Shipwreck, disease and Spanish attacks caused the deaths of 2,000 colonists, while the other activities of the Darien Company were nearly all failures. Of all its enterprises, the only profit came from a single trading voyage to West Africa.

Apart from the loss of life, thousands of Scottish investors had been ruined. Naturally, there was much ill-feeling against England, and for a few years the relations between England and Scotland were as bad as they had ever been. Yet the real lesson to be learned from the wretched Darien affair was that a union of England and Scotland would be an advantage to both. For the Scots held one strong card: as long as they remained a separate kingdom, they were not legally obliged to pay any attention to the English Act of Succession. At Anne's death, they might invite 'James III' to accept the Scottish crown.

On both sides, of course, there were opponents of the union. English merchants were far from eager to admit the Scots as equals and rivals. The Scots were anxious for the future of Presbyterianism. Crowds in Edinburgh and other places demonstrated wildly against union.

In the end, common sense won the argu-

A Highland Chieftain *by Michael Wright, about 1670. This magnificent chieftain is dressed for hunting, not for war. It is one of the earliest known portraits of Highland dress.*

ment. The Scottish parliament voted that the commissioners to discuss a possible union should be appointed by the queen. As Anne was in favour of union, she naturally appointed commissioners who shared her view. The commissioners for both countries showed tolerance and good will: for the negotiations were highly sensitive and could have been ruined by one bad-tempered speech. Finally, they produced their treaty of union, which left the Scots their own systems of law, education and religion. The treaty was voted into law early in 1707 by both the English and the Scottish parliament, which thus voted itself out of existence.

Union with England did not cure all Scotland's problems. Many people thought its immediate results were disappointing. Such feelings helped create support for the Jacobite rebellion of 1715.

# The Defeat of Louis XIV's France

In a sense, William III had two successors: on the throne he was followed by Queen Anne, on the battlefield by John Churchill, Duke of Marlborough (1650–1722), who became the leading general of the European alliance against Louis XIV.

From the peace of Ryswick in 1690, both France and England began preparations to renew the struggle, which was bound to break out on the death of the Spanish king, Carlos II. Last of his dynasty, poor Carlos was a wretched creature, misformed in mind and body. There was no question of him having children and in 1697 it was already clear he would not live long. He would leave a great prize behind him – not only Spain, but the vast Spanish empire in

*The Duke of Marlborough at the Battle of Blenheim, 1704, from a splendid tapestry at Blenheim Palace.*

the Americas, the kingdom of Naples, the Spanish Netherlands (Belgium) and other places. There were several possible claimants to Carlos's inheritance; the most suitable was a Bourbon prince, Philip, grandson of Louis XIV.

The prospect of Spain and the Spanish empire falling into the hands of the Bourbons filled the opponents of Louis XIV with alarm. A new European grand alliance was formed by William III to resist the French claim, and an Austrian archduke, Charles, became its rival candidate for the Spanish throne.

When Carlos II died in 1700, Louis XIV immediately accepted the Spanish throne on behalf of his grandson. Louis believed that his action was bound to provoke an attack from the Dutch and the British so, perhaps foolishly, he decided to strike first. He grabbed some forts on the Dutch border, he banned English trade goods from France and Spain, and he recognized 'James III' (son of James II, who died in 1701) as rightful king of England. That made war certain.

Jacobites used to drink the health of 'the little gentleman in black velvet' who caused the death of William III (the king died from a fall when his horse stumbled over a molehill). From the narrow viewpoint of military tactics, the death of William was no disaster, for it allowed Marlborough to take supreme command of the allied armies. An ancestor of Winston Churchill, Marlborough proved a brilliant general, perhaps the best (with the Duke of Wellington) that Britain ever produced. Like all successful generals, he was a good organizer and a good politician; for it is no less important for a supreme commander to keep on good terms with his allies than to work out the perfect battle plan. Marlborough spent much of his time travelling from one capital city to another, soothing politicians. The Austrians were only interested in Italy; the Dutch protested whenever Marlborough moved his army too far from the Nether-

*Detail of a grenadier from the Blenheim tapestry.*

lands – these were the kind of difficulties that he had to overcome. He managed to keep the alliance together and also win his battles.

On a white horse and in a scarlet coat, Marlborough won his first great victory, at Blenheim, in 1704. After that, the splendid French army was never quite the same, though Marlborough never again won quite so glorious a victory. But he had many triumphs – Ramillies in 1706, Oudenarde in 1708, Malplaquet in 1709 – and no real defeats. By 1708 the French were no longer capable of waging a dangerous campaign of aggression, and there were strong arguments in favour of peace. But greed, especially the desire of English merchants to seize trading advantages from Spain, kept the war going.

In general, the 'Whigs' wanted to carry on the war, while the 'Tories' wanted peace. Although we can speak of political parties at least as early as the reign of Charles II, it would be wrong to think of Whigs and Tories as 18th-century versions of the Labour and Conservative parties. They were not nearly so organized. In the 18th-century Parliament, power depended on family relationships, business interests and patronage (appointments to valuable posts or some other political favour), not on party loyalties.

However, there were genuine differences between Whigs and Tories. The Whigs stood for the interests of trade and the City of London. They were the heirs of Shaftesbury's 'Country' party, critical of royal government and the established Church.

The Tories, even less of an organized party, were more closely associated with the old land-owning aristocracy (though, of course, Whigs were also land-owners) and with loyalty to the monarch and the Anglican Church. The names of both began as insults: the original 'whigs' seem to have been Scottish Covenanters, the original 'tories' Irish bandits (though according to the staunch Tory, Samuel Johnson, the first Whig was the Devil).

In the political arguments about the War of the Spanish Succession, a large part was played by propaganda and by personal influence. A great writer, Jonathan Swift (his most famous book is *Gulliver's Travels*), wrote a powerful attack on the war, *The Conduct of the Allies,* published in 1711, which probably swung many people over to the side of the peace party. Daniel Defoe, author of *Robinson Crusoe* among many other books, was another brilliant writer employed by the Tories.

The Whigs, on the other hand, enjoyed one advantage in the great friendship that existed between the queen and the Duchess of Marlborough who, though not exactly a Whig (the Duke hated political parties), was certainly for going on with the war. Eventually, the Tory leader, Harley, managed to

*Marlborough discussing his campaign plans with a representative of the Dutch government.*

*The Treaty of Utrecht extended Britain's trade and her American colonies.*

replace the duchess in the queen's affection by a lady of his own preference and therefore, of course, a Tory. As Queen Anne had a mind of her own, this backstairs plotting may have been less important than the plotters believed.

In 1710 the Whigs made themselves very unpopular by impeaching Dr Sacheverell, a Tory preacher who had been denouncing the Revolution of 1688. The Tories came to power, and at once began talks for peace. The war dragged on for another year or two, but peace was finally signed in 1713 in the Treaty of Utrecht. Philip V kept the Spanish crown on condition that it should never be united with the throne of France. The Spanish people wanted Philip, and anyway the Archduke Charles had become Holy Roman Emperor in 1711, so there was little point in trying to win a Spanish crown for him as well.

Otherwise, Great Britain, as the country was now sometimes called, did very nicely out of the Treaty of Utrecht. The British kept many places that they had captured during the war, including Gibraltar (which has remained British ever since), Minorca, Newfoundland and Nova Scotia. They also gained the right to sell slaves to the Spanish colonies. This was thought of as the greatest gain of all: it was something the English had been after since the days of Hawkins and Drake. But it turned out to be less valuable than expected.

Although the British did well, their allies were not so fortunate. The Catalans of north-east Spain had fought on the allied side against Philip, but at Utrecht the British left them to Philip's revenge. The Dutch too had reason to feel they had been betrayed, and the legend of 'Perfidious Albion' – treacherous England – took root in Europe.

The war had confirmed some developments already taking place, and its really important results did not appear in black and white in the Treaty of Utrecht. In 1713 Britain clearly appeared as a great power, probably the greatest in Europe, although it was not yet certain that Britain had won the struggle for dominance with France. But if the French were still a powerful nation, it was equally certain that the great days of Spain were over; also, that the Dutch Republic, more exhausted by the war than any other country, had slipped from the position it had held at the height of its prosperity in the 17th century.

# The First Prime Minister

When the Hanoverian dynasty succeeded to the throne in the short, rather fierce-looking person of George I (1660–1727), the Tories fell from power. They were not to regain it for over half a century. Their most brilliant leader, Viscount Bolingbroke, fled abroad to the court of the Old Pretender, 'James III', in 1714, and with the Jacobite Rebellion of the following year, the Tories were tainted with Jacobitism for ever – or at least for as long as the Whigs could persuade the country that a Jacobite threat still existed.

In Scotland, the Jacobites were led by the Earl of Mar. The Hanoverian forces of the Duke of Argyll opposing them were much smaller, but they, like their commander, were veterans of Marlborough's campaigns. After several anxious months, the revolt was crushed. The Jacobite leaders were allowed to escape, while King George's soldiers raged through the Highlands.

Almost as big a worry to peaceful Englishmen as the Jacobite rebels was the National Debt. Although it had only been created – to help pay for war – in 1694, by 1713 it had risen to £54 millions. Today, the National Debt is about one thousand times that amount, and we have seen that a country can go very deeply into debt without actually becoming bankrupt. But in 1713 no one knew that. People were extremely frightened, thinking the country was on the edge of economic collapse. The end of war, as it always does, created other problems, such as unemployment. The Riot Act, giving more power to JPs, was passed to control the unruly crowds which so often appeared on the scene during most of the 18th century.

*The South Sea Bubble of 1714 resulted in people frantically buying and selling shares. Pawnbrokers had a good year, as people pawned many of their possessions to buy shares or pay off debts.*

To deal with the National Debt, one of the Whig ministers, Robert Walpole (1676–1745), devised the Sinking Fund. In theory, the Fund, which was supplied out of taxation, would have paid off the National Debt, though rather slowly. Some time later, another scheme for paying off the Debt more quickly was proposed by the directors of the South Sea Company, which would take the Debt on itself.

In financial circles, everyone gave a great sigh of relief. A terrific boom began. People invested in all sorts of business enterprise. The South Sea Company was a sound enough affair and well run; but many other companies were not. They popped up like mushrooms, promising vast profits to shareholders by extracting gold from seaweed or some equally crazy activity. Yet people invested dizzily in these concerns.

Of course the reaction soon came. But the crash, when it arrived in 1720, affected every business, good companies as well as daft ones. The South Sea Company collapsed like a pricked bubble: shareholders saw the value of their investments sink in a moment to zero.

One of the few prominent men not involved in the crash was Robert Walpole. As he already had a reputation as a financial wizard, he was the obvious man to put in charge of the wreckage. He managed to save a good deal from the South Sea Bubble, even getting a little back for the directors of the Company, and at the same time gaining for himself a dominant position in the government. He kept that position for about twenty years.

Walpole, who seemed a simple, red-faced Norfolk squire, possessed a deep knowledge of human nature, especially its less noble sides. He was an expert manager of men, working by influence and instinct. These were useful gifts for a politician, and earned Walpole the name of 'the first prime minister'. Perhaps they were not enough to make him a great statesman.

The political aims of Walpole were peace and prosperity – for himself, his friends and the whole country. On the whole he was very successful. He certainly became a rich man. Houghton Hall, his Norfolk mansion, was turned into a palace hung with as fine a collection of pictures as could be found in any private house.

In Walpole's day, politics were managed by influence and bribery. Walpole brought the Duke of Newcastle into his government chiefly because the Duke, by his influence and wealth, could control the results of a large number of elections. Walpole's opponents attacked him for corruption, but it was an age when everyone was in the business of buying favours; even some of his greatest opponents, when they eventually came to power, proved themselves no more virtuous.

Walpole's immediate aims were to increase the prosperity of trade and to reduce the Land Tax. After all, practically all MPs were landowners (many were also involved in trade), and had suffered from the increases in the tax which war had made necessary. Rather than raise taxation, Walpole preferred to raid the Sinking Fund. This type of expedient is normal practice for modern governments, but some of Walpole's friends, as well as his opponents, were shocked, since the Sinking Fund had been created for a quite different purpose. But in any case, it did not provide a permanent solution.

The solution that Walpole did find was the excise. Excise duties are taxes paid on goods sold in the country. All goods on which excise duty was to be paid passed through a government warehouse; if they were to be exported, no duty was paid. Walpole began this scheme in 1723 for one or two products, such as tea and coffee. It was a great financial success. Although the amount of duty was lower, the greater efficiency of the warehouse scheme meant that total income was greater.

As the quantity of goods was about the same, this result seems impossible. It is explained by the fact that Walpole's scheme reduced smuggling. In the 18th century smuggling was the biggest national pastime – in coastal counties at any rate. All kinds of people were involved. A Norfolk clergyman saw nothing wrong in ordering his tea from the local smuggler, instead of the grocer, and when someone in the House of Commons asked how many members had silk handkerchiefs, at a time when the import of such goods was forbidden, it turned out that nearly everyone had.

A nasty riot broke out in Edinburgh in 1736 at the execution of a well-known smuggler, and the officer in command of the guard, Captain Porteous, fired on the crowd. He was condemned, then reprieved, but some people came to the prison where he was held, dragged him out and killed

*Hogarth's interpretation of canvassing for votes, 1754.*

him. This type of lawlessness and violence was not rare in 18th-century Britain.

In 1733, Walpole tried to extend his excise scheme to tobacco and wine. He found himself facing furious opposition. The scheme would have raised a lot of money in a reasonably fair way (Walpole thought the Land Tax might be abolished altogether), and it would have assisted trade by cutting down on smuggling. Some of its opponents simply hated Walpole and wanted to break his hold on the government.

But there were other reasons for opposing the excise bill. People feared that armies of excise men would be constantly pushing their way into every little shop in the country to make sure that duty had been paid (some people today have a similar fear of VAT inspectors). Excise men in the 18th century were often rough characters, no more honest and no less violent than the smugglers they were after. Feelings about the excise bill were summed up in a verse:

> See this Dragon Excise
> Has Ten Thousand Eyes
> And Five Thousand Mouths to
>     Devour Us,
> A sting and sharp claws
> With wide-gaping jaws
> And belly as big as a Store-house.

*Sir Robert Walpole the Norfolk landowner, by John Wootton*

Walpole was never afraid of opposition. But this time he saw he could not win. He withdrew the bill.

From that time, his domination of Parliament began to fade. Young politicians like William Pitt made their reputations by speeches attacking him. Developments in Europe were not going Walpole's way. Just as it takes more than one to fight a battle, it takes more than one to keep the peace, and war could not be postponed for ever.

In spite of Newcastle's patronage, Walpole barely won a majority in the general election of 1734. With his position in the Commons so much weaker, he was forced into compromises: he could no longer go his own way, steam-rolling the opposition. A severe blow fell in 1737 when Queen Caroline (wife of George II) died. Walpole's power depended no less on the support of the Court than on his management of the Commons, and the intelligent queen had been a strong supporter.

Pressure was building up for war against Spain. The reason for it was mainly the old one of greed – the hope of rich pickings from the decaying carcase of the Spanish empire. But orators like Pitt made it appear a question of national honour. Even the nervous Newcastle wanted war, and in 1740 Walpole gave in. 'It is your war', he told Newcastle, 'and I wish you joy of it'.

Nowadays, a prime minister would (or should) resign in such a situation, but in Walpole's day ministers would hold on to power even if they were forced to carry out a policy they disagreed with. Not suprisingly, Walpole did not direct the war with much energy. Everyone was becoming very restless with his leadership until finally, in 1742, he did resign. He died three years later.

*Voters being 'entertained' by a Whig candidate, by Hogarth. Bribery was widespread.*

# New Wars against the French

*Private war in the West Indies: a Spanish vessel, claiming to be a coast guard but as likely to be a pirate, intercepts a British merchantman.*

The war which caused the defeat of Walpole was fought, like most British wars of the 18th century, over trade. The British had not been content with their gains in the Treaty of Utrecht (1715). They wanted far more than the one ship each year which was allowed to sell slaves to the Spanish colonies. A great deal of smuggling was going on all around the Caribbean, and British vessels often clashed with Spanish coastguards. Although the British were often in the wrong, the 'coast guards' were sometimes no better than pirates themselves. In 1738 a certain Captain Jenkins appeared in the House of Commons with one of his ears missing. It had been torn off, he explained, by the Spaniards, who had also robbed his ship. The war that broke out next year is known as the War of Jenkins's Ear.

It soon became mixed up with a general European war over the question of the Austrian succession. Britain played little part in the continental war, although some British and Hanoverian troops (for the king was still Elector of Hanover) fought on the Austrian side. At the battle of Dettingen in 1743 George II led his troops in person. It was the last time a reigning British monarch appeared on a battlefield. Times had changed since Agincourt.

The war did not go well for Britain, and the Jacobite Rebellion of 1745 made matters worse. When peace was signed in 1748, France was in a slightly stronger position, thanks to the victories of Marshal Saxe in the Low Countries and the British decision to hand back Louisbourg, which commanded the entrance to the heart of Canada, the St Lawrence River.

War began again less than eight years later, and lasted for seven years (longer in some parts of the world; but it is known as the Seven Years' War). This was to be the

decisive conflict between Britain and France for world empire, in which the British made themselves the most powerful nation in the world. The success of the British during the Seven Years' War was largely due to the leadership of a proud and lonely, half-mad statesman, William Pitt (1708–78), later Earl of Chatham.

Pitt had been one of Walpole's fiercest critics, and the chief reason why he did not gain power in the government until 1756 was that George II would not have him. Walpole had been the kind of minister, it was said, who read letters from his gamekeeper before foreign despatches. He was a country squire from an ancient landowning family. Pitt represented a different class, but one which had become increasingly powerful, the merchants and bankers

gained power to direct the war (with the indispensable Newcastle at his elbow). He took office then, when Britain seemed to be on the brink of disaster, with a famous statement, 'I know that I can save this country, and that no one else can'. It seems a foolish boast, but it was something that Pitt himself needed to believe. Perhaps it was also true. At any rate, during the four years when Pitt planned and directed the war, British arms and British ships won victory after victory and, in the process, gained a world-wide empire.

As far as Britain was concerned, the war was mainly a naval war. A powerful ally, the Prussia of Frederick the Great, tackled the French in Europe, while the British kept the French fleet bottled up and attempted to capture French trade in North America, India and Africa. Pitt was not interested in winning territory, only trade. That explains why some of his friends in the City thought the rich little islands of Guadeloupe and Martinique were more valuable conquests than the whole of Canada. West Indian sugar seemed likely to be more profitable than the fish, furs and timber which were all that Canada stood for in the City.

Ten years earlier, when Louisbourg was captured, Pitt had listed the advantages to be gained by conquering Canada. He had pointed out that the key to Canada was the city of Quebec. This plan he now put into action. The man he chose to lead the attack in 1759 was James Wolfe – a frail but inspiring general aged thirty-three. The attack came from the St Lawrence, which had been expertly surveyed and charted a year earlier by Captain Cook (later to gain greater fame as an explorer). Under cover of night, Wolfe led over 4,000 men single-file up cliff paths to the Heights of Abraham, just outside the city. They attacked at once and in a three-hour battle, in which both Wolfe and the French commander, Montcalm, were killed, the city was taken. Montreal fell the following year and Canada became British.

of the City. His family's fortune had been made by his grandfather, 'Diamond' Pitt, a rough, tough, East India merchant.

No two men could have been less alike personally than Walpole and Pitt. Walpole had worked through human interest and influence. His policy was for peace in which trade could prosper. Pitt seemed a much grander figure. He had little interest in individual people but inspiring visions of national greatness. His policy was for war in order to gain greater advantages for trade.

Pitt recognized that Britain had only one serious rival in the drive towards domination of world trade, and that was the old enemy, France. When war broke out again in 1756, Pitt's moment had come, or so it seemed. In fact another year of political bargaining and argument went past before Pitt

The capture of Quebec is remembered as a bold and brilliant victory. But it was only one among many in 1759, the year that the British, always ready to congratulate themselves, called *annus mirabilis*, 'year of marvels'. France's two main fleets were shattered, one by Admiral Boscawen off Portugal, the other by Hawke at Quiberon Bay on the coast of Brittany. French West Africa had been seized, and in India a remarkable general, Robert Clive, was destroying French power and influence by a succession of battles which left the British East India Company the greatest power in the Indian sub-continent. The fall of Manila gave Britain control of the China tea trade (all tea came from China then) and the French West Indian islands were captured one by one.

*Wolfe's men clambering up the steep path that led to the Heights of Abraham. Over 4,000 men reached the plain by dawn the next morning, where they won a famous battle against the French.*

Most people were cheered by all these successes. Yet there were also doubts. Men were being killed and – a much stronger objection in the 18th century – much money was being spent. In any case, what would be the result of it all? It was good to win battles and defeat the French. But if France were to be utterly defeated and her trade ruined, what would happen then? History proved that when one country became overbearingly powerful, as Britain seemed to be doing in 1760, the other countries of Europe would combine against it.

In that year also, George III came to the throne. Like all Hanoverian kings, he wanted a new policy, at least a new ministry, and though he admired Pitt, he was more ready to listen to his critics. In 1761, when ministers disagreed over the question of declaring war on Spain, as Pitt demanded, he was pushed out of office. (War with Spain did follow, and Pitt's plans were put into effect with complete success, although Pitt was no longer a member of the government.)

The Seven Years' War was officially ended by the Treaty of Paris. The terms

*In India, Clive won several remarkable victories against forces much larger than his own. British command of the sea, preventing French reinforcements, was a great help.*

were fairly generous to France. Britain kept its gains in India, but the important West African trading post of Dakar was given back, and so were the rich sugar islands of Guadeloupe and Martinique. Canada stayed British, but the French regained their Newfoundland fishing rights, which, in the eyes of Pitt, were the main reason for winning Canada in the first place. Gaunt, ill, and drugged to the eyebrows, Pitt denounced the Peace of Paris in the House of Commons in a speech that lasted longer than the battle of Quebec. He was not alone in his disgust. There were many in the City who agreed with the judgment of John Wilkes, the witty, though not very respectable, political reformer. The Peace of Paris, said Wilkes, was like the peace of God, for 'it passeth all understanding'.

## The King beyond the Sea

When Queen Anne died in 1714, 'James III', son of James II, might have regained the throne if he had been willing to turn Protestant. That he would not do, and the Hanoverian dynasty began its long occupation of the English throne. Yet James had many supporters in England, and more in Scotland, especially in the Highlands, where Presbyterianism had never been so strong. Scots of all classes were disappointed with the results of the union: if a referendum had been held in the early 18th century in Scotland, it would have resulted in a large vote for separation from England.

In 1715 James wrote from France to the Earl of Mar ordering him to raise the clans in the Stuart cause. The response was swift and eager, and if Mar had been a more spirited general, like Montrose, the revolt might have been more successful. As it was, he dithered too long in the north, then was checked by Argyll at Sheriffmuir near

*Bonnie Prince Charlie enters Edinburgh to the cheers of the delighted crowds.*

'pacified' a process that is not, as a rule, at all 'pacific'. The Gaelic language was forbidden in schools, and General Wade set about building military roads through the wild mountains and glens. Highlanders were attracted into the new regiments, like the Black Watch, which became the cream of the British army. Strongpoints were built at places like Fort William and Fort Augustus.

Almost nothing was done to make the Hanoverian government more acceptable to the Scots, and the Porteous case (*see page 166*) showed how English authority was hated. The government made matters worse by imposing a heavy fine on the city of Edinburgh for the murder of Porteous. The Scots were seething, and toasts were drunk more openly to 'the king over the water'. The outbreak of war in 1739 raised the hopes of the Jacobites: Scottish policy had always been to strike while the English were occupied elsewhere.

Although James was still alive, thirty years of idle exile in France had not made him any less depressing a leader, and his cause was taken up by his son, Charles Edward, known to legend as 'Bonnie Prince Charlie'.

The prince was a quite different kind of man. At twenty-four, he was handsome, brave and energetic. As King Louis XV of France did not seem eager to supply any direct assistance, and the Jacobites in Britain were unwilling to move without fair promise of success, Charles decided to force the issue. By pawning his mother's jewels, he raised enough money to fit out a couple of ships, and set sail for Scotland. A patrolling English warship intercepted him in the Channel, but he escaped and at the end of July, 1745, landed with five or six companions in the Outer Hebrides.

He was not very welcome. Some chiefs advised him to go away again, but he refused. In many cases reluctantly, the chiefs then swore their loyalty. Charles set out for Edinburgh, gathering support as he

Dunblane, in spite of the furious assault of the Jacobite MacDonalds against the Whig Campbells. By the time James arrived in Scotland in December, the cause was lost. Murmuring that his whole life had been 'a constant series of misfortunes', James hung about gloomily for a few weeks, then slipped back to France. The revolt collapsed.

The government had received a nasty fright. It tried to make sure that no such outbreak would occur again. Some Jacobites were hanged, many were transported to the colonies, and the Highlands were went, and brushing aside a couple of regiments of government troops who tried to stop him. With his large though ragged army, he rode into Edinburgh through cheering crowds. 'James III' was proclaimed king of Scotland.

The government's commander, General Cope, had discreetly backed away to Inverness, hoping that the Whig clans would join him. They showed no eagerness to do so: the Campbells had always tried to back the winning side, and it was far from clear which side that would be. Cope therefore advanced on Edinburgh, without much enthusiasm for battle himself. At Prestonpans, the wild charge of the Jacobite Highlanders made his men run, according to Prince Charles, 'like rabbits'.

Charles was a splendid leader and, though inexperienced, not a bad strategist. He saw that his only hope of success was in a quick, bold strike, though he waited several weeks in Edinburgh hoping for French aid that never came. It was November before he crossed the border and advanced into England. His objective was London, where the citizens quaked at news of his approach.

He chose a route through Lancashire, hoping to pick up more support. But only a few joined him, and meanwhile three English armies had taken the field, each larger than his. At Derby, only 225 kilometres from London, his officers advised a retreat to the safety of the Highlands. Charles wanted to press on to London, and though the risks were great, surely he was right. In the end, cursing furiously (he had a sharp temper), he gave in, and the Jacobite army withdrew.

The following spring, a large government army assembled at Aberdeen under the command of the Duke of Cumberland, son of George II, a fat and loathsome prince though a competent general. Better armed, better paid, better fed and twice the size of Charles's army, it advanced towards Inverness. On a bleak moor at Culloden, the Highlanders were practically wiped out. As they lay wounded, Cumberland's men bayoneted them to death, gaining for their commander his nickname 'Butcher'. Prince Charles, in tears, escaped. After many narrow shaves in the Highlands and Isles, he was picked up by a French frigate and carried away.

*Bonnie Charlie's now awa',*
*Will he no come back again?*

asked the song. The answer was no. Forty-two years later, drunken, disappointed, even more bad-tempered, he died, still an exile. But he had lived one great year.

The government's attempts to 'pacify' the Highlands after the rebellion of 1715 had not succeeded: Prince Charles provided the clearest proof of that. This time, the government made certain that the Highlands would never threaten it again. Cumberland's men tramped through the glens looking for Jacobites, burning houses and driving off cattle. Jacobite leaders were executed, clansmen exiled. The government's aim was nothing less than the destruction of the clan system. Even to wear a kilt or play the bagpipes was forbidden. Many Highland families left the country.

The policy was a success. Except for the odd act of revenge, the Highlands remained peaceful. But, as Dr Johnson said, it was not difficult to govern a country peacefully if you drove out the people.

The old clan system was not in every way admirable, but it did have virtues, among them the great bond of loyalty between a chief and his men. When Prince Charles was wandering among the poor Highlanders after Culloden, a huge reward was offered for his capture. Yet no one gave him away. All this was destroyed in the years that followed. The chiefs who remained became mere landlords who, like other landlords, were mainly concerned with making profits. That was often most easily done by clearing out the small farms in favour of

*Highland tragedy: the destruction of the clans at Culloden left the Stuarts without hope and ended an era in the history of Scotland.*

sheep. Tenants slow to leave when requested might have their cottages set on fire. More and more people left the Highlands. Some became fishermen on the coast, some joined the army, some emigrated to North America.

Although the history of the Highlands in the 18th century is a miserable story, things were different in the Lowlands. By the time of Culloden, Scotland was at last beginning to enjoy some advantages from the union with England. The tobacco trade made Glasgow a great business centre, while other towns grew rich on the linen industry (later changing to cotton). The coming of the Industrial Revolution was as vital to Scotland as it was to England, and released the genius for engineering for which the Scots became famous.

# Chapter 10

## New Crops and Fatter Sheep

In the 18th century, population began to grow very sharply and there was plenty of money about for investing in industry and trade. The country was thriving. And for the country to thrive, farming had to thrive. In fact, farming had to become more productive to provide food for the growing population. Changes do not occur quickly in farming, but in the 18th century it was as true to speak of an 'Agricultural Revolution' as of the 'Industrial Revolution' which followed it.

*Bakewell with his prize sheep.*

Although people had been complaining about enclosures since the 16th century, most of the country was still in big open fields. But it was impossible to experiment with new crops and new methods on the strips of the open fields. Enclosure was essential. To enclose common land, a landowner had to get permission through an act of Parliament, and the number of enclosure acts gives some idea of how much enclosure of that type was going on. In the ten years after 1700, there was only one enclosure act. In the ten years after 1800, there were 906.

For the poorest people in the country, enclosure was a hardship. They were entitled to compensation for the rights they lost when common land was enclosed, but they did not always get it. Even if they did, it was probably not enough. It was poor compensation to receive a small plot of land – some distance away perhaps – instead of the right to graze a cow on the common. When that happened, the cow had to go.

The great increase in production of food was the result of a new system of crop rotation, called the 'Norfolk system' because Norfolk landlords like 'Turnip' Townshend (who was an old colleague of Walpole) and Coke of Holkham made it popular. In the old, three-year rotation, the land had lain fallow for the third year. In the Norfolk system, the land was constantly in use during a four-year rotation. This became possible through the use of new field crops, such as turnips and clover. Farmers like Townshend would plant wheat the first year, turnips the second, wheat again or barley the third, and clover the fourth.

*Jethro Tull demonstrates his seed drill — not the first
ever invented, but the first to become popular.*

The new crops allowed farmers to keep
more animals through the winter. Under
the old system they had kept only enough
for breeding. The rest were killed, and their
salted carcases were stored in pits to provide
meat during the winter.

With good winter feed and enclosed
fields, experiments could be made in
improving the quality of livestock. Statis-
tics again tell the tale. In 1710 the average
weight of an ox sent for slaughter was 370
pounds (168 kilograms). In 1795 it was 800
pounds (363 kilograms). Sheep rose over
the same period from 38 pounds (18 kilograms) to 80 pounds (36 kilograms).

The most successful of the livestock
breeders was Robert Bakewell. Sheep were
his speciality, and he had one ram, called
Two-pounder, that earned him 800 guineas
(£840) during one season when it was hired
out to other farmers for breeding. So many
visitors came to Bakewell's farm, and he
entertained them so generously, that for all
his success he died poor.

Farm tools were simple in 1700 and had
hardly changed since the middle ages. New
machines, which were causing such great
changes in industry, were almost as important in farming. Jethro Tull invented the
first seed drill that worked properly. It
sowed the seed evenly in rows, where
before it had been scattered by hand. With
the new drill, the plants all ripened at the
same time, and a horse-drawn hoe could be
drawn between the young plants to remove
weeds and aerate the soil.

These rapid improvements made farming
a very different business on the great estates
of East Anglian and other rich farming regions. But for most ordinary people, the
changes were not so great. The women of
the villages still made their own clothes,
brewed their own beer, and baked their
own bread. The men worked in the field as
long as daylight lasted, made their own
tools and fences, cut firewood and turf on
waste land, and dug clay or cut stone for
building houses. Children worked also.
From an early age they did such simple jobs
as bird-scaring and wool-combing. There
was little education for them. Some quite
prosperous farmers could not read or write.

# An Age of Elegance

If the 17th century was the age of revolution, then the 18th century was the age of stability. The voices which had sounded loudly in Putney Church when Oliver Cromwell's army council met there, were seldom heard. Peace reigned and people grew prosperous. Nobody wanted to rock the boat. To get excited about anything, a new idea or a new dress, was not good manners: 'enthusiasm' was a dirty word. Cool reason was preferred to violent emotion. 'Avoid extremes', advised Alexander Pope, whose verse was typical of the age – finely polished, witty, and not very profound.

A parallel could be made with politics. It was a Whig age: the Tories, with their dangerous Jacobite enthusiasms, were out of tune with the times.

Saltram, Plymouth, Devon. In 1768 Robert Adam was called in to decorate the principal rooms, including this large drawing room.

It could be seen in architecture, where the simple classical style of ancient times gained supremacy over the Baroque style of the successors of Christopher Wren. The style could be severe: one famous example, Holkham Hall in Norfolk, might almost be a prison were it not so grand.

It was an age of towns, and town houses in what we call, rather vaguely, 'Georgian' style still survive in attractive rows and squares for there was some careful town planning too. The beautiful views of London along the Thames by the Italian painter, Canaletto, which today are so popular on calendars and postcards, catch the spirit of the age.

Yet it was also a time when the countryside was admired and enjoyed as never

*Handel conducting his* Water Music *on the Thames. The music was composed in honour of George I for a royal procession.*

before. Though tamer than it had once been, the countryside was not yet spoiled by the results of factories, chemical sprays and motor vehicles. The English manor house, amid its parkland, orchards and fields, was seen to be the most desirable residence for a gentleman. The landscape became, for the first time, a subject for English painters.

Another aspect of the love of nature was a new interest in landscape gardening. The English style of garden was less formal than the French, with more big trees and fewer neat hedges. People spent a great deal of money improving their property, under the advice of men like the architect William Kent and 'Capability' Brown ('I see great *capabilities* here', he would say to clients).

Nearly all objects were still made by hand, and the 18th century was the last and greatest age of English and Scottish craftsmanship. Pottery, glass, furniture – these were objects of art. Styles varied, especially later in the century, though 18th-century craftsmen were almost incapable of producing something ugly. There was a strong Chinese influence on furniture, which occasionally spread to architecture, while the ideas of architects like the Adam family, best known for their light and graceful interiors, also influenced pottery. Gothic made a surprising comeback in Twickenham, where Horace Walpole built his villa in the medieval style. Later, the 'Gothic Revival', with country houses built like medieval cathedrals, threatened to swamp all other styles.

Palladio was a 16th-century Italian architect. Chiswick House is a fine example of the English type of Palladian summer villa, fashionable in the 18th century.

An increase in wealth and leisure, which property owners enjoyed in the 18th century, often leads to a lively artistic literary scene. One exception was the theatre, for there were few good plays written except during a short period when Sheridan was writing *The Rivals, The School for Scandal,* and other classical comedies. However, the novel at last grew up. People had been writing stories in prose for centuries, but the first novelists who were concerned with character as well as plot were Samuel Richardson, author of *Pamela,* and Henry Fielding, a London magistrate whose knowledge of low life was put to good use in his most successful novel, *Tom Jones.* These books were popular, but the books to be seen on the shelves of the library that every large 18th-century house possessed were works of history by Gibbon, or of philosophy by Hume. Tobias Smollett and Laurence Sterne carried on the Fielding tradition, while Scotland produced the greatest poet of the age in Robert Burns, a farm worker's son.

After the death of Purcell in 1695, Britain had no great musicians. The best in the 18th century was probably Thomas Arne, who wrote *Rule, Brittania! The Beggar's Opera,* words by John Gay, might be called the first musical. Like so many works of the 18th century, its purpose was partly mockery – in this case making fun of Italian opera. Operas were also written by the greatest composer of the age, Handel, a German who settled in England and is best remembered for his oratorios (operas without acting), like *The Messiah.*

The outstanding literary figure of the age was Samuel Johnson. We know him best as a personality rather than a writer, thanks to the long biography of him by James Boswell. Though he wrote a lot, including an English Dictionary, he was at his best as a talker. He was the friend of many, including Oliver Goldsmith (author of *The Vicar of Wakefield*) and Joshua Reynolds (the painter who founded the Royal Academy).

English and Scottish painting became much more interesting in the 18th century. Portraits, by artists like Allan Ramsey, Reynolds and George Romney (a skilful flatterer) were still the most popular, and there was a fashion for group portraits, called 'conversation pieces'. The greatest artist of the first half of the century was Hogarth, whose popular work was to painting what *The Beggar's Opera* was to music or *Tom Jones* to literature. He was something of a comic-strip artist, producing stories in a set of pictures like *The Rake's Progress,* and showing terrifying evidence of the nastier sides of London life. An even greater painter was Gainsborough, a landscape painter by instinct who had to spend most of his time on portraits in order to make a living. There were many other great painters in this exciting period, like Wright of Derby and George Stubbs, the painter of animals.

Sculpture had always been a minor art in England, but in the 18th century it grew more popular (though the best sculptor in England was a Frenchman, Roubillac). As can be seen from church memorials, taste in sculpture was severe and classical. This attitude affected other arts. When Benjamin West was painting his famous picture of the death of General Wolfe at Quebec, Reynolds advised him to put the soldiers in Roman dress. That would be more 'heroic', but West wisely ignored the advice.

Elegant and orderly, the 18th-century world seems especially attractive now. But of course, only a minority of the population could take coffee with Dr Johnson or commission a portrait from Romney. And even among those people, life had some very unattractive aspects. There was much cruelty, mental and physical, much drinking and gambling, much wasting of time, money and talent. The expression 'as drunk as a lord' probably dates from the 18th century, and many a family was ruined by the stupidity of an heir with more money than sense.

*The 18th century saw a revolutionary change in garden design. The magnificent gardens of Stourhead, Wiltshire, with lakes, statues and ornamental trees, were laid out in 1741.*

# Below the Surface

Britain in the 18th century was still a country of small towns. Except for London and Bristol, no town had more than 50,000 people in 1750, though by the end of the century Manchester, Glasgow and several other cities were growing rapidly.

The towns were of all kinds. Some, like Bath or Cheltenham, were fashionable resorts, where 'society' – the fortunate few who did not have to work for a living – spent a part of each year before moving on to some seaside town, like Brighton. Sea bathing was becoming popular, and although there were no bathing costumes, the modest bather could hire a 'bathing machine' – a hut on wheels towed into the water – from which he or she could take a private dip.

Other towns lived on trade, acting as market centres for the surrounding countryside. In the wool areas there were industrial towns like Lavenham in Suffolk (which looks almost exactly the same now as it did then) or Devizes in Wiltshire. They were not at all like modern industrial towns, as the spinning and weaving of cloth was mostly carried on in cottages.

Thinking of London, people said that in England, 'the head was too big for the body'. London had close to a million people, a larger proportion of the population of Britain than it has even now. It was the greatest city in the world and citizens like Dr Johnson (who was not a Londoner by birth) were justly proud of it. Its shops and taverns, clubs and coffee houses, squares and gardens, were certainly splendid.

But London still had only one bridge across the Thames in George II's reign, and it was still as dirty as it had been in the Middle Ages. The river was the main highway, packed with boats of all sizes. The

*William Hogarth captured the seedier side of 18th-century London life:* The Orgy *is part of 'The Rake's Progress', a set of eight pictures depicting the downfall of a young man of fashion.*

narrow streets were no less crowded, and
the growing number of coaches and carriages caused constant traffic jams. People
walking on the pavement tried to keep close
to the buildings, to avoid being splashed by
mud and filth from the wheels of passing
vehicles. The noise was terrific.

We would not find it difficult to talk to
someone from the 18th century, not if he
were as tolerant and broad-minded as
Samuel Johnson. Yet Johnson lived in a
quite different kind of society. By our standards, there was a tremendous lack of
institutions – of government organizations
and departments to look after the various
aspects of ordinary life. In the towns, signs
of this were the lack of drains, the darkness
of streets, and the absence of police.

Today, there are parts of some cities
where certain people would not go. In

18th-century London there were many areas which no respectable person would enter. The fashionable world was constantly shifting farther to the west, to keep away from the rougher parts. Violence of some kind was difficult to avoid. The most

ly. While the rich drove their carriages out to a picnic, bands of poor children, taking a holiday from the thieving that was their best means of support, chased butterflies among the thistles.

Skilled workmen lived reasonably well in the 18th century. In some places they were almost as prosperous as shop-keepers, who in turn might, if successful, rival the local squire. But the poor suffered, as they

*Smugglers bringing French brandy ashore at dawn in a quiet cove on the Sussex coast.*

popular London entertainment was to watch prisoners being hanged at Tyburn (Marble Arch). Soldiers were publicly flogged in St James's Park.

Such bandits made the countryside around London more dangerous than the city itself. But at least it was possible for the townspeople to reach the countryside easi-

always do. The Poor Law had hardly changed since 1601. In some ways it was even more harsh. Workhouses were sometimes 'farmed out', which meant that a man would run them for a fixed sum on behalf of the parish. The more he could cut down on his expenses (such as the food of the poor), the more profit he could make.

The records showed that nine out of ten babies born to poor parents in the 1760s died before the age of three. This was horrible, but maybe they were better off dead. If they lived, they were bound as apprentices and might find themselves in the hands of someone like Mrs Brownrigg, who beat two apprentices to death.

It was very difficult for people who had fallen into the miserable ranks of the poor to get themselves out again. Their only comfort was gin, which was so cheap that a man could get drunk for a penny. Poverty plus gin led to crime, and in the first half of the 18th century, crime was increasing.

The government's answer to crime was savage punishment. A whole catalogue of crimes carried the death penalty, and decent people, serving on a jury, would sometimes refuse to convict a criminal because of the severity of the sentence. That in turn made the law seem foolish, so ordinary people became used to the idea of breaking it.

It was not only in the depths of London that law and order were non-existent. In a county like Sussex, which today has less crime than most, some parts were ruled by criminal gangs. The village of Hawkhurst was a famous example. It was inhabited by a tough group of smugglers who 'declared war' on a neighbouring village and attacked it, quite openly, in force (the villagers were also well organized and beat them off). On another day, the Hawkhurst men broke into the Customs House at Poole to take back a load of contraband tea that had been seized from one of their members.

Yet not many people were in prison in 18th-century Britain because, without regular police, law-breakers were not easily caught and convicted. The only laws that were firmly enforced were the severe and unreasonable laws against poaching; there, game-keepers acted as police.

Of those who were in prison at any time, about half were there for a 'crime' no more serious than debt. This seemed cruel and unnecessary to people like James Oglethorpe, who founded the colony of Georgia to give such unfortunate people a new start in life.

Many prisons were dark, uncomfortable and crawling with bugs. Prisoners had to pay money to the jailers. If they had none, their clothes were taken away and they were in serious danger of starving to death.

*Life was very cruel to the 18th-century criminal. Even the smallest crimes received savage punishments such as flogging or branding with an iron as shown here.*

People like Oglethorpe, or the prison reformer John Howard, made these dreadful conditions public. Johnson, Fielding and other public figures protested, and a few reforms were made. But the real improvements had to wait until the government took on greater responsibilities in the 19th century.

# Trade and the Colonies

By 1763 Britain had gained a world-wide empire, which included much of North America and parts of India, the West Indies, Central and South America and Africa. These various territories may have added up to an empire, but it was not an empire ruled from Westminster according to some universal system of government. As we have seen, the government did very little governing at home, never mind abroad. British responsibilities in India were in the hands of the directors of the East India Company.

*An East India Company ship in the Port of London.*

Even those parts held directly by the British were ruled by officials of the Company, not by the British government.

Many merchants built up vast private fortunes in India, often by fraud and exploitation, and this helped to turn public opinion against the Company in the later 18th century. Attempts to reform it from within revealed some nasty scandals, and the government reluctantly decided that it ought to have more control of the Company's actions. A governor-general was nominated as the supreme British official in

India, though the first man to hold the post, Warren Hastings, was later charged with corruption himself.

Britain's empire was the result of the country's commercial expansion. Trade was the only reason for its existence. That was true, not only of places like India or West Africa, where few Europeans lived, but also of the American colonies, where many of the people were of British descent. The purpose of colonies was to provide Britain with raw materials, like timber and tobacco, which it could not grow itself, and to provide a market for British-made goods, from hats to hairpins. All trade had to be carried in British ships, and the colonies were not allowed to trade with any foreign country, except through Britain. For a Virginia planter to sell his tobacco in France, it had to pass through England, and the man who made the profit was the English merchant who handled the deal, not the planter who grew the crop.

During the 18th century, the American colonists were beginning to feel angry at the way in which their activities were governed by what suited Britain. Stretching from Maine to Georgia, the colonies were no longer struggling settlements on the fringe of the wilderness. They contained prosperous cities, like Boston, New York and Philadelphia, which were as large as most English cities. The total inhabitants of the thirteen colonies in 1763 numbered about 2 millions (the population of England was about 7 millions). Many of them were German, French or Irish. Many others, though of British descent, had been born in America. Of those who had been born in Britain, some were criminals sentenced to transportation for their crimes (later, convicts were sent to Australia). Britain could not expect the American colonists to feel much loyalty to the mother country.

The Americans had reason to feel annoyed by Britain's hold on their economy, but they managed to get around the restrictions on trade by smuggling, which was as common a way of life in Massachusetts or Carolina as it was in Sussex or Cornwall. But if the British failed to understand the Americans' point of view, the Americans on their side knew – and cared – nothing about Britain's problems. During the Seven Years' War, Britain had defended the American colonies against the French. The colonists themselves had not paid their fair share of the cost of their defence, because the colonial legislatures (elected assemblies) would not vote taxes for it. This annoyed the British, but even more annoying was the smuggling that still went on. Several American merchants made quite large fortunes during the war by trading with the enemy.

After the war, the British government tried to control the American colonies more strictly, a policy which caused angry protests. The Sugar Act (1764), for example, tightened up the customs, and gave customs officers the right to go into any place to look for contraband. The government also forbade further expansion of the colonies to the west, because that brought them into conflict with the Indians of the prairies. This restriction was disobeyed, like others, but it annoyed men who hoped to make money from land deals in the west (they included George Washington and Benjamin Franklin). The Stamp Act (1765), a tax on documents and newspapers, which to the British government seemed a perfectly fair and moderate way of raising money for defence of the colonies, provoked furious outbursts.

The colonists had supporters among politicians in England, such as John Wilkes and the Earl of Chatham, and the protest against the Stamp Act on both sides of the Atlantic was so great that the government repealed it. But it refused to listen to the cry, heard in Ireland as well as America, 'No taxation without representation', which denied the right of the British government to levy taxes on the colonies.

# Chapter 11

## The Rebellion of the Americans

In spite of the repeal of the Stamp Act, the government was still determined to raise taxes in the American colonies somehow. In 1767 a series of import duties, known as the Townshend duties, was introduced, but again the opposition was so tremendous that they were withdrawn – with one exception. The tax on tea remained.

The quarrel had become so bitter that anything the government did was seen by the colonists as a blow against them. They had protested against the Townshend

*Bostonians disguised as American Indians hurled the East India Company's tea into the harbour as a protest against British colonial policy.*

duties, but when the duties were removed, they complained that they were being flooded with cheap goods to drive their own producers out of business. When the price of tea was sharply reduced so that, in spite of the duty, it was hardly worthwhile smuggling it, the Americans refused to accept the tea. A group of men dressed up as Indians threw the tea into Boston harbour. In many of the colonies royal government, represented by the governor, was collapsing.

Up to 1773, the policy of the British government towards the American colonies had been moderate, not through fear of the

Americans so much as fear of their supporters in England. After the Boston 'tea party', things changed. The port of Boston was closed and the charter of Massachusetts was suspended: economic prosperity and political freedom were both threatened. The colonists decided they must act as one against the threat, and the first Continental Congress was called.

At this time, very few Americans wanted to break away from Britain, however they might complain of British policy. But revolutions are not made by people in the mass. They are made by small groups of determined and dedicated people. After 1773, events swung in favour of American radicals, expert propagandists like Sam Adams, who was probably the man behind the Boston tea party.

War began in 1775 at Lexington, Massachusetts, when American militiamen tried to stop British troops on their way to seize an illegal ammunition store. Even then, more than a year passed before the Americans issued their Declaration of Independence.

The British did not seriously believe that the Americans would really become an independent nation. Nor did many Americans, even those who fully supported George Washington and his rather scruffy army. It should have been easy to crush resistance quickly, for the Americans had few guns and no navy; but the British did not try to do so. Gradually, the Americans became better organized, and through the diplomatic efforts of Benjamin Franklin, they gained assistance from France.

The British campaign was a muddle. Vital orders were delayed, mislaid, or ignored. One general did nothing while another tried to do too much. After a splendid advance from Montreal, General Burgoyne, surrounded and with no food, was forced to surrender at Saratoga (1777). The British defeat brought the French into the war, sniffing blood, and caused the prime

*George Washington, victorious general and first President, receives a copy of the US constitution.*

minister, Lord North, to offer his resignation, which King George III refused to accept. By 1779 the Spaniards had joined the French against Britain, and the British had lost the decisive advantage of supremacy at sea. When General Cornwallis, unsupported, was forced to surrender at Yorktown (1781) with 7,000 men, American independence was won.

Many people, including George III, believed that the Americans would never be able to form a united and prosperous nation. They found it hard to recognize that the colonies were lost for ever. Meanwhile, other dangers threatened, for the French were also active in India and the West Indies. But Rodney's defeat of the French and Spanish fleet in the Caribbean restored Britain's naval prestige, and peace came with the Treaty of Versailles (1783), in which Britain acknowledged the independence of the United States of America.

# Riots, Revolts and Wars

In 1770 Edmund Burke published his *Thoughts on the Present Discontents*. It was indeed a troubled time. The Americans were not the only people feeling dissatisfied.

Jeremy Bentham advised a complete reform of law and government on his 'utilitarian' principle of 'the greatest happiness of the greatest number'. Adam Smith argued in favour of new economic ideas: free trade (the removal of restrictions such as customs duties). Among his disciples was William Pitt the Younger (1759–1806), who became prime minister in 1784 at the age of twenty-four.

Other reformers were more concerned with everyday affairs. They were often religious dissenters, who were greatly strengthened by the preaching of Wesley and the foundation of Methodism. Radical reformers spoke of Liberty and Rights of the Citizen. They were sympathetic to the Americans and to the causes taken up by the politician John Wilkes. They called for reform of Parliament, the main political issue of the next fifty years.

The 'present discontents' were aggravated by the disaster of the American war and by the Gordon riots in London (1780), sparked off by an act removing some restrictions on Roman Catholics. But the

*On the deck of a British warship at Trafalgar: snipers high in the rigging tried to pick off the officers on an enemy ship. Nelson was killed by a sniper's shot.*

*The French Revolution degenerated into an orgy of executions in Paris: old women knitted as heads fell from the guillotine.*

most dramatic event, which turned many reformers into conservatives, happened abroad.

In 1789 the movement for radical reform in France, stifled by a government far more old-fashioned – in some ways still medieval – than Britain's, exploded in revolution. At first the revolution was welcomed in England by all liberals. But as it became more ferocious and bloody, there was a strong reaction against it. Edmund Burke, once a moderate reformer himself, clearly stated the dangers of radicalism in his *Reflections on the Revolution in France*. The government was naturally frightened that what had happened in France might happen in Britain. It

was especially worried by the strength of radical reform among the working class, and took tough measures against its leaders. Mass meetings were forbidden and the 'Combination Acts', which made associations of workers illegal, strangled the growth of trade unions.

The picture was not only of black reaction in England in the late 18th century. Slavery was declared illegal in 1772, and the campaign against the slave trade, led by William Wilberforce in Parliament, led to its abolition in 1806.

Except for one short break, Pitt was prime minister all his life after 1784. He restored the country's confidence after the

*The Congress of Vienna (1814–15) was dominated by Austria, Russia, Prussia and Britain (represented by Castlereagh). He sought to establish the balance of power and restored legitimate monarchs to their thrones.*

recent shocks and setbacks, and he vastly improved trade. Although some of his best measures were rejected by Parliament, Pitt was never troubled by the occasional defeat.

Pitt had built up a strong position for himself but, like all 18th-century ministers, he depended on royal support. George III was a very sick man and in 1787 he mistook an oak tree in Windsor Park for the king of Prussia. It was clear that the king was not in his right mind, so Pitt's opponents called for a regency, which would have meant the end of Pitt's power. But luckily George III recovered, and Pitt's position was stronger than ever. The outbreak of the French Revolution brought Burke and other powerful men over to his side, though it also signalled the end of his programmes of economic reform, because in spite of Pitt's hope of maintaining peace, in 1793 the French declared war.

Revolutionary France proved to be a formidable opponent. A British army in the Netherlands was defeated, and attacks on the French West Indies were beaten off, with heavy British casualties. Admiral Howe's naval victory of June 1, 1794, was some consolation, but in 1796 a new French general appeared on the scene – Napoleon. He drove the Austrians out of Italy, which

encouraged Spain to join France and forced the British out of the Mediterranean.

British fortunes were low. The navy was in a shocking state, and serious mutinies broke out in 1797. Poor harvests sent food prices soaring, the Bank of England was forced to stop paying out cash, Pitt's windows were broken by stone-throwing rioters, and the French refused a British offer of peace.

After 1797, the tide turned. The navy recovered its old form, defeating the Dutch at Camperdown and smashing a Spanish fleet at Cape St Vincent, where a captain named Nelson brought off a bold success without orders from his superior. Nelson (1758–1805) was then chosen to lead the British navy back into the Mediterranean, and he destroyed the fleet that had transported Napoleon's army to Egypt at Aboukir Bay (1798).

Peace came in 1802, but it did not last long. Napoleon, now ruler of France, dreamed of a great French empire. Again, an invasion of England was planned, and every French channel port echoed with the thump of hammers as an invasion fleet was prepared. But Napoleon delayed the order, and in 1805 Nelson won the last and greatest of his victories when he utterly destroyed a combined French and Spanish fleet at Trafalgar. Proud, unorthodox, charming, and extremely brave, Nelson was killed in the battle. The English were so shocked by news of his death that they failed to celebrate the victory.

The wars against Napoleon's France produced England's greatest admiral, and also its greatest general. In 1808 the Spaniards rebelled against Napoleon and asked Britain for help. A British force was sent to Portugal under the command of Sir Arthur Wellesley (1769–1852), later Duke of Wellington.

Wellington was not a dashing commander. He took no unnecessary risks and wasted no lives. Nor did he lose battles. In the Iberian peninsula he did not have to face Napoleon, who had defeated every other opponent with brilliant ease, but he did confront the best of Napoleon's marshals. The Peninsula War was a sideshow compared with Napoleon's great European circus, but it was a damaging wound in France's side.

After Napoleon had finally overstepped the mark by invading Russia, losing his army in the brutal Russian winter, and had been defeated by a European coalition at Leipzig, the long war came to an end. The victorious allies met in congress in Vienna to settle the much disturbed affairs of Europe. But Napoleon, escaping from imprisonment on the Mediterranean island of Elba, suddenly reappeared in France.

The final campaign was fought in Belgium on June 18, 1815, at a place called Waterloo, where Napoleon and Wellington came face to face at last. As the duke said afterwards, it was a close thing; but his men held on and the arrival of a Prussian army under Marshal Blücher sealed the fate of Napoleon. This time he was sent farther away, to St Helena in the South Atlantic. He never returned.

*Wellington on the field of Waterloo.*

# Chapter 12

## Painters, Architects and Inventors

In the late 18th century, there was a reaction against cool classicism in the arts. The Romantic movement, in literature especially, was a break with the past. Coleridge and Wordsworth thought of themselves as revolutionaries in poetry. With Byron (the most 'romantic' of the Romantics), Shelley and Keats, they put feelings higher than form. English poetry entered a rich period.

Plays remained in the doldrums, but the novel – domestic miniatures by Jane Austen, grand tapestries by Walter Scott, or early science fiction (*Frankenstein*) by Shelley's wife – sailed before a healthy breeze.

Painting equalled the achievements of poetry in the Romantic period. Landscape painting produced two great – though very different – geniuses in Constable and Turner; but there were many other fine landscape painters, mostly in watercolour, like Crome, Cotman and their fellows in the Norwich School. It was still easier to make a

*Charlotte Square, Edinburgh, the epitome of early 19th-century elegance.*

living as a portrait painter, like Raeburn in Edinburgh or Lawrence in the south.

In spite of the splendid terraces of Nash, architecture was already showing signs of a decline in taste, or at least a collapse of the strict standards of the earlier Georgian period, which soon overtook other arts as well. The most remarkable building of the Regency period (the early 19th century, so called because the Prince of Wales was regent for his father, George III) was Brighton Pavilion, also by Nash, a palace in a fairy-tale, oriental style which, however attractive it may be, is not regarded as 'serious' architecture.

Increased wealth made it possible for a larger proportion of people to take an interest in the arts, as in politics. Newspapers and magazines created a widening circle of readers. Literary and philosophical societies, mechanics' institutes and public libraries were founded in the growing cities, like Birmingham and Manchester. London University, the first university of England since Oxford and Cambridge, was founded in 1827. Unlike them, it admitted Dissenters and kept religion in the background.

In spite of all the difficulties caused by twenty years of war, the onward march of science continued. Scientific societies were founded in London and elsewhere. Chemistry made the greatest advances through John Dalton, Humphrey Davy (inventor of the miner's safety lamp) and later, Michael Faraday.

*Constable, one of the greatest of all landscape painters, making a sketch for his picture,* The Haywain.

# New Kinds of Transport

Before Britain could become a really prosperous country, something had to be done about transportation. No one had built decent roads in Britain since the Romans, and in the early 18th century the roads were worse than they were in the middle ages. Sunk deep below the surface of the surrounding country, some roads were muddy trenches which wheeled vehicles could use only in summer. One man who fell off his horse near Ipswich was drowned in an enormous pothole. The traveller and writer Arthur Young measured ruts over a metre deep in one main road.

Keeping up the road was the job of the parish through which it passed. This system had never really worked well, and as traffic increased, wearing down the roads more quickly, it ceased to work at all.

Improvement came in the later 18th century through the turnpike system. A group of men, usually local landowners, formed a company or 'turnpike trust' to look after one stretch of road, or build a new one. In exchange for this work they were allowed to levy a toll from road-users. The charge might be a penny for one man on a horse, or a shilling for a four-horse coach.

The turnpike system was not perfect. Even when the turnpike trusts were efficient, stretches of bad road were left between stretches of turnpike, and very often the trusts were not well organized. They collected the tolls at the toll houses (some old toll-houses can still be seen, now turned into cottages), but did not always keep the road in good repair.

The turnpike trusts could only improve the roads if they knew how to do it. In the early 19th century, two experts on road-

*A mail-coach preparing to depart. Introduced by John Palmer, they set new, high standards of passenger transport.*

Bridgewater had no easy way to transport the coal from his estates to nearby Manchester, so in 1761, with the engineer James Brindley, he dug a canal. At once the cost of transport was slashed. Other men soon saw the advantages of canals, and within a few years a network of inland waterways was built, stretching from Devonshire to Yorkshire and from London to South Wales. Gangs of men, many of them Irish, moved around the country building the canals. They were called 'navigators', later shortened to 'navvies', and like the railway navvies later, they were a tough lot.

Canals are easily built in flat country, but any rise or fall in the ground requires locks to stop the water running away. Yet canals were sometimes built in very hilly country, passing through hills via a tunnel and carried high over valleys by a viaduct. There were about 6,500 kilometres of canals by 1830, and although, like the roads, they suffered from the competition of railways, they never went completely out of use.

*James Brindley inspecting progress as a gang of navvies begin work on a new cut for a canal.*

building, Thomas Telford (also a great bridge-builder) and J L McAdam, rebuilt many of the chief roads. McAdam's method was the most popular because it was cheaper, and by the time Queen Victoria came to the throne (1837) many main roads and city streets were 'macadamized'.

The new roads allowed much faster travel. In the early 18th century it took a week for a London stage-coach to reach Edinburgh. In 1830, the mail-coach (which carried passengers as well as mail) completed the journey in forty-three hours, changing horses every fifteen kilometres or so. These fast coaches gave Britain the best system of public transport the world had seen, though it did not last long after the first railways were built.

For carrying goods in bulk, the best method had always been by water. But there were large areas of the country which boats could not reach. The Duke of

*James Watt gained his ideas for the better use of steam power when he was asked to repair an old, 18th-century steam-engine.*

# Machines and Mechanics

To change from a country of farms and villages to a country of cities and factories, the conditions for industrial expansion had to be right. We have seen that the country was prosperous, that farming could supply food for the workers, that transport was improving. The next step was more revolutionary than anything that had happened in Britain before. It was the change from handicrafts to mass production, the age of the machine.

Up to a point, industry could expand using the old methods. The mail-coach was not a new invention, just a better version of an old idea. But this kind of expansion was limited. For a real revolution in industry to take place, some technological invention was required – not a better coach but a railway locomotive. Coal mining was restricted to surface seams because the danger of flooding prevented miners going deeper. But in time, the surface seams were worked out. It became necessary to invent a

pump, to allow men to work at deeper levels. That was the reason for the steam engine.

Of course, there were many machines in use long before the Industrial Revolution, like water mills or spinning wheels. The new inventions arose from efforts to make old machines more efficient or to adapt them to new sources of power. The steam

engine itself is an example. In about 1760 James Watt invented the steam engine which, with later improvements, provided the power for the new industrial machines. But Watt's invention was simply a greatly improved version of an engine that had been in use for over fifty years.

There is nothing magical about the invention of new machines and new methods in the Industrial Revolution. Science had made great advances since the 17th century, and there was really no reason why the steam engine, for example, should not have been invented earlier, if it had been needed badly enough. Inventions usually occur because they are necessary. Those of the Industrial Revolution were developed by mechanics and engineers, not scientists, in workshops, not laboratories; and they were usually the result of an urgent need to speed up some step in the manufacturing process.

A machine that could do the work of ten or a hundred people caused unemployment, a more terrible thing then than now, for there was no unemployment pay. Machines, on the farm as well as in the factory, were often unpopular with working people. In the north Midlands especially, organized bands of masked men, the Luddites, went around smashing up factory machinery, around 1815. They took their name from Ned Ludd, a simple fellow who was said to have smashed up a machine in anger when he could not catch a boy who had been teasing him. That gave rise to a saying, 'Ludd did it', to explain any damaged machinery.

*Luddites at work: agricultural machinery angered them, as did factories.*

# Factories and Factory Workers

Anyone born around 1780 who lived for about seventy years would have seen Britain change from an agricultural country to an industrial country. So great a change, happening so fast, can be called a revolution even though, like most great changes, it did not happen as suddenly as it seems to have done from reading about it. We have already seen that steam engines were in use by 1710, and there were a few factories – using hundreds of workers, power-driven machines and mass-production methods – not much later. But they were exceptions. They hardly affected the basically rural character of society.

The Industrial Revolution happened in Britain earlier than anywhere else. That gave Britain a great advantage for a time, although it turned out to be a drawback in the long run. Other countries saved time and money by learning from Britain's experience; they could build the most up-to-date machines and factories when Britain still had to make do with creaking prototypes.

There is no simple reason why Britain should have been the first country to become industrialized. The conditions were right: prosperous agriculture, a strong position in world trade, a good banking system, easy transport, a growing population, plenty of coal and iron ore. Britain had some advantages which no other European country possessed. It had the largest home market (France had customs barriers between its provinces, Germany was not yet united), and it also had its colonies, all keen to buy British manufactures.

Increasing population is usually a sign of economic progress. Yet no one can say why the population of Britain should have begun to increase so rapidly in the late 18th century. Was it a cause of the Industrial Revolution or an effect? Probably both. The agricultural improvements meant better food for most people, so their health improved and they lived longer. Industrialization meant that manufactured goods were cheaper, so, again, the standard of living rose, allowing the population to grow.

Other reasons for Britain's taking the lead are harder to pin down. The political situation had something to do with it. Since the Glorious Revolution (1688), clever and enterprising young men had a better chance of getting ahead in Britain than in most other countries. People moved up (or down) the social scale more easily, and there was more contact between landowners and businessmen, between squires and tradesmen. The government itself looked kindly on the world of commerce and industry, waged wars to gain trade, and gave prizes for successful mechanical inventions.

The oldest industry in the world is probably the textile industry. And it was the textile industry, cotton in particular, that was the first to be industrialized.

There are four basic steps in the manufacture of textiles: preparation of the raw material, to form fibres; spinning, to convert fibres into yarn; weaving, to make yarn into fabric, and finishing, which includes processes like fulling and dyeing. In the old system, the spinners and weavers worked mainly in their own cottages, or in small groups. When growing demand made it necessary to increase production, the immediate technical problem was the slowness of the spinning stage – for one weaver could keep five or six spinners busy. The invention of the flying shuttle (1733) gave weavers an extra advantage.

The first major invention in spinning was the spinning jenny of James Hargreaves, which allowed several threads to be spun at the same time. Next came Arkwright's water frame, then (about 1779) Crompton's spinning mule, driven by steam power. The result of these inventions was that spinning

*A textile mill in Manchester. Power looms, manned by a few women and children, could do the work of hundreds of individual weavers.*

became a hundred times faster than before. Now the weavers could not keep up. For a time, the weavers were pleased, there was much demand for their work, but eventually the power loom came along to put the hand weavers (fine craftsmen, famous since the middle ages for their tough independence) out of work for ever.

The cotton industry is the classic example of industrialization (wool is not so easily handled by machine, and it took longer to find mass-production methods for woollens). In Lancashire, the centre of the cotton industry, the first industrial society was created. Cotton textiles played the leading part in Britain's economic expansion.

Although they never amounted to more than eight per cent of the total manufactures of the country, at one time they made up half of Britain's total exports. Cotton was the largest single industry; it was the first to expand, and it reflected the progress of the Industrial Revolution as a whole. Other industries followed the same kind of pattern, as they changed from craftwork to mass production.

The Industrial Revolution caused problems that no one had expected. The huge new cities with their masses of poor factory workers were something new in the world. They caused astonishment and fear. Though London contained slums as foul as any, no one had stopped to wonder if slums might be created also in Manchester and Glasgow. In any case, what could be done to prevent them? People did not believe it was the government's business to regulate town-building.

The living conditions of the new industrial working class were miserable. Homes had no proper drains nor running water. The hours of work were long, often twelve a day or more (an act of Parliament in 1819 made it illegal to employ children under sixteen for more than twelve hours a day). Conditions in factories were bad, wages small and insurance – against illness or unemployment – did not exist. One civilized Frenchman, visiting Manchester, exclaimed in horror, 'Civilized man is turned back almost into a savage'.

Here was a miserable existence. Yet it was probably no worse than the life of the poor in the countryside. It is the large number of people involved that makes it seem worse. For all the horrors of the early industrial town, factory workers were probably no worse off than their parents in a non-industrial society. Even child labour was not new, although if small children were to work, they were surely better off acting as bird-scarers in the fields than attending machines in a factory.

Employment was unreliable, especially during the wars with France and the rather silly little commercial war of 1812 against the United States (in which the British burned Washington). The end of the French wars brought a slump, and widespread unemployment. The price of bread was unstable: sometimes high, sometimes low.

*A coal mine: although young, poor children had always had to work on farms, long hours in a factory or a mine seemed cruel and unneccessary.*

*Houses for the new class of industrial worker. They were extremely small (the cut-away part shows two houses back-to-back), but perhaps no worse than what they replaced.*

When high, poor workers could barely afford to eat; when low, farmers went bankrupt. A Corn Law was passed in 1815 to help the farmers by keeping the price of wheat reasonably stable – and high. It ran into terrific opposition and was the cause of the fiercest political quarrels (except those over reform of Parliament) of the next thirty years.

If workers were not much worse off, they were no better off either. The benefits of industrialization meant nothing to them. It was the businessmen and the shareholders who grew rich.

There had always been rich and poor. But the effects of the Industrial Revolution split society into two – workers and bosses – in a way it had never been split before. As Benjamin Disraeli, a future Conservative prime minister, said in his novel, *Sybil*; the queen of England ruled not over one nation but over two – the rich and the poor.

# Coal, Iron and Steam

Among the essential conditions for Britain's astonishing transformation into the world's first industrial society, none was more important than the presence of coal and iron ore. Coal and iron were the basis of the new technology, in which machines and steam power replaced the old technology of wind and water power with machines made of wood.

Supplies of coal and iron were present in huge quantities. They were not too hard to get at. Nor were they too difficult to transport; and the new industrial towns tended to grow up near the mines that produced their fuel, making a pattern of development in England which has not changed much since.

Coal and iron ore had been mined in Britain for centuries on a small scale, but the two industries had been quite separate. The Industrial Revolution brought them together: coal was the fuel for making iron, and iron made the machines which, in turn, were driven by coal.

Iron is extracted from the ore by blasting in a furnace. The traditional fuel for this purpose was charcoal, but in 1709 Abraham Darby, member of a famous engineering family of Coalbrookdale, discovered a method for blasting with coke. Men had been trying to do this for many years without success, and Darby seems to have come upon his method by accident. He found it difficult to perfect the process, yet this was the first, most vital step in the expansion of the iron industry.

The increase in coal production depended less on the invention of new technology and more on a simple increase in the number of miners. The basic method of production has never changed much: a man with a pickaxe hacking away at a coal face. But the number of men rose from a few thousand at the

beginning of the 19th century to several million at the end.

Besides more miners, the coal industry had two main requirements. The first was cheap transport. Coal is bulky, and it is not worth mining if it has to be transported by air or, in 18th-century terms, by packhorse (although that happened in a few remote places). Britain was fortunate in its good water transport. It had rivers which could be navigated by boats and a sea that was never too far away (you can never be more than 110 kilometres from the coast in Britain). The canal system greatly improved water transportation, which, though slow, was quite cheap. But a really efficient transport system had to wait for the building of railways.

The other requirement of the coal industry was a pump. The need to dig deeper for coal had been causing flooding problems in the early 18th century. At one mine in the English Midlands 500 horses were kept busy hauling water up from the pit. The

*In the hold of a slave ship: slave-traders grew used to their job and treated the captured Africans like any other cargo, only caring that they stayed alive to be sold at the end of the voyage.*

neighbouring shaft. A system of safety doors was supposed to make sure that the whole mine was properly ventilated, but the job of opening and shutting the doors was often left to children of five or six years old; steam-driven fans were installed about 1840. The lamp invented by Davy gave miners some light at the coal face without the danger of an explosion.

Unfortunately, one effect of these improvements was to give the mine-owners an excuse to dig their pits still deeper. While the danger from explosion was less, the danger of collapsing tunnels and rock falls was greater.

We have to remember that when someone invents an improvement in some industrial process, it is not immediately adopted throughout the industry. Some factories were still using water power thirty or forty years after others had converted to steam although, in general, manufacturers were very quick to take advantage of new inventions. But to scrap a factory full of machinery just because someone has invented a better way of doing things may not always be possible: machines are expensive.

In later years, the problem of old-fashioned machinery and old-fashioned methods was one of the chief reasons for the industrial decline of Britain. It is a problem that has not been solved today.

Progress in any industry helped to set off progress in others. This was especially true of iron and coal, growing up together like sooty, gigantic twins. Iron manufacture needed carbon plus heat – provided by coal. Coal needed iron for its steam-driven pumps and a variety of other purposes.

Once the coke-blasting problem had been solved, the next step was to improve the draught in the blast furnace. Under the old methods, the draught was created by leather bellows; but they were not powerful enough for large furnaces. A breakthrough came in 1776 with the cast-iron, steam-driven, blowing cylinder of John Wilkin-

answer to the problem – and the answer, eventually, to the problem of power supply in all industry – was the steam engine.

The first steam engine that included a piston was invented by Thomas Newcomen in 1705. It was used in many mines throughout the 18th century, surviving in some places for a long time after the invention of the much better engine, with separate condensing chamber, of James Watt (*see page 198*).

Besides the necessities of cheap transport and efficient pumping, there were many other aspects of the mining industry in need of improvement, all connected with the shocking conditions in which miners worked. Iron cages and cables made transport from shaft to surface less dangerous. Fresh air was introduced by lighting a fire at the bottom of one shaft to draw in air down a son, one of the most devoted of the early iron-masters who wanted everything made of iron, including his own coffin.

The new methods made possible the production of cast iron in large quantities. But cast iron is brittle, and can only be used for certain purposes. To convert it to malleable or wrought iron, a new 'puddling and rolling' technique was needed, invented by Henry Cort in 1784. Iron then became a cheap and versatile material. At Coalbrookdale, the bridge over the Severn was made of iron, and so were the tombstones in the churchyard.

Any account of the development of an industry has to be simplified. Besides these big advances, many other changes and improvements in the manufacture of iron took place, most of them concerned with the blast furnace. In the case of steel, which is made from iron, progress was held up by one problem. All attempts to produce good-quality steel in large quantities failed until Henry Bessemer perfected his converter in 1850. Cheap production of steel then became possible for the first time. Steel began to be used instead of iron in industries like shipbuilding and railways.

The growth of the iron industry and the availability of steam power speeded up progress generally. Engineering became more precise. A steam engine, if it was to work efficiently, had to have a piston that fitted a cylinder tightly enough to make a vacuum. Such exactness would have been impossible in wood, the material from which the early textile machines were made, and it was not achieved without many failures. It represented a great step forward in engineering.

Equally important was standardization. If a piston rod on a steam engine broke, it had to be possible to replace it with an exact replica. Spare parts had to fit, and from this, efficient mass production developed. Thousands of articles, identical in every respect, were turned out at once. This development did not come quickly. 'Consumer goods' were not produced with real success until the second half of the century.

Besides textiles and the iron and coal industries, developments no less important, though less dramatic, were taking place in other industries. The chemical industry, for example, did not need huge amounts of money invested in it, nor did it employ a large number of people. Therefore it did not cause so much excitement and astonishment.

The advance of industrial chemistry was closely connected with textiles, for which dyes and bleaches were required in ever-increasing quantities. In the old days, these materials were obtained from plants of some kind. The chief advances made in the Industrial Revolution were in substituting minerals for vegetable materials. For example, sodium carbonate, a substance widely used in the textile industry, was obtained from such inconvenient sources as a Spanish plant or Scottish seaweed. But Nicolas Leblanc invented a method of obtaining it from common salt. Leblanc was a Frenchman, and most of the advances in industrial chemistry were made by the French or the Germans rather than the British, who were more mechanically minded. All the same, so powerful was Britain's position in the world market that it produced more industrial chemicals than any other country, until it was overtaken by Germany in the late 19th century.

The early industrialists had to be hard men if they were to be successful. They had to be ready to take risks, and they had to be able to deal with every aspect of their business, in a way which modern company directors do not. They had to understand not only the manufacturing process but also the marketing of the goods – two very different activities in modern industry.

Men like Matthew Boulton, partner of Watt in making steam engines, or Josiah Wedgwood, the maker of pottery, were

*The London stock exchange in the early 19th century.*

gifted in many different ways. Wedgwood made exquisite porcelain for the rich as well as cheaper earthenware for ordinary people. He introduced several new types of china and a vast number of new designs. He recognized the value of an attractive brand name and called his most profitable – and comparatively cheap – pottery 'Queen's ware'. Modern advertizing experts could have taught him little.

Wedgwood's versatility was typical of the best kind of early industrialist. He was versatile in matters far outside his business. At an early age, it was said of him, 'he distinguished himself by keen powers of observation and interest in all that was curious and beautiful'. He was involved in road improvement, canal building, founding schools, building chapels, forming learned societies, as well as producing the best earthenware the world had ever seen.

The ability and energy of men like Wedgwood are astonishing. Of course, he had a house full of servants, so he did not have to spend time washing up or shopping. Even so, it is hard to understand where he found time for all his interests and activities.

207

*The opening of the Canterbury to Whitstable line.*

# The Coming of the Railways

The trouble with rapid economic expansion is that at some time it must stop, and the faster the growth, the worse the slump that follows. There were already signs in the 1820s that the fizzing pace of industrialization was going flat. Just in time, the rate of growth was restored by the coming of the railways – the last and greatest performance of that superstar of the Industrial Revolution, the steam engine.

Railways were not a new idea in the 19th century. The first railway was probably built at a coal mine in Nottinghamshire in the year Queen Elizabeth I died. The rails were wooden, and the carts that carried the coal were drawn by horses. In the 18th century, this method of getting coal to the river or canal was widespread. It had disadvantages, however. For instance, the rails wore out in a year or two. In Shropshire, some

improvement resulted from adding a cast-iron plate to the wooden rail. By 1800 rails were being made entirely of iron.

The next step was to replace the horse with a locomotive. Richard Trevithick, a brilliant Cornish engineer, was probably the first to use a steam locomotive, in the Welsh coal mines. In 1809 he exhibited a steam locomotive towing a passenger carriage in Euston Square (which thirty years later became the site for one of London's main railway stations). Trevithick's train ran on lines in a circle, and a fence was built around the circle so that the public had to pay just to look at this strange new machine, never mind ride on it.

Trevithick's locomotive, and others like it built during the next ten or twelve years, were less efficient than horses. They also broke the rails on which they ran. Step by step, the track was improved, mainly by the use of wrought iron and the discovery, by trial and error, of the best shape for a rail.

So far, all railways had been built for

privately owned mines, for the sole purpose of shifting coal to the dockside. The first public railway was opened in 1825, running between Stockton and Darlington. This too was intended for freight, but anyone could use it to transport their goods and it carried a few passengers as well. At first it used a locomotive on part of the journey only. A stationary steam engine dragged it along by cable on one section, and horses were also used.

Surprisingly few people believed that the locomotive would prove to be the answer for future transport. Exploding boilers convinced some that it was far too dangerous. One man who did have faith in it was George Stephenson, engineer of the Stockton and Darlington Railway. Stephenson was also appointed engineer of the Manchester and Liverpool Railway, the first public passenger line, and although the directors of the company mostly favoured stationary engines, Stephenson argued successfully for locomotives. It was decided to hold a trial to see which of four possible locomotives performed the best.

The trial was won in splendid style by the *Rocket,* built by Stephenson himself and his son Robert, also a great engineer. The *Roc-* ket reached a maximum speed of forty-eight kilometres per hour, frightening the more nervous spectators, and although one of its competitors seemed equally fast, the *Rocket* alone did not break down.

The Manchester and Liverpool Railway was opened by the Duke of Wellington in 1830. In spite of an unfortunate accident, when a former cabinet minister was struck and killed by the train, the railway was an immediate success. There were more passengers than the company could carry. The railway boom was under way.

In 1836, a peak year, acts of Parliament were passed to authorize the formation of twenty-nine railway companies which, between them, were to build over 1,600 kilometres of track. The total capital of these companies was to be £23 million, a vast sum even now, when a pound is worth a fraction of what it was worth in 1836.

A slight slump in trade in the late 1830s was followed by an even greater railway boom in the 1840s. In 1846, 272 railway companies were sanctioned by acts of Parliament; between them they covered about 7,242 kilometres of track and had a capital of £133 million. The country went wild for railway shares. It was like the South Sea

*Euston station: entrance portico and lodges (1836–9).*

*A blast furnace in an iron foundry. Technological advances in the manufacture of iron made possible the building of locomotives and steamships.*

Bubble all over again, but this time, fortunately, there was no bubble.

Gangs of navvies moved slowly along the routes, digging cuttings, blasting tunnels, raising embankments and laying down tracks. They ate and drank vast quantities, fought each other in large gangs, and terrified the local population. When Matthew Brassey, a great railway builder, finished one of his lines, a great feast was thrown for the navvies, with whole oxen roasted on spits and a troop of cavalry to keep order.

*Stephenson's* Rocket *showing its paces: the barrel behind contains water for the boiler.*

Nothing the world had ever seen – not the pyramids of ancient Egypt nor the Great Wall of China – could compare for size and speed of construction with the railways. Themselves the result of the growth of the iron and coal industries, they made those industries grow even faster. They directly affected all other industries too. By making transport so much quicker and cheaper, they lowered the cost of manufactures. The British were able to reduce their prices and to undercut their competitors throughout the world. Perishable goods were moved faster and reached larger markets.

Railways themselves were a valuable export. Other countries imported British locomotives and railway equipment. British contractors like Brassey and engineers like Robert Stephenson travelled all over the world building railways.

The railways also had an effect on society. For the first time it was possible for poor people to travel long distances. From the beginning, trains had three classes (the standard of comfort varied enormously between first class and third). On stagecoaches, this division, even if possible, would not have been worthwhile, because poor people could not afford the fares.

The government had nothing to do with the building of the railways and, obeying the ideas of the time, interfered very little with their construction or their workings. The lack of central planning caused some muddles. Brunel, on the Great Western Railway, used a larger gauge than Stephenson, whom most other railway companies copied, so the early lines could not be joined up in a single system. Rival lines served the same town in some parts while another town of the same size was left without a railway at all. Landowners could be difficult too. The reason the line to Wick, Scotland, takes such a great curve through Sutherland and Caithness is that the Duke of Portland refused to have his deer disturbed by the daily passing of any 'infernal machine'.

Landowners were not the only people who disliked the railways. Some cities, Oxford for one, tried to keep the railway away, which they later came to regret. The authorities at Eton College gave the Great Western Railway a very hard time. They insisted that the part of the line near the college should be patrolled by the railway company in case any of the Eton boys should wander on it. The patrol was not stopped until 1886.

*Brunel's influence extended beyond railways. His* Great Britain *was a famous iron-hulled, steam-driven ship.*

# Religion and Reformers in Industrial Britain

Well-meaning people in the 18th century were worried by the distress caused by the new industrial society, and as the years passed all kinds of schemes were suggested to improve the standard of living. None of these plans for the improvement of society had much effect on the country as a whole. At the same time, no one believed that the government should do anything about social welfare, any more than it should plan the railways.

Nor was the Church of England much help. The trouble was that the national Church lacked leadership. There were no meetings of Convocation (the assembly of the clergy) between 1712 and 1741; bishops often did not live in their bishoprics; many parish priests were more interested in fox hunting or a fine claret than in the care of souls. They hired curates, at very low pay, to do the necessary parish work for them.

The religion of 18th-century society was restrained and orderly. When the Dean of Peterborough preached a sermon at court he did not like to use the word 'Hell' because it was not, he thought, quite polite.

John Wesley (1703–91), one of nineteen children of a Lincolnshire rector, did not fit this picture. Wesley was an *enthusiast,* and an enthusiast for religion. Though he once thought of joining the Dissenters, he remained loyal to the Church of England. After a spell as a missionary in Georgia, he underwent a kind of religious conversion – a sudden, warming feeling of complete trust in Christ. For the rest of his eighty-eight years Wesley put all his energy into preaching that faith to the working people of the British Isles.

At first he preached in churches, but the Established Church was suspicious of him, and eventually he was forced to preach in the open. He attracted huge crowds all over

the British Isles, from Cornwall to Scotland. He crossed the Irish Sea forty-two times.

The Church of England became steadily more hostile, and Wesley formed the congregations, with ministers ordained by himself, that became the Methodist Church, although it did not break away from the Church of England completely until after Wesley's death.

Methodism brought hope to thousands of people who had little else to live for except the prospect of a better life after death. It was not liberal in its ideas, doing almost nothing (for example) to make working conditions easier. Wesley believed that idleness was a sin, and constant work was the thing to prevent it. Though he disliked the aristocracy, Wesley believed in the order of society: his preaching was the opposite of revolutionary. The scientist and Unitarian minister, Joseph Priestley, who was no admirer of the Methodists, admitted that Methodism was responsible for 'the

*Wesley preached in the open air because he was not allowed in church. His congregations soon grew so large no church would hold them anyway.*

civilization, the industry, and sobriety of great numbers of the labouring part of the community'.

Wesley and his disciples were not intellectuals, and believed that a lot of prayer and Bible reading were the most important aspects of education. Yet Wesley, for all his contradictions, was a kind and generous man. He defended the restrictions on Roman Catholics, but he also defended the Irish. He was concerned not only with the souls of his people, but also their food and clothes, even their lavatories (or lack of them). He lived to see a great change in the public attitude towards him. Once he had been jeered at, pelted with eggs, even attacked. Yet in his later years, the arrival of the old preacher was the signal for a public holiday. Children followed his carriage in crowds. He preached his last sermon at

Leatherhead, Surrey, in February, 1791, and wrote his last letter to William Wilberforce, urging him to carry on the fight against the slave trade.

The Methodists were not interested in changing society, except in small ways. But it was clear to many people that drastic changes in the way society was organized were necessary to cope with the enormous changes brought about by industrialization. Some of the men who, to their credit, recognized the need for reforming society, were themselves successful industrialists. The most remarkable of them all was Robert Owen, who was born in a Welsh village in 1771.

When he reached the ripe old age of ten, Robert Owen's father gave him £2 and a stage-coach ticket to look for a job. He became a shop assistant in Stamford, later moving to Manchester. At eighteen he went into business for himself, borrowed £100 and hired forty textile workers. Somehow he made a profit and got himself a job managing a much larger business, most of which he knew nothing about, at a high salary. At twenty-two he was an important person in booming Manchester. Three years later he became the manager of the huge New Lanark mills, after marrying the boss's daughter. Here he meant to try out his plans for a new form of industrial community.

Owen had to make money – that was his job. But money was not what interested him. He was an experimenter by nature, and society itself was the subject of his experiments.

Owen did not believe that the poor and ignorant must always remain so. At New Lanark, he immediately ended the beastly system of hiring poor orphans from the parish as labourers. He would not employ children under ten, and would have fixed the age limit higher if he could. He stopped all fines and punishments (factory foremen used to carry leather straps for beating child

*Owen's New Lanark Mills. The mills prospered in this model community where conditions were improved and where schools were provided for workers' children.*

workers), he shortened hours of work, and when he was forced to lay off workers due to a temporary cotton shortage, he went on paying their wages. Owen built larger homes for workers, provided decent food and made sure children went to school.

Education was perhaps his greatest interest, and though some of his ideas on the subject – and on other subjects – were quaint, others were very modern. He believed that education should be *fun*; there should be no parrot-fashion learning and no punishments. The children should wear comfortable clothes, do plenty of exercise, singing and dancing, and if possible have their lessons in the open air.

Owen's methods at New Lanark were a success, and visitors streamed north to see the proof of his belief that it was possible to run a successful business without exploiting the workers. In 1813 he began to publish his ideas in books. They caused some dismay, for it soon appeared that Owen did not believe in God and appeared to be some kind of socialist. That lost him many of his friends in the establishment, though the Duke of Kent (father of Queen Victoria) said that Owen's private opinions did not

matter. His support for a Factory Bill, which would have improved industrial working conditions, earned him the hostility of fellow-manufacturers. But Owen insisted that higher wages meant larger profits, as the workers were also consumers and, if better paid, would buy more goods.

As time went by, Owen became more visionary and less practical. He held great open-air meetings in London to publicize his plans for a new type of society – 'villages of co-operation'. He attacked the Church, which was honest but not wise. In 1824, on the spur of the moment, he sailed to America and set up a Utopian settlement in Indiana. But New Harmony, as he called it, fell apart after a few years. Yet he was not discouraged, in spite of losing his fortune in it. As the radical paper, *Black Dwarf,* said, if Owen could have made the people who were to live in his paradises, 'there can be no doubt that he would manage everything extremely well'. But like most Utopian schemes, Owen's communities were wrecked on the knobbly rocks of human nature.

while it did not outlaw unions, denied them the right to strike.

Property owners often regarded the working class with fear and distrust. Their leaders were seen as dangerous threats to society. 'Look at them', said Lord Grey, who was not a reactionary. 'Is there one among them with whom you would trust yourself in the dark?' On the other hand, the workers had their defenders, several of them disciples of Owen, who preached the doctrine of the value of labour and insisted that capital was merely stored-up labour.

Owen himself for a time played a leading part in the Grand National Consolidated Trades Union, which could be called a remote ancestor of the TUC. Though it attracted many members, it was not a success, and Owen was not by nature a trade unionist. He was more interested in getting workers and employers working together in one body.

One effort towards a more just society which was supported by Owen was the Co-operative movement. The simplest form of co-operative is a group of people who get together to buy goods at wholesale prices. Families can get their food cheaper, craftsmen their raw materials. But as Owen pointed out, a whole community could be run on Co-operative principles – food, education, medical care, etc. Many Co-operatives were formed in the 1820s, although they were mostly more limited in scope.

Owen was also involved with the development of trade unions. In 1824 the Combination Act, which made it illegal to form trade unions, was repealed. Trade unions leaped into existence in many different industries, startling Parliament (which, of course, still represented only employers, not workers) into passing a new act which,

*A 19th-century certificate of trade union membership.*

# Sports, Pastimes and New Games

Between 1800 and 1900 many of the sports and games popular today were developed, or were invented, to fill the growing leisure hours of the British middle classes. Many sports in 1800 were chiefly an excuse for betting – the favourite vice of the rich and (when wages rose) of working men also.

The part played by the horse in early 19th-century Britain, both in work and play, was larger than the part played now by the motor car.

Horse-racing was well established when King Charles II and his brother escaped the Rye House plotters on their way back from Newmarket in 1683. A hundred years later, horse-racing had become more popular, but it badly needed regulating, in spite of the founding of an organizing body, the Jockey Club, in 1750. A meeting might be held on any piece of waste ground. There were few rules, no regular programme – extra races might be run to decide bets between rival

*A prize fight: bare fists only, and the fight to end only when one man could no longer stand.*

owners – and the standard of riding was low. The whole affair was decidely rough and ready. One jockey angrily complained that he had nearly been killed by a crowd of toughs at Margate after riding his horse to an unpopular win. Only in the mid-19th century, when keen aristocratic owners like Lord George Bentinck took a hand, were dishonesty and fraud stamped out, and the 'sport of kings' properly organized.

Fox-hunting was popular in the north of England by 1700, though some people felt that the hare was a better quarry. We tend to think of hunting as the exclusive sport of the landowning upper class, but in fact there was more social mixing in the hunting field than almost anywhere else. The most famous fox-hunting hero in fiction is not some lord in a pink coat but Mr Jorrocks, the cockney grocer created by the sporting writer R S Surtees.

Leaping the Brook:
*fox-hunting became popular in
the 18th century.*

Shooting, the modern equivalent of the medieval sport of falconry, was more exclusive than hunting. Shooting rights were protected by the harsh Game Laws, which caused great bitterness among ordinary country people who were forbidden to take game on the land they worked. Fishing was, as it always has been, a classless sport. It required more skill 150 years ago than it does now, as the fisherman had to make his own rod and tackle. On the other hand, some methods which are now considered unsporting, if not illegal, were allowed.

People were less squeamish then – we could say more brutal. They were not protected from the harshness of nature as we are today, and some of their entertainments, such as cock-fighting (extremely popular), badger-baiting or bull-baiting, or watching public executions, seem disgusting to us. During the course of the 19th century, when society was rapidly becoming, in this respect at least, more civilized and gentler, such unpleasant sports became illegal, along with prize fights, in which the contestants wore no gloves and fought to a finish, and duelling with cudgels, which is described in Thomas Hughes's novel about Rugby

school, *Tom Brown's School Days* (1857).

As these crude old sports gradually disappeared, other games arose to replace them. Most of the new games were not really 'new' at all, although the old forms from which they came would have been hard to recognize.

Cricket may have begun as some bat-and-ball game of the Anglo-Saxons, although it is not mentioned by name until the 16th century. In the reign of James I we hear of cricketers being fined for playing on Sunday, and the first county match (London v. Kent) was played in 1719. Up to that time, the game was played mostly by humble folk, like the shepherds of the Sussex and Hampshire downs, but in the 18th century, the aristocracy and gentry became interested. In 1751 the Prince of Wales died after being struck by the ball at cricket practice. But the rise of cricket owed no less to the Hampshire village of Hambledon, whose team, captained by Richard Nyren, landlord of the Bat and Ball Inn, was good enough to beat an all-England team by an innings.

Cricket bats were curved, like the blade of a scythe, and spectators sometimes sat on the field, nearer the wicket than the deep fielders. The ball was bowled underarm. Overarm bowling (as it is done today) became general practice only in 1864. By that time the game was being played all over the British Empire, and county cricket was well established.

As it was played a hundred years ago, cricket would have been easily recognizable to a modern cricketer. But the grass was kept short by grazing sheep, and the fielders turned out in top hats and black boots.

In 1800 football was even less like its modern descendant – soccer or rugby – than cricket was. Yet, like cricket, football can be traced back a long way. There is a legend in Chester of the citizens using the head of a conquered Viking as a football, and boys in the Middle Ages used to play with a cow's bladder or stuffed animal skin. These 'games' were more like friendly fights. The whole village might take part, and the 'pitch' might cover several kilometres. In the Orkneys and one or two other places,

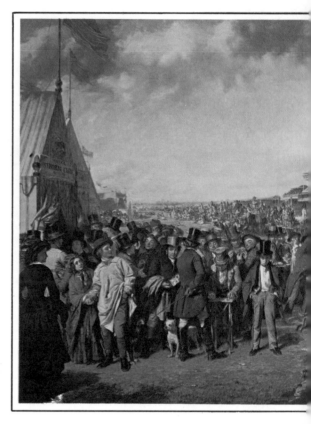

*Girls playing tennis, about 1890. There were no special clothes and racquets still looked like 'real' tennis racquets.*

and at some old public schools such as Eton and Winchester, old forms of folk football are still played in the traditional way.

Football games were probably used as an excuse for a riot, for example by villagers who wanted to tear down the enclosure fences put up by a reforming farmer. They were therefore unpopular with the authorities and, like most old ball games, were frequently forbidden by law.

In the 19th century football was played at many boys' schools, but each school had its own rules for the game. When students from different schools came together at university, they wanted to go on playing, so they worked out a set of rules which everyone could agree with. These rules, the fore-runners of the modern laws of the game, were drawn up at Cambridge in 1846. Unfortunately, they have since been lost, and we do not know exactly what they said. We do know that knocking the ball down with the hands was allowed, and that

*William Frith's famous painting,* Derby Day *(1858). By the mid-19th century 'the sport of kings' was a well-organized, social affair.*

the goal had no crossbar and no penalty area. Then as now, each side had eleven players. Nine of them were forwards: it was an attacking game then all right.

At that time, football was mostly played by those who had plenty of free time. The FA Cup of 1882 was won by Old Etonians. But by that time, the professionals, mainly Scots players, were appearing on the scene, and the professional football match soon became the favourite Saturday afternoon entertainment of working men.

According to an old legend, rugby football was invented at Rugby School when someone called William Webb Ellis, getting tired of kicking the ball, picked it up and ran with it. The earliest rugby club was at Blackheath, founded in 1860, but it was not until after the foundation of the Football Association in 1863 that soccer and rugby finally split into two different games. An argument concerned with professionalism later caused the division between rugby league and rugby union.

In the Victorian Age there was a demand for games that could be played by smaller numbers of people in an ordinary garden (the gardens of middle-class people were larger then). Several old games were adapted to meet these conditions. In the process they became quite different games. Croquet grew out of the old game of palle malle, played in the 17th century in streets now called Pall Mall or The Mall.

Croquet was enormously popular until swept into second place about 1880 by another new invention, lawn tennis. Lawn tennis developed from the older and more complicated game of 'real' tennis, which requires an expensive indoor court. As played on the lawns of Victorian suburbs, it was a duller game than now. Ladies wore clothes that would have been equally suitable for tea with the queen; men took off their jackets but always kept on their stiff collars and ties.

# Chapter 13

## Britain in the Victorian Age

Queen Victoria reigned for such a long time (1837–1901) that most of the 19th century is covered by the 'Victorian Age'. Such names can be misleading, because they suggest a period which was different from the time before and the time after, and was somehow unique and unchanging. But the rapid pace of change continued in the 19th century; it did not pause because Queen Victoria happened to be on the throne.

When the seventeen-year-old Victoria became queen, railways were a novelty: the Birmingham-London line had not yet been opened. Before she died at the age of eighty-one, she had seen motor cars chugging along the streets of London. In 1837, sending a letter was an elaborate, slow and expensive business, though the penny post

was soon to be introduced. Before 1901, Queen Victoria had sent telegrams and had used a telephone (which she did not like). The young Victoria knew the Duke of Wellington in his prime. She also knew the generals who were to command the British forces in the First World War. How surprised, shocked even, Wellington or Lord Melbourne (Victoria's first prime minister) would have been to read the works of Charles Darwin on evolution in biology, or of Karl Marx on the coming dictatorship of the working class, or of Sigmund Freud on human psychology. Yet all those writers were 'Victorians'.

Perhaps the most obvious change was the growth of towns. In 1837 most people still lived in the country. In the census of 1851 town-dwellers overtook country-dwellers for the first time. By 1901 there were 25 million people living in towns in England and Wales. That number was more than half

*Victorian Britain saw an increase in the number of manufactured household goods.*

*A Victorian engraving of industrial Bradford, Yorkshire.*

again as many as the total population fifty years earlier.

At least we can say that growth was a characteristic of the Victorian Age. It was also a period of peace. There was one international war in which Britain was involved, but it was fought far away (in the Crimean peninsula) and did not last long. There were also some small colonial campaigns, while Britain was gaining what is sometimes called the 'Second British Empire'. But none of these wars seriously affected developments at home. In spite of the winning of a new empire, the most interesting events happened in Britain.

Another characteristic of the Victorian Age was the much greater part played by the government in everyday affairs. In an industrial society, it was impossible to let things go on in the old way with as few rules and restrictions as possible. The government had to step in, if only to prevent chaos. Although it moved slowly and not far enough in the right direction, government action did lead to a less brutal, more just society.

The hardest thing to grasp about the age is the Victorian state of mind. People today sometimes describe a person or an idea as 'Victorian', meaning old-fashioned in the sense of conservative, or even puritanical. This can be a little misleading as a guide to the way most people thought in the 19th century.

There was a reaction against the cynical, careless spirit of the 18th century. Victorian people – especially middle-class people, who set the tone of the age – took life seriously. Religion was important, and so was a serious attitude to life. That included making a successful career. Drop-outs were treated with severe disapproval: they seemed little better than criminals.

The Victorians believed in virtue, although their idea of what is virtuous was different from ours. We do not put so much importance, for example, on those great Victorian qualities, self-discipline and self-help. But we should never condemn another society for its ideas about how people ought to behave without considering all the circumstances of that society. The Victorians were certainly very puritanical in their outlook, although less puritanical in practice than in what they wrote or said. However, they were primarily governed by their strong belief in the value of the family unit.

Queen Victoria herself was a symbol of her age. She had many 'Victorian' qualities, so that one of her prime ministers said that when he knew what the queen thought about any question of the day, he had a very good idea of what her subjects thought – at any rate, her middle-class subjects. Her husband, Albert, a German prince, was almost equally 'Victorian', in the best sense of the word: serious-minded, hard-working, honourable.

The time had passed when the reigning monarch was also a ruling monarch. Although George III (Victoria's grandfather) had managed in his early years to play a powerful part in government, the power had fallen almost entirely into the hands of the prime minister and his cabinet, who depended on a majority in Parliament.

As an old lady, Victoria had considerable influence on politics, but no actual control. When she was younger and influenced by Albert, the monarchy did seem to have at least a shred of real power. If Albert had not died at forty-two in 1861, it might perhaps have regained more.

Prince Albert was the driving force behind a great display of the Victorian belief in progress, the Great Exhibition of 1851. The idea of international exhibitions was then quite new, and Albert had to overcome a lot of opposition, some of it extremely silly.

The exhibition building was an enormous glass hall – the Crystal Palace – in Hyde Park. Inside were machinery and manufactures from Britain, the Empire and other countries. Among all the useful and productive exhibits, there were some odd ones too – a garden seat made of coal, rhubarb 'champagne', and a stuffed frog holding an umbrella. The exhibition was a tremendous success, truly a 'great conception', as the queen said. And it is impossible to think of the Victorians as conservative after looking at what the novelist, Thackeray, called a 'blazing arch of lucid glass' – that genuinely

*Opening Day at the Great Exhibition, 1851, which started the fashion for international exhibitions. Prince Albert organized it.*

revolutionary building, the Crystal Palace.

It was designed by Joseph Paxton, himself a good illustration of the Victorian belief in self-improvement. He began as a gardener, but his talents were noticed by his employer, the Duke of Devonshire, for whom he built iron-and-glass greenhouses. He sent in his design for the Crystal Palace unasked. Not only was it the first glass building, it was also the first prefabricated building, made in pieces which were put together on the site.

# The Struggle for Reform in Politics

Social improvements came very slowly to 19th-century Britain, making a contrast with the speed of industrial development. When the government did begin to accept some responsibility for the conditions of the new factories and passed Factory Acts which limited the number of hours worked by children, the new laws were widely disobeyed because no authority existed to enforce them. The Industrial Revolution continued on its haphazard way, its worst problems resulting from the lack of civil servants. There were no factory inspectors, housing officers, health officers or even regular police, until the formation of the London police force in 1829. Welfare depended on charity, and although many people gave a lot to charity, it solved none of the basic problems.

These problems could only be tackled by political reform. In the 1760s and 1770s John Wilkes had been the leading figure in a number of famous causes, which protected the rights of voters, stopped the government arresting people without charging them, and ensured the freedom to report debates in Parliament. But these were victories of the Common Law. They had no effect on the institutions of government, some of which had hardly changed since the Middle Ages.

Members of Parliament were still elected according to a system which had existed in the days of Elizabeth I, with the result that different parts of the country were represented in an absurdly uneven way. For example, the county of Cornwall elected forty-four men to the House of Commons. The total population of Cornwall was less than the population of Manchester or Birmingham, yet neither of those cities had a single MP.

Qualifications for voting had hardly changed in 400 years. In the counties, a man could vote if he owned freehold property worth £2 a year. That was not a great deal even in the early 19th century, but what made the system ridiculous was that a man who held his property on a lease could not vote, though he might well be a far richer man than the £2 freeholder. The system in the towns was worse. There, voting qualifications were more complicated but equally illogical. In several seats, the number of qualified voters was extremely small: in Old Sarum, for example, there were seven voters. In practice, the election was decided in these 'pocket' boroughs by the local bigwig, who had the electors 'in his pocket'.

There were various other ways in which an election could be managed, with a little skill and bribery. In the early 19th century about half the seats in Parliament were actually controlled by some patron – perhaps by the king, some aristocratic magnate or by a local squire.

In Scotland the situation was worse. The number of voters in the whole country was not much over 4,000, and a skilful operator with plenty of money, like Pitt's friend Henry Dundas, could almost wrap up the whole contingent of Scottish MPs for whatever interest or party he represented.

Voting was not secret. A man who promised to vote for Candidate X, and perhaps accepted a bribe as the price for voting for him, could not very well vote for Candidate Y because his treachery would be known.

Although the system was so obviously out of date and corrupt, it was not reformed

*One of the first London 'bobbies', named after Sir Robert Peel, who as home secretary was responsible for creating the force.*

*In 1820 a plot to murder the foreign secretary and other ministers was revealed. The conspirators were arrested at their headquarters in Cato Street, where one was killed.*

without a struggle. From the time of the Younger Pitt, politics were dominated by the Tories. They included intense conservatives like the Duke of Wellington, as well as liberals like George Canning, the ablest of Pitt's disciples. But even Canning was not a supporter of reform. Like most politicians of the day, he thought 'democracy' was a dirty word, no better than the despotism of Spanish rule in South America, where Canning aided the new republic in revolt against the Spaniards.

Canning died young in 1828, and two years later, with the demand for reform rising to a deafening pitch, Wellington became prime minister. Less skilful at politics than at war, Wellington annoyed the Canningite wing of his party by his stiff conservatism, but equally annoyed the conservative wing by accepting a bill to admit Roman Catholics to Parliament. Lord Winchelsea accused him of deceit, which led to a duel (neither was hurt). Politics were soon in complete confusion.

The confusion at Westminster reflected the situation in the country. It was an unsettled time, with new outbreaks of machine-breaking and riots. A new election, caused by the death of George IV in 1830, drove the Tories out of power. With a Whig government installed, reform seemed inevitable. Yet two years, marked by one crisis after another, went by before the Great Reform Bill was finally passed into law.

The Reform Act was a victory for the middle classes. It redistributed parliamentary seats more fairly, and it introduced new voting qualifications. The effect of these was to give the vote to most people living in towns who could be called 'middle-class', including a few skilled craftsmen and small shopkeepers.

After all the fuss, the effects of the long-awaited reform turned out to be rather slight. The type of man elected to Parliament remained much the same, and the great mass of the people were still left without a political voice. The real importance of the act, as its opponents were the first to recognize, was that it made the first small break in the wall of privilege which protected the interests of the land-owning ruling class. Once reform had begun, the next step was easier. The vote was distributed more widely by later reform acts in 1867 and 1884. By 1885, nearly all males over twenty-one could vote, although women had to wait much longer.

The reform of Parliament was followed by a reform of local government in 1835. By that time most people, even those who had resisted reform almost to the point of civil war, had come to accept the act. But not everyone was satisfied.

Another cause of discontent was the Poor Law of 1834. It was well-meaning, but harsh and stupid. In order to discourage people from seeking refuge in a workhouse, the workhouses were deliberately made unpleasant. Husbands were separated from wives; tobacco was forbidden.

Dislike of the new Poor Law together with disappointment at the results of the Reform Act partly explained the rise of Chartism. Chartism was a working-class movement for radical reform. It took its name from a charter, drawn up in 1838, which demanded six changes: the vote for all males; parliamentary constituencies of equal size; voting by secret ballot; a salary for MPs; no property qualification for MPs; annual Parliaments. All these reforms except the last have long since come to pass, and to us the demands of the Chartists seem very moderate. But in 1839 they seemed revolutionary.

The Chartist movement gained a great deal of support from working people. Its leaders included some fine men, but also, unfortunately, one or two rogues. What chiefly worried the ruling class was that the movement appeared to be a cover for even more revolutionary ideas and for protests of all kinds against the established order. Governments in the 19th century were always especially nervous of any kind of political secret society. In them they saw the seeds of conspiracy and rebellion. That fear was the main reason for the acts against trade unions, and for the fate of the 'Tolpuddle Martyrs' in 1834. These workers in Tolpuddle, Dorset, had formed a 'Friendly Society of Agricultural Labourers'. Six men were prosecuted for 'administering an illegal oath' and were transported to an overseas penal settlement.

There were riots in many parts of the country in 1839, and Chartism had a sharp revival in 1848. That was the 'year of revolution', when Britain was almost alone among European countries in avoiding a violent revolutionary upheaval.

At many times up to 1848, revolution had seemed possible, even likely. But during the second half of the century the threat of social violence grew less. The reforms of the Whig government of 1832 and its successors were partially responsible for this. The Factory Acts improved working conditions, though not enormously. An attempt was made to stop brutality to chimney-sweeping boys. The game laws were reformed, with the result that poaching decreased instead of – as opponents forecast – increasing. Customs and excise duties were reduced, which almost ended organized smuggling. The armed gangs of poachers or smugglers which had once roamed the countryside to the terror of ordinary people disappeared, never to return.

*There were regular Chartist meetings in the 1830s and in 1848 the movement was revived, when a large meeting was held on Kennington Common.*

# The High Price of Bread

Besides reform, the greatest argument in Britain during the first half of the 19th century was over the Corn Laws. Unlike many political arguments, this one affected ordinary people in a simple, direct way, because in its simplest form it was an argument over the price of bread.

The great improvement in farming methods during the 18th century allowed farmers to grow more corn, some of it on land which would once have been too poor for a decent crop. That was fine so long as demand was high. But when the French wars came to an end, causing a sudden slump, the price of corn fell so far that farmers were selling it at a loss. They demanded protection.

Protection was granted by the Corn Law of 1815, which said that no foreign corn should be imported to Britain until the price rose higher than £160 a ton. The idea was that farmers should be able to make a profit but, when the price of bread went too high, foreign corn would be imported to keep the price down to a level which people could afford.

The law of 1815 did not work. In general, the price of bread was too high; as a result

*Famine: the Irish peasants, always poor, starved when the potato crop failed in the 1840s.*

even the farmers suffered as people had less money to spend on other foods. When a bad harvest then sent the price soaring higher, foreign corn was suddenly imported in such large quantities that the price fell sharply, creating more problems for the farmer.

In 1828 a new Corn Law was introduced. Instead of a single level of £160 a ton above which foreign corn could be imported, it restricted imports of corn by a sliding scale of duties. The higher the price of bread rose in Britain, the lower the duty on imported corn. The government hoped that this would keep the price of bread at a reasonable level for both producer and consumer, and – no less important – that prices would not suddenly go jumping up or down.

This clever scheme did not work either. Smart dealers held their imported corn until the price went up and the duty came down. Then they flooded the market with it, and that in turn sent the price spinning downward.

There were more important questions at issue in the Corn Laws debate than technical fiddling with prices and duties. Everyone wanted *stable* prices, but the landowners, who still dominated Parliament, wanted stable *high* prices. The factory owners and businessmen wanted stable *low* prices. They were wage-payers, and if the price of bread was high they had to pay higher wages.

Just as reform of Parliament was the spearhead of a movement for reforming all the institutions of government, so the Corn Laws argument was the vital factor in a wider argument about economic policy: Free Trade or Protection? The Free Trade movement wanted the duties removed from corn and other imports, and to reduce the influence of landowners – nearly all of them Protectionists – in government.

During the 1840s Britain had one of the best governments of the century, under Sir Robert Peel (1788–1850) as prime minister. Although a Tory, Peel was sympathetic to Free Trade. He removed import duties on

PEEL'S CHEAP BREAD SHOP,
OPENED JANUARY 22, 1846.

*Famine in Ireland convinced Peel that the Corn Laws should be repealed in 1846. This contemporary cartoon was one of many which showed that the repeal was popular.*

many goods and reduced them on others. But the Corn Laws remained. No leader of the landowners of England, as Peel was, could be expected to move against the system which seemed to defend farmers' profits.

But in the end Peel did so. His reason was famine in Ireland, following failure of the potato crop. To keep the price of bread high by artificial means while Irish peasants were starving, Peel thought, was absurd and inhuman. With the votes of the opposition (most of his own party voted against) he repealed the Corn Laws in 1846. It was the final, greatest victory of Free Trade. It also split the Tory party into two parts, which were never reunited; however, in spite of the gloomy forecasts of Peel's opponents, it did not harm British farming.

## Education for Everybody

The reforming spirit of the 19th century was nowhere more effective than in education. Schools were as important to the new society as railways, and although some bosses preferred their workers ignorant, many people agreed with the historian and philosopher, Thomas Carlyle, that education is 'a prime necessity of man'.

They were also aware that English education was backward. Technical education was far better in Germany, for example, and that was one reason why Germany overtook Britain as an industrial power.

In 1837 about one-third of working-class children never went to school. Others left at eleven. Many could not read or write even then, because teachers were few and untrained. Older children often taught younger ones.

Education was grim by our standards. Lessons were mostly a matter of learning by heart and the cane and the strap were freely used. Jeremy Bentham said, quite seriously, that his design for a modern prison would do equally well for a school. Of course others, like Robert Owen, had kinder ideas of how to treat schoolchildren.

A movement for national education was growing. Education for everyone seemed especially important after the Reform Act of 1867 had given many working-class men the right to vote. In 1870, education was made compulsory for children from five to twelve. Parents who could not afford the fees did not have to pay, but free education had to wait until the 1890s.

The 1870 act also provided for schools to be run by local school boards and supported by rates. This was an important step towards removing education from the exclusive control of religious bodies such as the Church of England.

Secondary education was for the middle and upper classes only, and mainly for boys, although some girls' schools and colleges were founded. Except in Scotland, which had a different, and in most ways much better, system of education, secondary schools were divided into grammar and public schools. Most public schools were grammar schools which had taken boarders in order to survive, but many new ones were founded later in the century.

Some of these schools taught only Latin and Greek. They were old-fashioned in other ways too. When the Duke of Wellington said that the battle of Waterloo was won 'on the playing fields of Eton', he was not thinking of British sportsmanship but of the violence and fighting that went on at places like Eton College.

The public schools were transformed by reforming headmasters like Arnold of Rugby, who 'civilized' them. But, unfortunately, public schools helped to harden the division of people into classes which was a strong characteristic of Victorian society.

Universities were even further out of date than grammar schools, more tightly in the grip of the Church, and harder to reform. They were still what they had been in the Middle Ages: vocational training centres for priests and lawyers. Change came gradually: Oxford had no scientific laboratories until 1855. The example of Scotland, where the universities were less troubled by religious quarrels and took in a wider variety of students, encouraged reforms in England, and so did the foundation of new universities in London, Manchester, Durham and other places.

Adult education improved in the 19th century. The great success was the Mechanics' Institutes. They had been founded by Professor Anderson of Glasgow in the 18th century, and though they spread enormously, they became less working-class and less rigorous in their instruction.

*The playing fields of Rugby in 1870.*

# Literature, Art and Music

Literature and the arts do not exist in some compartment separated from the rest of life. The novels, paintings and music of Victorian Britain were influenced by the type of society in which they existed – a society that had changed greatly as a result of the Industrial Revolution. The new engineering and new materials had their effect on the design of buildings, and of other objects too. The forms most suitable for iron and steel were different from those more suitable for wood and stone.

Another, more important effect of the Industrial Revolution was the creation of a new class of patrons of the arts – buyers of novels, spectators at art galleries and theatres. The new middle class of factory owners, merchants and businessmen had plenty of money to spend, but not much education. We are all blinded by our own prejudices, but it is fair to say that the Victorian middle classes often showed a taste that, by the standards of almost any earlier age, was simple and shallow, if not vulgar.

It is in the Victorian age also that we find, flourishing vigorously, the attitude called Philistinism. A 'Philistine' (the name comes from the people in the Old Testament) is someone who is interested only in common, everyday matters, like food or money, and cares nothing for art or ideas. The poet and critic Matthew Arnold (son of the head of Rugby School) recognized two kinds of Philistine, one who liked 'fanaticism, business and money-making', and another, less ferocious, who liked 'comfort and tea meetings'.

Victorian writers attacked other aspects of society which they disliked. Charles Dickens exposed the social evils of the times in novels like *Oliver Twist*, *Nicholas Nickleby* and *David Copperfield*. He was the greatest novelist of the age, overflowing with talent, enormously popular in his own time and ever since. His novels were usually published as weekly serials, and Anthony Trol-

*Dickens not only wrote novels. He gave readings of them, which were hugely popular.*

lope came even closer to the idea of today's TV serials by writing several novels about the same place, with the same characters.

Dickens excelled at depicting characters from the seamy side of London life. Trollope was happier in the middle-class countryside, and so was Thackeray, who was as sharp as Dickens when it came to exposing middle-class hypocrisy. Both suffered from the puritanical attitude of the times, which made it impossible for Dickens to discuss openly the shocking problem of child prostitution in London.

It was a great age for novels – a middle-class form of literature anyway. They came out in three fat volumes. Not until late in the century did people think that a one-volume novel was enough.

The popularity of the novel allowed women writers to flourish as never before. One Yorkshire vicarage produced three sisters who were all published novelists – the Brontës. 'George Eliot', whom some regard as the greatest novelist of her time, chose to write under a man's name, but Mrs Gaskell admitted to being a married woman.

The novel went through great changes before the end of the century, becoming more concerned with psychology. Thomas Hardy and Henry James were both 'Victorian' novelists, though as writers they were vastly different from Thackeray or Dickens.

The English drama remained sunk in failure until rescued, towards the end of the century, by the Irish (who also produced the best playwrights in English of the 18th and perhaps the 20th century). Oscar Wilde wrote one brilliantly entertaining comedy, *The Importance of Being Earnest*, but his career was cut short when he fell foul of public puritanism. He was convicted of homosexuality, was sent to prison, and died five years later. Bernard Shaw was a more serious figure, although his plays are as witty as Wilde's. He was an idealistic socialist, who

*Henry Wood conducting his first promenade concert in the Queen's Hall, 1895.*

wished to reform the world while he amused it, and he remained a brilliant and provoking critic of British society until the mid-20th century.

Some poets, such as Browning, wrote plays which read well but are hopeless as theatre. A greater poet was Tennyson, a splendid and very Victorian figure, confident, honourable, religious, but not always concealing moments of doubt. By the end of the century, Gerard Manley Hopkins was experimenting with quite new forms of poetry.

The Victorians produced plenty of critics, like Matthew Arnold or the art critic Ruskin, who attacked the sentimentality of much Victorian art. Ruskin gave approval to the group of painters who were called the Pre-Raphaelite Brotherhood. Their paintings were painstakingly true to life, with bright, natural colours and accurate detail. Their group name was a reference to Italian painting of the early Renaissance ('before Raphael'), and they tried to capture the simple sincerity of that time.

Greater than any of the Pre-Raphaelites was James Whistler, born before his time. Even Ruskin failed to understand what he was aiming at with his subtle assemblies of shapes and colours.

Associated with the Pre-Raphaelites was William Morris, whose wife was their favourite model. A socialist, Morris reacted fiercely against the Industrial Revolution, with its heartless mass-production processes. He was the leading force in a revival of individual craftsmanship and design – the arts and crafts movement. Many a suburban home today has 'William Morris' wallpaper in the front room.

The Pre-Raphaelites were one example of the great Victorian nostalgia for the Middle Ages. In architecture this took the form of an astonishing comeback for the Gothic style. Victorian architects revived a great variety of old styles, including Classical Greek, but Gothic was most favoured after 1850. It appeared not only in stone churches, like Pugin's church at Ramsgate, but in brick town halls and railway stations all over the country. Many of these buildings have gained charm over the years, and we are no longer irritated by their phoney quality, which is the mark of a 'second-hand' style.

Even the Crystal Palace was Gothic in feeling. After the Great Exhibition it was re-erected at Sydenham in south London and put to good use as a Saturday concert hall. In a time when there were no radios or record-players, concerts had a very important purpose, like art galleries before the days of good colour printing. There was a great musical revival in the later 19th century, signalled by the foundation of the Hallé Orchestra in Manchester in 1857. Grove, compiler of the famous musical dictionary, still in print, became first director

*Three Pre-Raphaelite painters (Millais, Rossetti and Holman Hunt) discussing Millais's* Death of Ophelia, *now in the Tate Gallery.*

*One of the most spectacular achievements of the 'Aesthetic Movement' was Whistler's remarkable Peacock Room. In 1904 it was taken to America.*

of the Royal College of Music. Parry, Stanford and, later, Elgar, were better composers than any England had produced since Purcell.

The jolly, tuneful operettas of Gilbert and Sullivan, like the increasingly popular music hall, were enjoyed by people with more spare time and money than their grandfathers. As the reading public grew larger (especially after the Education Act of 1870) there was more demand for popular literature. R L Stevenson (*Treasure Island*), Conan Doyle (the Sherlock Holmes stories) and the tales of Kipling and H G Wells represented the best end of the market. Many writers, popular then, are now forgotten.

In the 1890s a reaction against Victorianism began. The 'Aesthetic Movement', with which Wilde and Whistler were connected, was once rudely described as an affair of pale young men with dreamy faces thinking nasty thoughts. A prime example was a brilliant artist, Aubrey Beardsley, who completed many cruel and exquisite drawings before dying of tuberculosis at twenty-six.

The new style in art was called Art Nouveau ('new art'). Its main features were its elegant line, borrowed from the world of plants, and pale colours. In what are called the 'useful arts' (glass, pottery, etc.) Art Nouveau produced fine objects. It had at least one architect of genius in Charles Rennie Mackintosh, whose best-known building is the Glasgow School of Art. With Mackintosh and others, Britain at the end of the century seemed ready to take the lead in the new architecture of the 20th century. But that never happened. The British failed to build on their native resources, and the lead was taken by Germany, France and the United States.

# Victorian Science and Medicine

During the 19th century, the population of Britain was growing fast. In 1800 there were about 10 million people. In 1900 there were nearly 40 million, although the rate of increase had already begun to slow down.

It was not just that more people were being born, nor that immigrants were arriving from abroad, although those causes played a small part. The main reason was that people were living much longer. The average life of a man born in 1800 was thirty years. By 1900 it was fifty years. (Today it is about seventy.)

Of course that did not mean that in 1800 a man was old at thirty. With good luck and good health, people lived as long then as they do now. But the general health of people improved so much as time passed that an ever-increasing number lived to be old.

Standards of health were raised in two ways: first, through the advance of medical knowledge; second, through the improvement of living conditions. Medicine was

still a rough and ready business in the early 19th century. No-one went into a hospital except as a last resort. Doctors were ignorant of the dangers of infection and did not know that germs existed. Surgeons were hardly more than skilful butchers: anaesthetics were unknown.

In the slums of Lancashire, anyone who reached the age of twenty-one could be considered lucky. Overcrowded and overworked, people had less resistance to disease, and in the filthy streets deadly fevers lay in wait. Bubonic plague had disappeared in the 17th century, but other plagues like typhoid or cholera lived on. In the year of the Great Reform Act (1832) over 50,000 people in Britain died of cholera. Prince Albert, husband of Queen Victoria, died from typhoid which he quite likely caught from foul drinking water at Windsor Castle.

Industrial slums made disease worse. But industry also brought improvements. Cheap cotton and soap meant that clothes

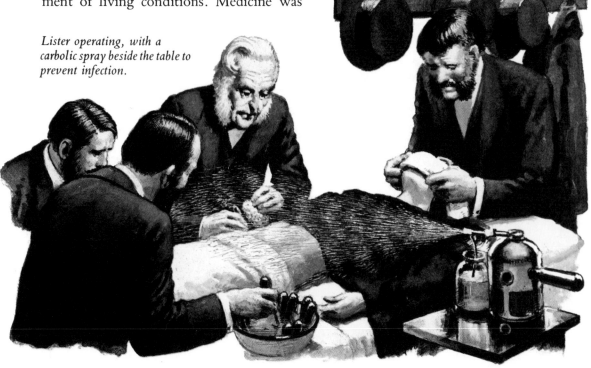

*Lister operating, with a carbolic spray beside the table to prevent infection.*

could be washed more often. Cheap iron production made it possible to lay good drains and sewers, which probably saved more lives than any other improvement.

Progress was not made as quickly as it could and should have been. Not until 1866 did Parliament force towns to install a proper water supply and sewage system. Attempts to clear the slums often ran into opposition from landlords who regarded their profits as more important than the health of their tenants. Vaccination against smallpox, which killed as many as 10,000 people one year, was not made compulsory for babies until 1853. It had been discovered, by Jenner, fifty-seven years earlier.

A great advance in surgery was the discovery of anaesthetics. Chloroform was first used by James Simpson. It was a godsend for all who needed operations and for women in childbirth, although it was opposed by people who seemed to think that childbirth ought to be painful (Queen Victoria, who had nine children, was not one of them: 'That blessed chloroform!' she called it).

Chloroform allowed surgeons to undertake more complicated operations, but the immediate result was more deaths from infections caused by dirty operating conditions. In the 1860s the Frenchman Pasteur showed that disease was caused by germs, and after that conditions rapidly improved. Joseph Lister (1827–1912) discovered that germs were killed by carbolic acid, which he sprayed freely around his surgery. The death rate in surgical operations dropped dramatically. If you had a leg cut off in 1860, you had only an even chance of living. Under Lister's methods, your chances were better than nine out of ten.

A stay in hospital became less dangerous. It was also more comfortable, thanks to the revolution in nursing brought about by Florence Nightingale (1820–1910).

Living conditions generally were improving. Better pay for working people meant

*The development of the sewers was perhaps the most important factor in the improvement of 19th-century hygiene.*

more food and better transport meant fresher food. By 1900 meat was being imported from as far away as Australia and New Zealand in refrigerated holds of ships.

Refrigeration was only one of the many benefits of electricity. If all the uses of electricity in its various forms are lumped together, they add up to a revolution as great as steam power. Before the end of the 19th century, electric trams were running on city streets, and in some places electric lights were replacing gas lamps – themselves an invention of the 19th century.

The greatest advances in science do not always have an obvious practical value. Ideas can be more important than inventions and may, in the long run, cause greater changes than the most spectacular advances in technology. During the 19th century three men were born whose ideas have been hugely influential on the modern world. They were Karl Marx (1818–83), founder of modern Communism; Sigmund Freud (1856–1939), founder of psycho-analysis; and Charles Darwin (1809–82), founder of the modern theory of biological evolution. Although Marx and Freud were German-speaking Jews, both died in England as political refugees (Marx lived in England for many years).

It is hard for us to understand the shock – even horror – which the idea of evolution

*Darwin making notes about the iguanas of the Galapagos Islands.*

once aroused. But the Victorians firmly believed in the truth of the Bible's saying that God created man 'in his own image', and most people took literally the story of Adam and Eve in Genesis.

Some thinking people had their doubts. Fossils showed that some animals had become extinct; also that some extinct animals looked very like surviving species. This did not square with the idea that each creature was created, once and for all, by God. Geologists had shown that the Earth was much older than most people believed,

*Two of Darwin's finches, which illustrate how species adapt to their environment. The greatest variation is in their bills; one eats seeds, the other insects.*

and that it had gone through immense changes, being destroyed and reborn again and again.

Many earlier scientists laid the groundwork for the theory of evolution. Darwin's achievement was to prove that the theory was correct.

Although his book *On the Origin of Species* was not published until 1859, Darwin's ideas were formed during a scientific voyage on the ship *Beagle* in 1831–36. As he studied animals and plants around the world, Darwin began to wonder about their relationships. Why do all birds have wings although some cannot fly? The ostrich uses its wings as sails, the penguin as fins. Why not grow extra legs or flippers?

The strangest animals were on the Galapagos Islands. Darwin observed that the animals there were very like the animals on the nearby mainland of South America, yet were not the same. Why were they not either identical, or completely different? He noticed that a certain bird on one island had a strong beak with which to crack shellfish. On another island there was a bird exactly the same except that its beak was long and thin. There were no shellfish there, and the long-beaked bird fed on insects picked from cracks in tree trunks.

The reason, Darwin concluded, was 'natural selection'. The individuals of any species are more likely to survive and breed the better they are adapted to their environment. Their characteristics are passed on through generations, and gradually the species evolves. The reason for the resemblance between different species is that they are all descended from the same ancestor in the distant past.

Darwin deliberately said nothing about one animal – Man. But the conclusion was obvious. Man too had evolved over the ages, and the reason why he looks so much like a monkey is that Man and monkey share the same ancestors.

This upset the whole Biblical explanation of the creation of Man. Many people refused to accept Darwin's theory (a few still do). It was not the first, nor the last, blow that Christian beliefs were to receive from science. But it was the heaviest.

# High Church, Low Church and Broad Church

In the 18th century, religion had ceased to be a burning question. Certainly, no one would fight for religion as in the 17th century, and most people thought it hardly worth arguing over. But the 19th century was a time of religious revival. For the Victorians, whether they were Anglicans or Presbyterians, Methodists or Quakers, religion was a highly important matter.

Religion required regular attendance at church, prayer and Bible-reading at home, and good conduct in life generally. In people's minds it was associated with the belief in self-improvement. The Victorians believed that human nature could be made perfect, and the way to do it was by education and prayer.

The Church of England receives great attention in history books, yet only about half the Christian population of England belonged to it. According to the census of 1851, 7,261,915 people went to church on March 30 of that year. Of that number, 3,488,411 went to non-Anglican churches or chapels.

By the end of the century the grip of religion on society was breaking, partly through the growth of materialism – the result of scientific thought following Darwin – and partly through the growing desire for relaxation and amusement, an end to Victorian seriousness. Another cause was divisions inside the churches themselves.

In religion, as in politics or education, reform was in the air. The old Church of England establishment was unpopular. The bishops had voted against the Great Reform Bill in the House of Lords, and as a result their carriages were stoned in the streets by angry crowds. It was said that the Church could not long survive.

Reform, however, saved it, as reform probably saved Parliament. A cleaning-up programme was put in motion: some of the excess wealth was trimmed from fat bishoprics, and the lower orders of the clergy were rescued from desperate poverty. New churches were built in industrial districts.

The religious revival produced new religious movements. One of the most influential in the Anglican Church was the Oxford Movement, led mainly by Oxford scholars like Pusey, Keble and Newman. It was extremely 'High Church', very close to Roman Catholicism in ritual and belief. The High Church movement clashed with the Evangelical movement, which had been an extremely powerful missionary force since the days of Wilberforce (1759–1833). The Evangelicals were 'Low Church', closer to the Non-Conformists than to Roman Catholics – or to High Anglicans like Pusey. Many Evangelicals drifted into Non-Conformity, while J H Newman, the most brilliant member of the Oxford Movement, became a convert to Roman Catholicism.

The quarrel inside the church was fierce, but eventually the victory was won by what was called the 'Broad Church' party,

*The Salvation Army was founded when the great dock strike of 1889 had made life in the east end of London even more wretched than usual.*

although it was not really a party, simply a label for the groups and individuals not tied to either of the two extremes.

The Oxford Movement and other High Church movements like the 'Christian Socialism' of Charles Kingsley (professor of history at Cambridge University and author of *The Water Babies*) were another example of the disgust felt by many sensitive people at the philistine materialism of the age, sometimes coupled with nostalgia for the supposedly pure and simple life of the Middle Ages.

High Church religion had some effect on political life. The great Liberal leader, Gladstone (1809–98), would have been a very different kind of statesman without his powerful religious convictions. Gladstone, and the people who voted for him (mainly Non-Conformists as it happened) believed that religion had as much to do with politics as with any other part of life.

Divisions between members of the same church caused more dramatic changes in Scotland. The Scottish Church had always been more democratic than the Church of England, but during the more easy-going times of the 18th century, the appointment of ministers had fallen more and more into the hands of patrons, who sometimes appointed unsuitable men. In the 19th-century religious revival, efforts were made to improve the quality of the ministry, which led to local quarrels when a congregation refused to accept a minister nominated by some aristocratic patron.

Various plans were tried as a compromise. But the government was not willing to accept that local congregations should control the appointment of ministers. The final result was a permanent split in the Church. In 1843 the Free Church of Scotland was formed as a separate institution from the Church of Scotland. Initially it had 474 ministers, and within four years, by a tremendous effort of zeal, it had built over 650 churches.

# Victorian Politics and Statesmen

We tend to think of politics as a battle between two parties, with one or two small parties on the fringe. That is how it has been for the past hundred years or so. But not always.

When Peel resigned in 1846 after his repeal of the Corn Laws had lost him the support of his own party, party politics became a muddle again. The old Tory party was divided into 'Peelites' and the larger group of 'Protectionists', who had opposed ending the Corn Laws.

The old Whig party was changing too. The progressive, or 'Liberal' wing, whose members were closer to the Peelites than to old-fashioned Whigs, was gaining in strength. But it was the presence of Lord Palmerston at, or near, the top of the government that ensured parties would remain in a state of confusion.

He was not a party man. Although he had been a member of many Whig governments, the Conservative leader Lord Derby saw nothing odd in asking him to join a Conservative government in 1852.

Palmerston was born in 1784 and first held a post in the government as early as 1807. In 1830, under Grey, he had been foreign secretary, the post he held for the longest time. He became prime minister in 1855 and, with one short gap, he continued as leader of the government until his death in 1865.

It was almost impossible for a government to exist unless it contained Lord Palmerston. When he was dismissed from office on one occasion, the government collapsed soon afterwards. For Palmerston seemed to represent, in his personal ideas and behaviour as well as his politics, the new, prosperous middle class of industry and business. In spite of the Reform Act of 1832, which gave that class a more powerful

*A portrait of Palmerston, a bluff, jaunty man, liked even by those who disapproved of his policy.*

voice, it still had rather few spokesmen in Parliament.

Palmerston's policy was conservative at home and liberal abroad. He was not interested in reform, and in spite of the shortcomings of the act of 1832, no further act of parliamentary reform could be passed until 1867, after Palmerston's death.

His foreign policy was, as a rule, to support the future against the past: for example, he supported Garibaldi and the Italian nationalists fighting to make Italy a united and independent country. The reasons for this liberal policy were the reasons for any foreign policy: the best interests of Britain. He was not so much concerned with Italian independence as a just cause as with the likely profits for Britain in an independent Italy. Hated by all the old-established powers in Europe, Palmerston loudly proclaimed British rights and British superiority. In a famous speech, he compared the rights of a British citizen with the rights of a Roman citizen in ancient times, when everyone else was a 'barbarian'.

Palmerston's foreign policy was continued by the Conservative leader, Benjamin Disraeli, who was prime minister in 1868 and in 1874–80. 'Jingoism' – the word for extreme, flag-waving patriotism – though encouraged by Disraeli, was loathed by his still greater rival, the Liberal leader, William E Gladstone.

By 1870, when the Disraeli-Gladstone contest was in full swing, two-party politics were firmly established. Although Gladstone, like Peel, eventually split his own party, and Labour rose to replace the Liberal party, two-party politics has been the rule in Britain for most of the time since then.

Gladstone and Disraeli were both middle-class men, as Peel had been. In all other respects they could not have been more different. Disraeli, son of a Jewish writer, was elegant and witty; Gladstone was thunderous and righteous. They disliked each other thoroughly, as well as disagreeing about politics, and that made their battles in the House of Commons (where the standard of debating was very high) all the more spectacular.

*In 1880 Gladstone succeeded Disraeli as prime minister. A contemporary Punch cartoon read: 'Ex-head gardener: "Well, William, yer don't seem to be makin' much progress — do yer?"*
*New-head gardener: "Why no Benjamin; you left the place in such a precious mess!!"'*

# Europe and the Eastern Question

The foreign policy of the bigger European countries – the 'powers' of Europe – was (or seemed to be) often concerned with something called the 'balance of power'. This was the notion that the distribution of power among the different states should remain more or less unaltered. The balance had often been upset in the past, most recently by Napoleon. The settlement made after Napoleon's defeat at the Congress of Vienna (1815) had restored it.

Of course if each of the powers really wanted to keep the balance steady between itself and its neighbours, the 'balance of power' would never have been in danger. It was one of those ideas which do not mean very much in practice. Obviously, Napoleon did not believe in a 'balance of power', unless it were one heavily weighted towards France. Later on, the same could be said of Bismarck and his overpowering German empire.

But when one country became so powerful that its neighbours felt threatened, out of self-defence they combined against it. That had eventually caused the defeat of Napoleon. In that respect, the 'balance of power' was a reality in Europe's affairs.

The balance could be threatened by countries becoming more powerful or by countries growing weaker, or by the appearance on the scales of powers that were altogether new. All three of these factors were involved in the longest-running of all diplomatic troubles in the 19th century, the 'Eastern Question'.

At the heart of the Eastern Question was

*During the Crimean War Florence Nightingale brought what little comfort she could to wounded soldiers at Scutari.*

the feebleness of the Ottoman Turkish empire. Turkey was called 'the sick man of Europe', and one or two large vultures were circling impatiently, waiting to pick the sick man's bones. The largest was Russia, which had already gained some outlying parts of the Turkish empire and had certain rights to interfere in the Turkish provinces of southeast Europe as protector of the Christians under Turkish rule (the Turks were Muslims).

Other European powers wished to prop up the 'sick man' and pump new life into him so that he would be able to resist the attacks of the Russian vulture. The chief of these pro-Turkish powers was, for most of the 19th century, Britain (in the 1890s the Turks began to look to Germany for assistance).

This dispute resulted in the only European war in which Britain was engaged between 1815 and 1914 – the Crimean War. The immediate cause of its outbreak was a Russian quarrel with the Turks, leading to a Turkish declaration of war in 1853. The Russians swiftly destroyed the Turkish fleet and Britain, in alliance with France, sent ships to the Black Sea to prevent the invasion of Turkey. War followed, and in September 1854 French and British forces invaded the Crimea.

The war was not a glorious one. The most famous military event was the charge of the Light Brigade at the battle of Balaclava (1854), when British light cavalry charged the Russian artillery as a result of a misunderstood order. Even worse than the leadership in battle was the terrible organization behind the lines. It was typical that a load of army boots sent out from Britain should have been all for the left foot.

The horrors of the Crimea were worst for the wounded. Some of them, at least, received help and comfort in the hospital at Scutari from the thirty female nurses who were led by Florence Nightingale. The 'lady with the lamp', the soldiers called

*Prince Bismarck meets Disraeli in his hotel before the Congress of Berlin. The British prime minister was to return in triumph.*

her as, by the light of an oil lamp, she made her nightly rounds tending the wounded.

The Crimean War, which ended in 1856, solved nothing. In the 1870s Russian pressure on Turkey was renewed, with the help of the nationalistic Slav peoples still under Turkish rule. A short war followed in which the Russians reached the outskirts of Constantinople (Istanbul). The British became so alarmed at Russian expansion that they insisted on an international conference to settle the whole business.

At the Congress of Berlin (1878) Britain was represented by Disraeli, ageing but still crafty enough to trick his opponents into giving way by pretending to make preparations to leave the conference. The Congress saved Turkey from being carved up and, incidentally, gave Britain rights over Cyprus. Disraeli returned in triumph saying he brought back 'Peace with Honour' from Berlin. The Duke of Argyll, Gladstone's lieutenant, might sourly complain that it sounded more like 'Retreat with Boasting', but in fact the agreement reached at Berlin preserved the peace in Europe until the outbreak of the Great War in 1914.

# British Exploration and Empire

In the 18th century Britain had become an imperial power, only to lose the major part of its empire when the United States declared its independence. In the 19th century, Britain gained another empire, taking control of large areas of land in every part of the world. That empire, the largest the world had ever seen, was a reflection of the enormous power that Britain possessed through its command of trade, finance, and manufacturing.

Yet the British in the early 19th century cared nothing for colonies. The only use for Australia that they could think of was as a place to dump criminals after it became impossible to send them to America. Governments regarded colonies as expensive and dangerous, likely to lead to war with rival powers. More than once the government flatly rejected the offer of a new colony, even when a native ruler begged for British protection. Disraeli in the 1850s described colonies as 'a millstone around our necks'. But, like others, he changed his mind later.

The colonies that did exist in 1815 looked impressive on the map because they covered large areas. But they were less important than they looked. The total white population of Canada, South Africa, Australia and the British West Indies was less than the population of Birmingham. The colonies were scattered around the world. Each one was quite different from the others and each was governed differently – or not governed at all. There was really no such thing as an 'empire', if that word means a group of colonies brought together in a system of government common to all.

And yet the colonies were united in some ways. They were united by English law and by trade. They were linked to Britain by the British obligation to protect their inhabit-

*Famous meeting: the journalist Stanley greets Livingstone, unheard-of for six years, near Lake Tanganyika.*

ants even against British settlers. Of course, the British put their own interests first. But the tradition of protecting non-European people, although it was often broken or carried on in a half-hearted way, did exist. One of the causes of the American War of Independence had been British efforts to protect American Indians from the expanding colonists. One reason why Britain fell out with the South African Boers (descendants of the original Dutch colonists) was its attempt to safeguard the interests of African peoples.

Emigration from the British Isles to the colonies (and the USA) went on throughout the 19th century. Many of the early emigrants were ex-soldiers, without a job. They were joined by Highlanders who had been driven off the land, Irish families fleeing famine, English and Welsh who were poor or unemployed and sought a better chance in a new country. Emigrants were often helped by wealthy patrons, or by religious institutions and charities. In the early days they received no help from the government, which was not yet interested in colonies. New Zealand would not have become British had it not been for Gibbon Wakefield, and others as keen as he, who founded a company to colonize the country.

What began as private enterprise often ended under government control. New Zealand was an example. Wakefield's colonists soon clashed with the Maoris, whom they tried to cheat out of land. Fighting broke out and the British government was forced to step in (there were fears that the

Maoris would be wiped out, as the Aborigines of Tasmania were – to the last person). In 1850 the government bought out all the company's rights in New Zealand, which then became the responsibility of the Crown.

By that time the attitude towards colonies was changing. As Britain gained new lands, by war or other means, it had to consider how such very different places might be governed. The ideas of the new breed of colonial administrators were much more liberal than those of their predecessors, whose rigid thinking had resulted in the loss of America. The Navigation Laws were thrown out, allowing the colonies greater freedom of trade. Government support was given to settlers in certain areas – South Africa (to balance the Boers), parts of Canada and Australia (to keep out the French).

The Colonial Office, which had once been a humble little limb attached to the great body of the War Office, became a large and important ministry on its own. People began to think that an empire consisting of many different communities, under varying degrees of British control and owing final allegiance to Britain, might after all be not only possible but grand and desirable. Yet most people, at the beginning of the Victorian period, still thought that colonies would become self-governing and, in time, independent.

A rebellion in Quebec province, which was populated mainly by people of French descent, was one cause of an investigation into Canadian affairs carried out by Lord Durham. He issued a famous report in 1839 which recommended something close to self-government. His recommendations were not immediately carried out, being too advanced for the government of the day, but his report represented the hopes and ideas of the 'liberal imperialists'. In 1867 the British North America Act laid the basis for the Dominion of Canada as a federal state,

independent in most matters. It marked the birth of a new nation.

Australia and New Zealand were slightly easier to deal with because the settlers there were mainly British. New South Wales gained some self-government in 1842, only fifty-four years after the first convicts had landed in Botany Bay and founded Sydney. The population expanded rapidly after 1850, because gold was discovered, attracting many immigrants. By 1861 there were four self-governing colonies: New South Wales, South Australia, Victoria and Queensland.

The Cape Colony of South Africa was a bigger problem. Like Quebec, it had mainly non-British colonists. The Boers (the word meant 'farmers') were restless under British control, and many of them set out on the Great Trek to get away from British rule. They founded new republics farther north

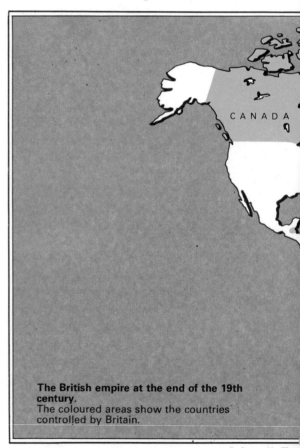

**The British empire at the end of the 19th century.**
The coloured areas show the countries controlled by Britain.

and east, on the Orange River and in Natal. The British later took over Natal, and the three-way clash of interests between British, Boers and Bantu (Africans) threatened serious trouble in the future.

British power in India continued to grow in the 19th century, and new territories were added. In 1857 the Indian Army mutinied. The immediate trouble was the use of animal fat as grease for guns, which offended both Hindu and Muslim soldiers; but there were deeper causes too. Horrible acts were committed on both sides.

One result of the Mutiny was the ending of the authority of the East India Company, making the British government responsible for all political affairs. As a sign of the new status of India, Queen Victoria browbeat Disraeli into giving her the title Empress of India, though he had a hard time getting Parliament's agreement. The 'Queen and Empress', as she signed herself in future, thought India her most glamorous possession; she also wanted to win a title equal to the emperors of Russia and Germany.

In the last quarter of the 19th century, the British came to think of their empire in a more selfish and aggressive way. In common with other European countries, Britain suddenly began grabbing colonies like a greedy child let loose in a cake shop. Within a few years, almost the whole of the vast continent of Africa was divided up among the powers of Europe. Britain also added part of New Guinea and Burma to its growing Asian empire.

The 'new imperialism' was certainly a dramatic change in British colonial policy. In the past British governments had often avoided new colonial responsibilities: when missionaries or merchants tried to persuade the government to support British settle-

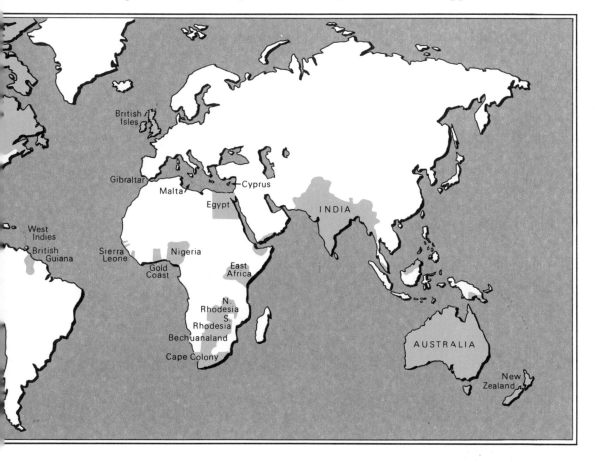

ment in some part of Africa, they had usually been told that their schemes were impossible or undesirable. Then there had been a feeling of trusteeship: Britain had a responsibility to people who (the British thought) were less fortunate than themselves, to bring them the benefits of Christianity, economic development, and a modern form of government. What kept Dr Livingstone marching across Africa until he dropped dead in his tracks was his desire to help the Africans, not to prepare the way for a new British empire.

By 1880 such ideas were no longer dominant. Imperialism had become popular with the middle classes. J R Seeley, a history professor, said in a famous lecture that the mere idea of giving up the colonies was 'fantastic'. The sun did not set on the empire – and if the new imperialists had had their way, it never would have set.

We can hear a note of coarseness sounding among the patriotic trumpets of the new imperialism. Men like Cecil Rhodes (founder of Rhodesia) and the German-born Alfred Milner spoke as though the British were a superior race, certainly superior to Africans or Indians.

Some of the unpleasant jingoism of the time was the result of fear. Soon after 1870 Britain passed its peak as a great power and began the downward slide which has been going on ever since. The aggressive spouting of imperialist propaganda was, to some extent, a defiant reaction by men who no longer felt confidence in the future.

In general, British colonies were well governed. They were certainly governed better than those of other European powers, though French methods were more effective in certain ways. The British could easily have been thrown out of most of their Afri-

ment forbade it. Although it was not the sole reason, the 'Opium Wars' were fought to enforce that right – a case of the 'unacceptable face' of free trade.

The scramble for colonies in Africa reached a crisis in the north and south of the continent at about the same time. At Fashoda, on the upper Nile, a French force, moving east from the French West African possessions, came face to face with a British army under Kitchener (1850–1916), moving south after conquering a religious uprising in the Sudan. Suddenly, France and Britain were on the brink of war. Fortunately for both countries, the French decided to withdraw.

In the south, the long conflict between Boers and British smouldered on. In 1895 Cecil Rhodes, then prime minister of the Cape Colony, acting with the secret approval of the British Colonial Secretary, Joseph Chamberlain, had tried to overthrow the legal government of the Transvaal republic. An armed expedition led by a Dr Jameson had been supposed to set off a rising against President Kruger's government; but the plan failed (Chamberlain's guilt was not discovered for sixty years.) Full-scale war with the Boers did break out four years later.

The Boers were surprisingly successful against the might of Britain. They had the sympathy of almost all Europe and of a section of the British population.

The British were thoroughly shaken by the South African War. The empire began to seem much less glorious when a bunch of guerilla fighters could keep the British army on the hop for over two years. Suddenly aware that they had no allies in Europe, the British began to feel a chilly draught. They looked about, and eventually found allies in France and Russia – for a long time their traditional enemies. Though no one could see it yet, the lines were already being drawn up for a far more serious conflict – the Great War of 1914–18.

*Two powerful and aggressive nations — the British and the Zulu — clash in South Africa.*

can and Asian colonies if the inhabitants had hated them enough to try. But British rule was not unpopular with the mass of people, and the old idea of service never died. Even the Indian Mutiny was not so much a rebellion against British rule as a reaction against modern methods of education and economic management.

Yet there were many nasty incidents, large and small, which were due to British imperialism. A whole chain of small colonial wars were fought for reasons which, to the other side, looked like pure aggression by Britain. The most dishonourable were the 'Opium Wars' against China. British merchants wished to sell opium, a dangerous drug, to the Chinese, whose govern-

# Home Rule for Ireland

After an unsuccessful rebellion in 1798 the Irish Parliament was persuaded to vote for an act of union with England. Pitt the Younger promised that Irish wrongs would be righted and that the restrictions on Catholics, which prevented them sitting in the British Parliament, would be lifted. As things turned out, nearly thirty years passed before this promise was carried out.

Representation in the British Parliament was no cure for Ireland's sorrows. The country was in a wretched state, poor and backward. Riots and murders were a common feature of life in the countryside. Land-ownership was at the root of the problem: the mass of the people were poor peasants, holding small plots of land as tenants and living close to the edge of disaster. The landlord often lived in England and never visited his Irish estates, which he left to a local manager. All the power and most of the money was in Protestant hands.

In Daniel O'Connell (1775–1847), 'the Liberator', the Irish found a redoubtable leader. He deserved much of the credit for the Catholic Emancipation Act of 1829 which allowed Catholics to become members of Parliament, and he was no less determined to end the union with England. A great orator, he aroused devotion among his supporters, but his Catholic Association was suppressed by a government nervous of violence, and in 1843 he was arrested. Much fiercer opposition to Britain came from the Young Ireland Movement.

Hatred flourished in the terrible times of the famine, when many starved as a direct result of a diseased potato crop and an indirect result of the injustice of the land-owning system. Some died; many fled. Up to 1845 the Irish population had been growing steadily and had reached 8,500,000. In the next five years it dropped by a quarter.

Thousands of desperate people struggled to escape to England and, in growing numbers, to North America.

From the American Irish came support for the revolutionary movement known as Fenianism (from the word *Fianna*, ancient Irish heroes). Fenians carried out a few terrorist acts in England in the 1850s and 1860s, blowing up a prison and trying to capture Chester.

An agricultural crisis brought bad times again to Ireland in the 1870s. Some reforms were made, for English politicians (especially Gladstone) were becoming aware that something had to be done to improve the situation in Ireland. The Disestablishment Act of 1869 ended the privileges of the Protestant Irish Church, which had been supported by the taxes of poor Catholics. Land reform acts allowed more small farmers to own the land they lived on, so that they could no longer be turned out of their homes at a moment's notice because the landlord wished to get rid of them.

But many were still evicted. About 1,000 families were turned out in 1879, a bad year, when there were new outbreaks of violence, including murder, 'land-grabbing' (seizing vacant farms illegally), and deaths from starvation. The practice of the boycott – refusing all contact with someone who has offended the community – grew up at this time. The name came from an unpopular land agent in County Mayo, Captain Boycott, who was one of the first to receive the treatment.

At Westminster, Ireland had about a hundred MPs out of a total of about 600. About thirty of the Irish members, most of them from the northern province of Ulster, came to be counted with the Conservatives because, unlike the rest of the Irish members, they were against Home Rule (self-government in internal affairs) for Ireland. The leader of the Home Rule party was one of the most brilliant politicians of the age, Charles Parnell (1846–91).

The Irish members were mainly solid, middle-class property-owners. They were moderate nationalists who had no sympathy with the Irish Republican Brotherhood, the secret society which had organized the unsuccessful Fenian revolt in 1867. They were not particularly anti-British.

In Parliament, the Home Rule party was more powerful than it looked on paper. For one thing it had the leadership of Parnell. For another, it was able to extract promises from the two major parties (Liberal and Conservative) because, in a close election, it held the balance between them. Parnell's filibustering (preventing other members speaking on other subjects) forced the British Parliament to give more attention to 'the Irish Question'.

The Irish Question was made especially difficult, someone once said, because as soon as the British thought of an answer the Irish changed the question. Certainly, the reforms of Liberal governments only encouraged the growth of Irish nationalism, as a taste of water makes a thirsty person even thirstier.

In 1882 the great Liberal prime minister, Gladstone, came to the decision that Home Rule for Ireland was right and necessary. It is impossible to imagine a modern prime minister making such a decision, which was to destroy the Liberal party, at least for a time, just as Peel, also doing what he thought was right, had wrecked the Tories over the Corn Laws. But Gladstone was as determined in his seventies as he had been in his thirties (he was born in 1809). Having decided that Home Rule was the right policy, he stuck to it.

*In 1881 Parnell was imprisoned for inciting the Irish in their struggle for independence. After his arrest the disorders grew worse and Gladstone released him.*

Gladstone brought his first Home Rule bill before Parliament in 1885. The Liberals were split in two, the bill was defeated, and the government resigned.

A few years later Parnell fell into disgrace as a result of his love affair with the wife of another MP. He lost his leadership and died soon afterwards. The Home Rule party itself was split by this affair, and it was never quite such a force in politics again, although it was reunited after 1900.

Meanwhile, Gladstone had returned to power in 1893 and brought in another Home Rule bill. The 'Grand Old Man' fought it through the Commons, but it was defeated in the House of Lords, which at that time had more power in law-making.

There followed a long period of Conservative rule, under Lord Salisbury. In 1905 the Liberals won a surprisingly big victory (their last to date) and it seemed that Home Rule would soon become a reality. But with their large majority in Parliament, the Liberals no longer depended on the votes of Irish members, and they were in no hurry to pass Home Rule. Not until 1912, when their majority had been seriously reduced at new elections, was the third Home Rule bill introduced. It was passed into law but never went into effect because of the outbreak of the Great War in 1914.

The truth was that Home Rule was already out of date. More extreme nationalists were preparing Ireland's future – in which Britain was to play a smaller part than the Home Rulers imagined.

In the late 19th century Ireland experienced what can be called a 'renaissance' – a great revival of Irish culture. One example of the movement was the foundation of the Gaelic League, a learned society which encouraged the study of the Irish language and literature. Among the great figures in Dublin literary society were the poet Yeats, the playwright Synge, and the founder of the Abbey Theatre, Lady Gregory. (Bernard Shaw had left for England; Sean O'Casey and James Joyce had not begun writing.) But it was a sign of the times that the chairman of the Gaelic League was a poet who also happened to be a dedicated revolutionary, Patrick Pearse.

The press gave birth to some lively nationalist newspapers, including *Sinn Fein* ('Ourselves') which represented a new nationalist organization with that name. Nationalism was a growing force in the labour movement, through the leadership of James Connolly. In 1913 Connolly founded the Irish Citizen Army, which together with the Irish Volunteers of Eoin

MacNeill and Patrick Pearse was to form the fighting force of the coming rebellion against the British.

The Irish problem was made additionally complicated by the attitude of a large minority, mostly in Ulster, who were violently opposed to the idea of Irish independence. These Ulster Unionists, skilfully led by a brilliant barrister, Edward Carson, were descendants of the Scottish and English settlers planted in Ireland in the 16th and 17th centuries to help keep the Irish in order. They had more to lose if Ireland became independent: most industry was in Ulster,

*In 1916 Pearse and his colleagues captured the General Post Office in Dublin. The rebels held out for a week under bombardment, but finally surrendered.*

and would have been handicapped if Ulster ceased to be part of the economic unit of Britain. Also, they were Protestants, with an instinctive hatred for the pope.

The Great War, which began in 1914, kept Britain occupied and gave an opportunity to the nationalists in the south. At Easter 1916 a rising began in Dublin. But planning was poor: after a few days' desperate fighting, the rebels were defeated by British soldiers. Pearse, Connolly and several others were executed by firing squad.

Although the Easter Rising received small support from the public, it proved to be the spark that was needed to set Irish nationalism aflame. The old policy of Home Rule was not enough. Redmond's party was heavily defeated in the election of 1918, nearly all its members losing to Sinn Fein candidates, who refused to take their seats in the British Parliament.

British regulations and restrictions angered the Irish. In 1919 Sinn Fein formed its own, Irish Parliament, and elected Eamonn de Valera (1882–1975) as president. A very nasty type of civil war began, with murders, treachery and torture committed by both sides. Finally, an agreement was reached which created the Irish Free State, self-governing but with a British governor-general. Six counties of Ulster were cut off to form the British province of Northern Ireland.

The agreement was not accepted by all parties in Ireland. Yet more horror followed with an all-Irish civil war, which lasted until 1923.

Over the next ten years, the connection with Britain gradually withered. During the Second World War Ireland remained neutral, and in 1949 Britain at last formally acknowledged the fact that Eire (Ireland) was an independent republic. Northern Ireland remained part of the United Kingdom, creating an undying grievance for republicans and nationalists and carrying on the violent traditions of the years of 'troubles' which had followed the Easter Rising.

# The End of an Era: New Rivals

Britain's influence on the rest of the world in the 19th century was enormous. It was due chiefly to Britain's domination of world markets with its factory-made goods, and the part played by British investment in economic developments overseas. Even the American railways were built to some extent with British money. By 1870, the amount of British capital invested abroad was about £800 millions.

Another influential British export, almost as important as manufactures or capital, was people. Between 1850 and 1880 about 2.5 million people left Britain for other countries (the United States, Canada, Australia, New Zealand, South Africa). Some emigrants later returned, but there were also many people, mostly young men, who served temporarily in foreign countries as missionaries, merchants or colonial officials.

In the last quarter of the century, the tide of British influence turned and began to go out. Fewer people emigrated, though many still did. The population, which had been growing extremely fast for a hundred years, was still growing, but less quickly. In 1876 thirty-six babies were born for every thousand people; by 1911, the number had fallen to twenty-three per thousand.

Foreign investment continued to grow but at a slower rate. There was no longer extra capital available which could be invested abroad. In fact, some of the profits from earlier investment had to be used to pay for current expenses where, before, it would have been reinvested. At the same time, it had become a custom for the British to invest abroad, and no one wanted to invest in home industry when foreign investment promised greater profit. Capital was taken out of Britain to be reinvested in the Dominions (Canada, Australia, New Zealand, South Africa) and various foreign countries.

Between 1850 and 1870 Britain's exports more than doubled. But so did imports. By 1870 Britain had an 'unfavourable balance of trade' (imports costing more than exports are earning). In reality the situation was better than it seemed because of the contribution made by 'invisible earnings' such as insurance, for which London was the world centre. But by 1880 Britain was suffering from the growing competition of other industrial powers like Germany and the United States, which were already larger in population and were growing greater in mining, steel production and other industries. Soon, the unfavourable trade balance had to be made up by capital – leaving even less for investment.

Agriculture was ruined in the 1870s by cheap food from abroad, especially American wheat. Prices slumped. Free trade, for which British manufacturers had fought so hard, no longer worked. While Britain had no major competitors, free trade had enabled British manufactures to sweep the world, but by 1880 things were more complicated.

The new industrial powers, keen to encourage their own industries, slapped duties on British imports. Britain was shut out of what had once been its most profitable markets. New opportunities were found in the Far East, but even there competition was increasing: Japan was already launched on its own industrial revolution.

Living conditions had been improving for nearly everyone in Britain during the second half of the 19th century. But by 1900 this general development had almost stopped. Wages were no longer rising, and in some industries, such as mining, they actually fell. Although the number of people near the starvation line was less than it had been a hundred years earlier, millions were still very poor. Half the population of Scot-

*Queen Victoria in old age. Her reign saw Great Britain as the most powerful nation in the world. By her death in 1901 Britain's power was declining.*

land lived in homes of one or two rooms. One-third of the men who applied to join the army were rejected on grounds of poor health. Many people still worked ten or more hours a day. In spite of the advances made in public health, housing and education, much more remained to be done in social welfare.

People in Britain were aware that the tide of history was no longer running so strongly in their favour in the late 19th century, although they could not understand exactly what, if anything, had gone wrong. They could dimly see that a great age was passing, and few people prefer an unknown future to a familiar past.

Disraeli, after tottering around the salons like an elegant, oriental ghost, finally faded out in 1881. He left the Conservative party to the care of the reserved and bearded Salisbury, a member of the famous Cecil family which had provided Elizabeth I with her best ministers. Tennyson, the poet laureate, made a peer by his admirer, Queen Victoria, lived until 1892. Gladstone, the most honourable statesman of the age (and

of most other ages) lasted magnificently until 1898 (to the extreme disgust of the queen whom Disraeli, with his remarkable gift for flattering elderly ladies, had made into a firm Conservative).

The long lives of these giants of the age concealed the fact that times were changing fast. Queen Victoria herself, after the longest reign in English or Scottish history, died in 1901 at Osborne, Isle of Wight. Her coffin, which was white (the best colour for funerals, she had always said), was taken by special train to Windsor. On a chilly January day, people knelt bare-headed in the fields as it passed.

Few people were old enough to remember a time when Victoria had not been queen. News of her death in the first month of a new century caused shock, even a kind of fear. People felt, uncomfortably, that many things which had seemed solid and reliable in Victoria's England would vanish for ever. For a moment, the vast self-confidence of the British was seriously shaken. If they had been able to see into the future, they would not have been reassured.

# Chapter 14

## Britain in the Edwardian Age

When Edward VII (1841–1910) came to the throne there were still plenty of people, apart from foreigners, who were exceedingly rich. Income tax was only 5 pence in the pound. However, Britain had become a democratic country, and the Labour movement was growing fast. Time was running out for the small minority of people at the top who owned such a large proportion of the national wealth.

It may have been the fear, perhaps an unconscious fear, that the privileges of the old ruling class were about to start crumbling away that made the Edwardians so snobbish. Snobbery was not of course new. But the kind of snobbery which condemned a man because his fortune was made in trade, rather than something 'respectable' like property, had only developed during Victorian times. Like all beliefs which con-

*The 'age of elegance': the Edwardian upper classes still had the time and the money for extravagant fashions in clothes, and for lengthy holidays in luxurious hotels.*

demn other people for their class or nationality or skin-colour, snobbery was a way of protecting privileges which could not be justified by any moral standards.

It was difficult for a grocer to be accepted in fashionable society, even a grocer like the great tea merchant, Sir Thomas Lipton. But the upper class no longer consisted of old landed families who could trace their pedigrees back to the Middle Ages (and preferably to the Normans, who, people seemed to think, were more aristocratic than the Anglo-Saxons). The people who set the tone in Mayfair and Park Lane were descendants of railway barons, Indian *nabobs* (an Indian word for a ruler, which came to be used for rich Englishmen), South African diamond kings and the like. They spent their money freely, extravagantly. There was a fashion for exotic (and expensive) parties, like one given by a man to celebrate a gambling win where everything – curtains, carpets, tablecloths, even the food –

*Police arresting a suffragette: in their determination to win the vote, the suffragettes broke windows, attacked politicians and set fire to buildings.*

was coloured red (he had been betting on red at roulette).

Perhaps it is not surprising that people who gave parties like that also had a love of practical jokes (often a sign of a lack of real humour). There really were people like the peer in Anthony Powell's novel, *The Kindly Ones*, who rode horses up staircases and put clockwork mice down people's coatsleeves. King Edward VII himself shared this taste. A friend of his, having been put to bed drunk, woke up next morning to find a live rabbit in the bed beside him.

It is always difficult to compare prices in an earlier age because some things which we take for granted were luxuries then, and vice versa. In 1910 you could rent a large house in one of the best suburbs of Birmingham or Manchester for about 50 pence a week. Scotch salmon cost 10 pence a pound, cod 2 pence or 3 pence. A simple meal at one of the new Lyons cafés in London cost 3 pence or 4 pence. A tailor-made man's suit cost about £5; hand-made shoes £1.50 (but a good pair of factory-made shoes cost no more than 75 pence). A middle-class family lived comfortably on £500 a year. (The leading character in E M Forster's beautiful Edwardian novel, *Howard's End*, has £600 a year and does not have to worry about paying for house-servants, concert tickets, foreign holidays, etc.)

But most people had to live on very much less. When Charles Booth (1840–1916) was conducting his long and revealing investigations among the London poor, he estimated that over one-third of the population of the capital could be classed as 'poor' or 'very poor' – with family incomes of less than £1 a week. There were many people, he said, who would not go to bed in hot weather because 'you can't get a wink of sleep for bugs and fleas'.

Edwardians in London could travel by underground, though most of the trains were drawn by steam engines, which made breathing difficult. But the new lines being built to the fast-growing suburbs were run on electricity.

Entertainment was cheaper then. There were theatres in nearly every large suburb, and in many provincial towns. Even so, London had more theatres than it has today. The West End was gayer than it had been since electric light and plate-glass windows for shops had brightened it up. On the other hand, small crimes and prostitution were at a high level, probably higher than at any other time.

*The living room at Hill House, Scotland. Charles Rennie Mackintosh was responsible for both the stylized interior design and the architecture* (see page 235).

The music hall was still popular. Performances sometimes ended with a ten-minute film show – a shadowy, flickering, jerky invention which was put on at the end so that people who had already seen it could leave. Even when the first cinema opened in 1906, no one realized that this new medium would put the music halls out of business.

Music lovers queued for concerts, but they could also listen to their favourites, like the Australian soprano, Dame Nellie Melba, on a gramophone. The earliest records were wax cylinders, but by 1914 they had been replaced by black discs.

The gramophone had not yet replaced the piano, which was a feature of every middle-class home. It was soon to gain another rival in the wireless (radio). By 1910 it was possible to send messages by wireless all around the world. The murderer Crippen, who had killed his wife and made – he thought – a safe getaway to Canada, was caught when a wireless message was sent to the ship he was on.

Democracy, which still seemed a disastrous idea to many people, had arrived for men, but not for women. No woman could vote. Over this question, feelings ran high. Queen Victoria was violently opposed to women voting, and her son, Edward VII, also disliked the idea. Like many of his male subjects, he believed that women should be beautiful and amusing and not much else. But women's suffrage had male supporters too, like the great 19th-century thinker, John Stuart Mill, and the founder of the Labour party, Keir Hardie.

In 1903 a small, attractive woman called Mrs Emmeline Pankhurst started a militant women's suffrage movement. Her followers, known as Suffragettes, interrupted debates in Parliament, smashed windows, slashed paintings in the National Gallery, chained themselves to railings, and generally caused as much disturbance as possible. Winston Churchill (1874–1965) who had voted in favour of votes for women, was attacked with a whip simply because he was a Liberal, and the Suffragettes thought the Liberal party had let them down.

The authorities reacted with severity. Mrs Pankhurst and others were roughly treated, given long prison sentences, and fed by force (a brutal technique) when they went on hunger strike in prison.

The Suffragettes were disliked by moderate reformers, including many women who were as keen as they were to get the vote. Whether their violent tactics were necessary or not, they certainly made their demands well known. But it was the Great War which finally broke resistance to female suffrage. Thousands of women did men's jobs in 1914–18, and men recognized the absurdity of refusing them the vote. Women over thirty gained the right in 1918, women over twenty-one in 1928.

*Edwardian 'Gaiety Girls' were the forerunners of Hollywood's film stars; they were beautiful dancers at the Gaiety Theatre and untouchable for their adorers.*

# A Second Revolution in Transport

Motor cars were on the roads in Queen Victoria's time, but in 1901 motoring was still nothing more than an out-of-the-way sport. For transport, the horse and carriage was cheaper and more reliable (until 1896 it was also quicker, as vehicles had to obey a speed limit of six kilometres per hour).

The Edwardian actress Mrs Pat Campbell once said that you could do anything you liked in England as long as you did not do it in the streets and frighten the horses. Motor cars disobeyed this sensible rule. Not only did they frighten horses, they made unpleasant noises and smells, they churned up clouds of dust, and they slaughtered careless chickens; while female passengers took their sewing along to have something to do during breakdowns.

*Early motor cars, like this Rolls, had to run on roads made for horse traffic — rough and dusty. Trams, like this London tram of 1908, ran on tracks laid in the streets.*

*This type of bicycle was called a 'penny-farthing': a penny was a very large coin and a farthing a very small one.*

By 1914 the motor vehicle had won a decisive victory over the horse. The horse-drawn vehicles that had cluttered city streets only fifteen years before had almost vanished. Motor taxis replaced the old hansom cabs, motor buses replaced the old horse omnibuses. The world of fashion no longer paraded on horseback in Hyde Park.

But the most remarkable change in those fifteen years was in the motor car itself. When Edward VII came to the throne in 1901 it was a clumsy, slow and uncomfortable contraption. By 1915 it had become (in its most expensive form) a smoothly luxurious, powerful, silent conveyance. Goods vehicles had appeared, and so had motor-bicycles, which were within reach of the better-paid working man's purse. Petrol was six pence a gallon.

The internal combustion engine caused a revolution in transport. And not only on the ground.

Man first took to the air in the late 18th century – in a balloon. Early balloons were simply bags of hot air with baskets attached, in which the brave balloonist was blown about by the wind, unable to control his direction.

By 1900 many improvements had been made. Steam engines were used for a time, but they had a nasty tendency to set fire to

could fly without a clumsy, dangerous bag of gas to keep him airborne.

At this time HG Wells (1866–1946) was writing his stories about space travel and air warfare. The aeroplane seemed to hint that Wells's stories might one day prove to be more than fantasy. Public interest in aviation was intense, and the Frenchman, Blériot, became an international hero when he flew across the English Channel in 1909.

While a few specialists experimented with flying machines, and a larger, but still quite small, number drove about in motor cars, the ordinary working man needed a cheaper form of transport. The bicycle gave him one.

The history of bicycles goes back to the beginning of the 19th century. But early cycles were dangerous, uncomfortable, and required a great deal of effort to move along. A Scots blacksmith, Kirkpatrick MacMillan, was the real inventor of the modern bicycle. He was the first to build pedals driving the back wheel. That was in the 1830s, but it was not until the 1890s that his invention came into its own with the chain-driven bicycle, which was the direct ancestor of modern bikes.

the balloon, or rather, airship. Electric motors were safer, though they had other drawbacks. But in 1905 the Wright brothers in America kept their aeroplane, which was fitted with a motor-car engine, in the air for over thirty minutes. They proved that man

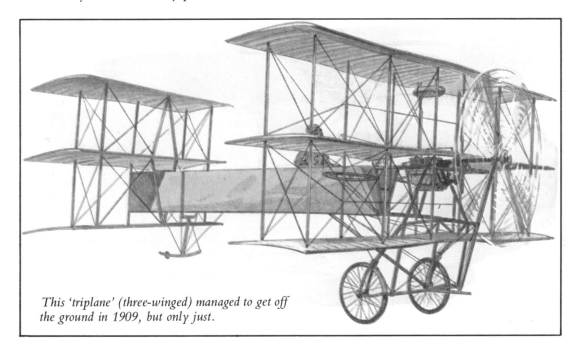

*This 'triplane' (three-winged) managed to get off the ground in 1909, but only just.*

# Britain and the Great War

The Great War of 1914–18 marks the end of an age: the end of the old order, when Britain led Europe and Europe led the world; the beginning of a more democratic age when British society became fairer and the lives of most people became easier, more comfortable. These changes would have happened anyway, but war, like any big disturbance, acted as a catalyst, speeding up the process of change.

The war, which is also called the First World War, thus had some good results eventually. But it was still the most horrible war in European history.

Long before it began, people were saying that war was bound to happen, and if people keep on saying something will happen, it often does. The war grew out of the dangerous and out-dated European system of nation-states, all fiercely competing against each other. To those who like to think of the idea of a 'balance of power', the trouble began in the late 19th century when the balance was upset by the creation of the Prussian-led German empire. That was the great achievement of Bismarck.

Bismarck was not afraid of war if it were necessary to advance German power, and several short, sharp wars were fought in the process of creating the German empire. The German people, once thought of as homely, simple folk, began to appear, in British eyes, as a nation of jack-booted, thick-necked bullies.

Europe formed two armed camps: Germany, with Austria-Hungary (successor of the old Holy Roman Empire) and Italy were lined up against Britain, France and Russia. Economic and imperialist rivalry had got all these powers entangled in a web of military alliances and weapon-building programmes. The British, long accustomed to think of themselves as 'rulers of the waves', were especially worried by Germany's new fleet of battleships.

In 1912–13 two wars were fought in the Balkans (south-east Europe). Several countries gained land from the Turkish empire, and Serbia emerged as a considerable power in the region.

The Slav nationalists of the Balkans were encouraged by their fellow Slavs in Russia,

*Trench warfare was as foul, depressing, and deadly as any form of fighting yet invented. Men prayed for a wound bad enough to take them back to England.*

and strongly opposed by Austria, which also ruled a large Slav population. Austria's desire to come to the aid of Turkey was checked by Germany for the time being, but in June 1914 the heir to the Austrian throne, Archduke Franz Ferdinand, was assassinated by a Serbian terrorist. War became inevitable. Austria attacked Serbia and Russia, fulfilling its promise, came to Serbia's aid. The allies of both major powers were quickly drawn in. Britain had no choice but to declare war on August 4, 1914, after Germany, on its way to attack France, had invaded neutral Belgium.

The war in Europe very soon fell into a dreadful pattern from which no general on either side could break out. The soldiers dug themselves into trenches which stretched across western Europe. The ground between was turned into a desert of mud, in which wounded men might die of suffocation, by the pounding it received from heavy artillery.

Defence was simple, but attack was almost impossible, although both sides kept trying. The machine gun, a deadly new weapon, and tangles of barbed wire made any attempt at advance by infantry a suicidal

*On Christmas Day, British and German troops played football in No Man's Land, between the trenches. Next day they went back to killing each other.*

business. Neither aeroplanes nor tanks were used with any effect until the closing stages of the war, partly because they were too primitive and partly because the commanders were too conservative to give whole-hearted support to new military methods.

The outbreak of war had been greeted with enthusiasm in Britain by people who knew no better. They expected – and were promised – a short campaign like the campaigns of Bismarck's Prussia, fought by a small, professional army and having no directly unpleasant effects for civilians. But the war dragged on, and the casualties were horrifying. In a single day – the first day of the battle of the Somme – 20,000 British men were killed and 40,000 wounded. In 1916 conscription (compulsory military service) had to be introduced for the first time in Britain. Unfortunately, by that time, many of the country's best young soldiers were dead.

Other symptoms of the new 'total war' were the use of poison gas on the battlefield and hysterical anti-German hate-campaigns at home: dachshunds suddenly became unpopular as pets; Beethoven's music was seldom played.

At sea, the mighty battle fleets of Britain and Germany cancelled each other out. Neither side was eager to risk its precious 'dreadnoughts' (new, heavy battleships), and only one major sea battle was fought in the four years of war. That battle in the North Sea, off Jutland, ended without a definite result, in spite – or because – of the fact that twenty-five admirals were present.

Much more effective were the German submarines. They proved that in wartime there are drawbacks, as well as advantages, in being an island. Britain was dependent on merchant ships bringing food and raw materials, especially from North America. The German submarines came near to breaking that vital link. Between February and April, 1917, over two million tonnes of merchant shipping, most of it British, was lost. Britain had only enough bread for six weeks. At the insistence of David Lloyd George (who became prime minister in December 1916) and in the face of opposition from the Admiralty, the convoy system was intro-duced. Losses were immediately and dramatically reduced.

From the German point of view, the successes of the submarines were a mixed blessing. They sunk ships of neutral countries, including the United States, as well as British vessels, and that brought the Americans into the war against Germany in 1917.

In the same year Britain lost an ally when the government of the Russian tsar was broken by revolution. The Bolsheviks (Communists) came to power. They regarded the war, with some justice, as the work of the capitalist class in Europe, having nothing to do with the interests of the working masses. They arranged peace with Germany, signed in March 1918.

The war was also fought in other continents. When Turkey entered the conflict on Germany's side, the British and French sent an expedition to the Dardanelles (Gallipoli).

*Women making weapons in an arms factory during the Great War: this was heavy industrial labour, previously done by men.*

*A German U-boat (submarine) comes to the surface to finish off an Allied merchantship, which it has torpedoed.*

It was a costly failure, and the allied force had to withdraw. The man who took most of the blame for this failure was the First Lord of the Admiralty, Winston Churchill.

An Arab revolt against the Turks, in which a romantic and mysterious Englishman named TE Lawrence took part, helped British forces under General Allenby to advance in the Middle East. They entered Jerusalem in 1917.

On the Western Front (Belgium and north France) Germany could not hope to win once General Pershing's Americans began to arrive. In a final effort, the Germans advanced to the River Marne, but a counter-attack by Foch (France), Haig (Britain) and Pershing drove them back. The *kaiser* (emperor), William II, a grandson of Queen Victoria, abdicated in November 1918, and an armistice was signed.

Britain and its empire had lost about a million men and about three million were permanently injured. And there were other debts to pay, not least in simple cash. Britain had paid for the war partly by higher taxes, but mainly by borrowing – from the United States, the Dominions, and European countries – at high rates of interest. Britain had also lent large sums to other countries, dipping deep into its pockets to find the money, and had made rash international promises, which were to prove impossible to carry out. Much equipment had also been lost, especially ships.

No one can measure such a vague thing as the 'quality of life', but in many ways the experiences of the war – the disgusting propaganda, the horrific and almost pointless slaughter, the centralization and regimentation that produced the national 'war effort' – made life seem cheaper, less noble. It is not easy to understand the attitudes of ordinary people at that time – like the young women who would present a white feather, a symbol of cowardice, to any man of military age not in uniform.

# Lloyd George, Pensions and the Dole

In the early 20th century most people were better off than ever before. As often happens in prosperous times, the very poor were actually poorer, but the number of people who could be classed as 'very poor' was much smaller than it had been fifty years earlier. Once, people had supposed that nothing could be done about the very poor: 'the poor are always with us', they said. By 1900 this attitude was out of date. Poverty seemed not so much a permanent condition of society, but a fault, something unnecessary in a prosperous country which could be cured by government action. Socialists pointed out that profits should go to the people who did the work, not to idle shareholders. Higher wages, they demanded, not higher dividends.

Socialists were still rare creatures. The Independent Labour party, for which Keir Hardie had won his seat (he had arrived at Westminster wearing a worker's cloth cap and escorted by a brass band) was founded in 1893. The modern Labour party got underway in 1906 when it won twenty-nine seats in the House of Commons, drawing its chief support from the trade union movement.

Labour remained a minority party in Parliament until the 1920s, serving as the ally, often a reluctant ally, of the Liberal party, whose decline into creaking old age was halted for a time by a brilliant politician, David Lloyd George (1863-1945).

The 'Welsh wizard', a country lawyer who entered Parliament in 1892, began his career as the spokesman of Welsh nationalism and as a leader of the radical Left. He was a pacifist during the South African War of 1899, which made him extremely unpopular.

But Lloyd George never lacked moral courage (though he was not physically

*A contemporary cartoon of David Lloyd George.*

brave, being frightened by air raids), and opposition only turned him into a more determined reformer when the Liberals came to power in 1906.

Between 1908, when he was appointed

Chancellor of the Exchequer, and the outbreak of war in 1914, he was chiefly responsible for a series of reforms in British society which foreshadowed the welfare state of today.

A pension for people over sixty-five had been discussed during the 1890s, but it turned out then that most of the people who needed help were dead by that age. As Lloyd George said, there were still 'conditions of poverty, destitution and squalour . . . that would make the rocks weep'. Old-age pensions were started in 1908, but like other social reforms put into effect by the Liberal government, they had to be paid for. Lloyd George's budget of 1909 greatly increased taxes, especially taxes on property, which infuriated Conservatives.

The House of Lords refused to vote for Lloyd George's budget, challenging the principle (which had been established by the Civil War) that the Commons were supreme in financial matters. A long constitutional battle followed, ending in the Parliament Act of 1911 which sharply reduced the powers of the House of Lords, a victory for Lloyd George.

Lloyd George's greatest reform was the National Insurance Act (1911), which was based on a scheme already in use in Germany. The act ended the worst menaces to ordinary working families by providing insurance against loss of earnings through sickness or unemployment. Again, a huge amount of money had to be raised – £27 million. For each worker, 4 pence a week was paid in: 1 penny out of taxation, 1 penny by the employer, and 2 pence by the worker. But it was a great step in making Britain a more just and kinder place to live in.

By 1914 Lloyd George was recognized as the most likely successor to Asquith (1852–1928) as prime minister. In 1915 he became minister of munitions – supplying the weapons of war – and then minister of war. At the end of 1916 a political crisis

*At the end of the First World War thousands of men found themselves out of work, as they poured back from Europe. They returned to build a new world, but there was no room for them.*

blew up over Asquith's uninspiring direction of the war effort. An expert at tricky manoeuvring, Lloyd George emerged from the crisis as prime minister.

He was a dynamic war leader, but his personal position was weaker than Churchill's position in the Second World War. He had lost the support of his own party, he was disliked by most established authorities, from the king downwards, and he was unable to get rid of military commanders, like Haig, whom he disliked and distrusted. His leadership won him a great personal victory in the general election of 1918, but he was still a leader without a party.

At the peace negotiations, public opinion made Lloyd George demand tougher terms from Germany than he thought was wise. He worked for better relations with the new Soviet government (some British troops had fought against the Bolsheviks in 1918), and he made the agreement with Irish leaders that created the Irish Free State in 1921.

In 1922 the Conservatives withdrew their support from Lloyd George. The Liberals had never forgiven him for betraying Asquith, and anyway they were in decline as a party. He had also lost the support of Labour. He fell from power. 'He will be back', said King George without much enthusiasm, but strange to say, this brilliant politician never again held government office.

Peace, so much desired by people during wartime, sometimes proves a disappointment. So it seemed after 1918. Unemployment was high, especially after the economic slump of 1921. Returning soldiers had been promised 'homes fit for heroes', but the housing shortage was as bad as ever. Yet some men were making money out of such shortages. There was much sharp practice in high places. Lloyd George's government awarded peerages to those willing to make a large contribution to party funds. The smell of corruption was in the air.

*Clydeside strikers battling with the police in 1919. The strikers were demanding a forty-hour week.*

There were strikes by workers, including – to everyone's alarm – the police. A demonstration in India ended in a panic and the death of nearly 400 people, many of them shot by British troops. The Indian leader, Gandhi (1869–1948), began his campaign of non-violent resistance to British rule; but not all his sympathizers were non-violent. The British were put in charge of Palestine by the newly formed League of Nations, but found the task of reconciling the Palestinian Arabs with the Jewish immigrants more difficult than they had calculated. In Egypt a revolt made the British anxious to get out of the country, which was officially a British protectorate. But no agreement could be reached which made the Suez Canal safe for British ships. In the end British control over Egypt was tightened.

By about 1925 the skies were much brighter. The international scene appeared settled and peaceful after the treaty of Locarno when the major powers undertook to submit disputes to arbitration. A 'Locarno spirit' of mutual tolerance and forgiveness

*Children playing outside a block of council flats in the 1920s.*

seemed to be growing. The main, white-inhabited countries of the Commonwealth became self-governing dominions, and Gandhi accepted a promise that India would become a dominion eventually. In 1924 the first Labour government, though short-lived (it had no majority in the House of Commons) had shown that British socialists were not a gang of desperate revolutionaries, as some people feared.

The economic situation was improving. The 'Bright Young Things' enjoyed themselves at the Ritz and the Café Royal, and were commemorated in the early novels of Evelyn Waugh. Life, for the lucky, was gay, if sometimes rather silly – a reaction, partly, to the grimness of war. If people had been able to see what lay ahead, they might have found other reasons to enjoy themselves while they had the chance.

# Literature and the Arts after the Great War

A British explorer in Africa before the Great War once disturbed a cloud of butterflies, which rose in a brilliant mass of fluttering colour from the road ahead of him. When he drew near, he saw that they had been feeding on a pile of camel dung. Filth giving birth to beauty.

So too may art spring from horror. The Great War produced or inspired many very fine poets. Rupert Brooke, everyone's idea of a romantic Englishman, died early in the war. His poetry is now admired less than that of Wilfred Owen, killed in the last week of fighting, Robert Graves, Edmund Blunden, or Siegfried Sassoon, who won the Military Cross for bravery but later refused to fight in protest against the failure of the government to hold peace talks.

None of them quite reached the stature of

*An illustration from one of HG Wells's science-fiction stories,* The First Men in the Moon.

the American born T S Eliot in the 1920s, or even that of W H Auden from the 1930s onward. Auden was the most accomplished of a new group of poets, most of them sympathetic to the political Left (socialist or communist), as many sensitive people in Europe were in the 1930s. They included the poets Spender, MacNeice and Day Lewis.

English traditions in music were revived by Delius, Vaughan Williams, Walton and Holst, as well as Elgar. But in art and architecture, Britain lagged behind developments on the continent. When Roger Fry had put on an exhibition of French post-Impressionist painters (Cézanne, Gaugin, etc.) in 1906, many respectable critics had thrown up their hands in horror. Wyndham Lewis, an angry, talented man, led a curious little movement called Vorticism, which had something in common with Cubism and Italian Futurism, and painted semi-abstract, machine-like pictures. The sculptor Epstein was linked with the Vorticists for a time. He hoped to prepare the way for the acceptance of sculpture as a major art, as it became in England with the appearance of Henry Moore, England's one truly great sculptor, and Barbara Hepworth in the 1920s.

For ordinary people, the new styles in art often seemed hard to understand, if not deliberately obscure. The period of the Great War marks a dividing line, but a very rough one, in all the arts, including literature. The 'man in the street' may not have understood all the ideas and ambitions of Victorian painters, but he could appreciate their paintings without difficulty. He was not bewildered by them as he was by Cubist or any other non-realistic work of art. As Lord Shortcake (one of Beachcomber's characters in his *Daily Express* column) thought it wise to advise the artist sent to paint his portrait, 'I'm not a three-cornered tomato on a yellow banjo, even if I look like that to you'.

The Edwardian period was the last period when the best in literature was also popular. Writers like Hardy, Kipling, Wells, Arnold Bennett, even the Polish-born Conrad, are not especially hard to read; but James Joyce's *Finnegan's Wake* (1939) is a gigantic word game incomprehensible to most people.

D H Lawrence, however, whose first novel was published in 1913, is easily readable while being no less 'revolutionary' than Joyce. Lawrence, son of a Nottingham miner, believed in the vital importance of instinct over intelligence, emotion over reason, and he wrote with a rare passion.

Neither Joyce nor Lawrence seems to have much in common with the most famous literary and artistic 'school' of the 1920s – the Bloomsbury Group (named after the London district where some of them lived). The leading novelist of Bloomsbury was Virginia Woolf, but it also included Lytton Strachey, who led the reaction against Victorianism with his witty but unfair *Eminent Victorians,* and E M Forster. Among others associated with the group were the economist Maynard Keynes and artists and critics like Roger Fry, Clive and Vanessa Bell and Duncan Grant. To those more in sympathy with the world of Lawrence, the Bloomsbury Group sometimes seemed to lack red blood and muscle.

The decade of the 1930s was a time of political upheavals and growing international tension, which finally exploded in war. It was also a revolutionary period in architecture. 'Modernism' at last caught up with Britain: new buildings were designed on functional principles. That meant they were supposed to look appropriate to the job they were meant to do, as a carpenter's

*In 1922 Howard Carter, a British archaeologist, uncovered some steps leading to a royal tomb of ancient Egypt. The tomb was found to belong to Tutankhamun, and had not been disturbed for over 3,000 years. The discovery led to a new interest in ancient civilizations.*

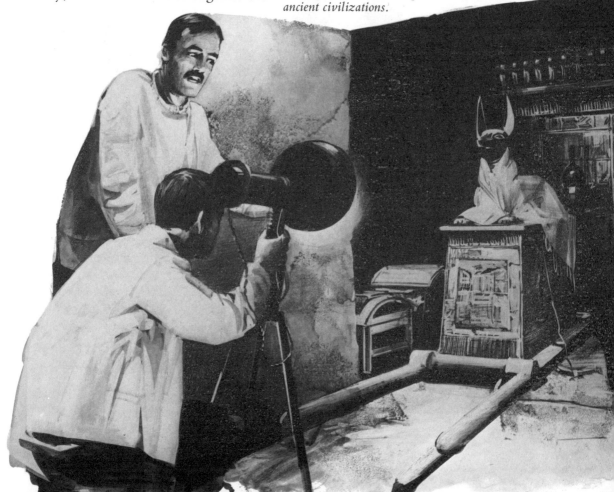

*Doing the Charleston at a dance hall in the 1920s. Jazz was popular, skirts were short: young people wanted a good time.*

tool does; decoration for its own sake was condemned. Concrete, a highly functional material, came into its own. Steel and glass were used for offices and shops.

This movement affected all the arts. Sculpture and painting became less realistic and more abstract – arrangements of colour and form with no obvious resemblance to objects in nature.

Another continental art movement, Surrealism, had different roots. The Surrealists liked to make ordinary things appear odd, mixing the everyday world with the world of dreams (they owed much to the work of Freud). To us, the Surrealists are most familiar as artists (Magritte, Max Ernst, Dali, etc.). But Surrealism affected the whole intellectual world. It has remained a powerful force in, for example, films. It also aided the growth of interesting new art forms like *collage* (a composition of odd bits and pieces – bus tickets, scraps of material, magazine advertisements, etc.).

Popular entertainment became big business in the 1920s. The first football cup final at Wembley in 1923 attracted a crowd so huge that the police were taken by surprise. Nearly half the adult population filled in football pools and greyhound racing became popular in working-class areas.

The cinema provided welcome relief from the dullness or grimness of life, especially when the 'talkies' began in 1929. By that time, the cinema had produced at least one British genius in Charlie Chaplin. More than 3,000 cinemas were built by 1930, splendid palaces in the style of decoration called Art Deco (a more angular version of Art Nouveau). The BBC established its great reputation as a kind of national aunt: entertaining, but also instructive and very respectable (announcers, though unseen, wore evening dress). Radio brought music into the homes of those who could not attend concerts. Good music, especially opera and ballet, was increasingly popular, thanks partly to such enthusiastic professionals as Sir Thomas Beecham, a great showman as well as a great conductor (though he once complained that the British do not like music, they only like the noise it makes).

Many people took up more energetic entertainments, like hiking or bicycling. Green Line coaches took weekend parties from London on rambling tours in the countryside. Rock-climbing, mountaineering, fishing, skiing and similar sports became more popular and better organized.

The printed word was, for once, fairly profitable. Newspapers battled each other for new readers, offering prizes and special offers. The *Daily Express* was the first to sell over two million copies, but even *The Times* made a profit. The market for 'pulp' fiction, already large in Victorian times, was bigger than ever. Some pulp writers, Edgar Wallace for one, turned out gripping stories. But there were a lot of middle-class detective stories in which bodies were regularly discovered in libraries and the butler was a likely suspect. Comics, supposed to be for children but read by many adults, had grown out of funny cartoon strips in newspapers, where they had first appeared before 1900. The name 'comic' stuck, although some of the picture stories were not comic at all.

In spite of the continuing housing shortage, home life was becoming easier in the 1920s and 1930s, except for the unemployed or unskilled worker. The middle classes could no longer afford servants, or not so many of them, but they had things like electric irons and perhaps a vacuum cleaner. The gap between rich and poor was still large, and the gap between north (badly hit by the economic slump) and south was growing. Cars and buses made people more mobile (by 1930 there were about a million private cars), and the wireless kept them better informed (nine houses out of ten had a set in the 1930s). There was much happening in Europe of which they needed to be informed: it would soon affect them directly.

*A family listening to an early radio. One member prefers the comics, then printed only in black-and-white.*

# A General Strike and Economic Slump

The climate of better understanding and greater co-operation in the mid 1920s was, as far as Britain was concerned, a mirage. In 1926 it vanished suddenly when the Trades Union Congress (an association representing most trade unions) called a general strike. Industrial workers downed tools and the country came to a stop.

The indirect cause of the General Strike was the insistence by the Conservative government on fixing the value of the pound at the same level as before 1914. It was much too high, and had a disastrous effect on exports. At a time when industry should have been racing forward, as it was in other countries, British industry was limping painfully. Unemployment remained high.

Among the worst hit were the coal miners. Their employers, whom even the Conservative leader, Stanley Baldwin, described as 'stupid and discourteous', decided to cut wages and lengthen hours of work because of the high value of the pound. The miners naturally protested, and efforts by the government to get an agreement failed. At the end of April the miners struck (today we would say, more clumsily, they 'took industrial action'). The TUC called for a national strike of workers in sympathy.

The General Strike lasted nine days. Ernest Bevin, head of the big Transport and General Workers' Union, was the man who did most to keep the workers together. But the government's emergency measures worked quite well, and the final result was not a victory for anyone. The miners were left out on their own, and although their strike lasted six months, they were finally forced to surrender.

The General Strike was an important event in British history. In some ways it hardened the political division between Right and Left, bosses and workers, and it left some 'bitterness behind. But it also demonstrated that there was no profit in extremism. All-out industrial warfare did no one any good. Employers and workers gained more understanding of each other, although the illusions of those who saw Britain as one big happy family, all seeking a common goal, were swept away.

There were also some amusing, friendly moments. Football games were played between strikers and police.

The after-effects might have been worse if Baldwin had not chosen a policy of easygoing tolerance. There are times when a

*Miners playing cards during the General Strike. In the end, they were forced back to work.*

*When the shipbuilding yard at Jarrow closed down in 1936, the MP for Jarrow led a march to London to seek government help for the unemployed.*

government's best policy is to do nothing, and Baldwin realized that this was one of them. Tempers slowly cooled.

Led, as before, by Ramsay MacDonald, Labour returned to power in 1929. It was an unlucky moment. In October a dizzy slide in share prices on the New York stock exchange set off the worst economic slump of modern times. Millionaires were ruined overnight, businesses collapsed, and the numbers of unemployed grew to enormous and horrifying proportions.

The Labour government could not cope with the crisis, and in 1931 a national coalition was formed. (Britain has had many coalition governments in its recent history whatever politicians today may say.) Mac-Donald remained prime minister, and although most of the Labour members rejected the new arrangement, most of them also lost their seats at the 1931 election (every member of MacDonald's Labour cabinet was defeated bar one). In 1935 MacDonald was succeeded by his colleague, the Conservative leader, Baldwin.

The national government rejected the good advice of the economist Keynes that unemployment was curable, but by 1933 the situation was improving as a result of other conditions, such as a boom in the building industry and falling world prices. Unfortunately, the areas of Britain most in need of help, like the industrial north of England, received less relief than more prosperous parts. Unemployment stayed high in the north and living standards, in spite of unemployment pay, were dreadfully low.

Communism came nearer than at any other time to gaining a firm footing in Britain. This was partly due to resentment at the condition of society – too big a gap between rich and poor. But it was also encouraged by the rise of fascism in Europe.

# Hitler and the Approach of War

The treaties and 'pacts' between nations signed in the years after the Great War did not satisfy everyone. Nor could the League of Nations (founded in 1919) guarantee peace. Some countries (Germany and Italy were two) felt strongly that they had been cheated or exploited.

These feelings of resentment opened the door for fascism, a political movement of the extreme Right. The first successful fascist was Mussolini, who seized power in Italy in 1922. His regime made the country in certain ways more efficient – at the price of freedom. Anyone who dared criticize *il Duce* ('the leader') was brutally treated.

*Hitler in full cry: as head of the nastiest government Europe had ever seen, Hitler conquered most of the continent.*

A similar but even nastier movement was National Socialism in Germany. The Nazis, as they are better known, gained power in 1933. Their leader, Adolf Hitler (1889–1945), gained office by legal means; but once there he overthrew the constitution and made himself dictator. He preached a hysterical, racist nationalism: Germans were superior to all others, said Hitler, and millions believed him. Communists and Socialists were not proper Germans, it seemed, and nor were Jews. They were viciously persecuted.

The Nazis were interested only in power – power at any price. Hitler promised to

*'Dad's Army': the Home Guard was formed in the Second World War from men too old or too frail to join the regular forces.*

make Germany great again, and his idea of greatness was being in a position to kick everyone else around. He set out to break down the conditions laid down in the Treaty of Versailles (1919), which had aimed to keep Germany weak after the Great War.

From 1933 to 1939 the affairs of Europe revolved around Hitler. The governments of the democratic countries, Britain in particular, could not make up their minds whether to give in to Hitler's demands, none of which were completely unreasonable, or to resist them. Britain and France remained neutral during the Spanish Civil War (1936–39), while Germany and Italy gave the Spanish dictator, General Franco, the support he needed for a fascist victory. When Hitler's troops marched into Austria

and declared it part of the *Reich* (empire), Britain and France protested but did nothing.

In 1938 Hitler demanded part of Czechoslovakia, where many people were of German descent. Naturally, the Czech government refused. Hitler's powerful propaganda machine went into top gear: his ranting speeches inspired enormous enthusiasm among the German masses. By September, a European war seemed on the point of breaking out. At a hurriedly arranged meeting in Munich, Neville Chamberlain, who had succeeded Baldwin as prime minister, together with the French premier, awarded Hitler part of Czechoslovakia. Without support from France or Britain, the Czechs were forced to agree.

Chamberlain thought the Munich agreement meant 'peace in our time'. He was wrong. Six months later, on the feeblest of excuses, Hitler's forces marched into Prague, the Czech capital.

*Chamberlain returned from his meeting with Hitler waving a copy of their agreement which, he said, stood for 'Peace with Honour'. He was wrong.*

# Britain and the Second World War

When he ordered his troops to march into Prague, Hitler tore up the Munich agreement. It was clear that the British policy of 'appeasement' – trying to keep peace in Europe by giving in to Hitler's main demands – was a failure. Hitler could not be tamed with treaties. Up to this time, Britain had steered clear of treaties and alliances in Europe (except with France). This policy was reversed in 1939, as the government began to make promises of support to the other countries, such as Rumania and Poland, which were threatened by Nazi aggression.

An attempt was made to rebuild the alliance which had fought against Germany in 1914, but the third member, Russia, distrusted the Western democracies. The Russians shocked their friends in the West by signing an agreement with Hitler in August 1939. The United States, although sympathetic to Britain, was not willing to become involved in another European war. Although the dominions were loyal to Britain, the British and the French could expect no help from a really powerful ally.

Hitler had added Austria and a large part of Czechoslovakia to the *Reich*. He also had designs on Poland. During the summer of 1939, Nazi propaganda was turned against the Poles. Hitler's threats became fiercer and fiercer; international tension was screwed to breaking point. It was Czechoslovakia all over again. Hitler believed that the British and French, however loudly they might protest, would not help Poland any more than they had helped Czechoslovakia.

But this time there was no Munich. No one wanted war, least of all a man like the prime minister, Chamberlain, who remembered with horror the slaughter of the Great War. But Britain had a clear obligation to defend Poland, and the British people, who would not have gone to war willingly at the time of Munich, had come to realize that no alternative was possible. When the Germans invaded Poland on September 1, 1939, the British and French

*Evacuation: children were sent away from London, chief target of Hitler's bombs, to greater safety in the country.*

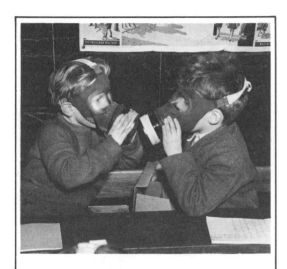

*Children learning how to put on their gas masks. Poison gas had been used in the First World War, but it was not used in the Second.*

governments declared war. There was little they could do to help the Poles, but the time had come to halt German aggression before all Europe was overwhelmed.

Chamberlain hung on to power until May 1940. That was the time of the 'twilight' or 'phoney' war, when very little actually happened. But in April Germany embarked on a new burst of conquest, and a new leader was required, someone not con-nected with the dead policy of appeasement. Winston Churchill, who had for years been warning the government of the danger of German aggression, became prime minister of a national government which included Labour leaders like Clement Attlee and Ernest Bevin.

This was a time of disaster. The British Expeditionary Force was driven out of Europe, escaping by the skin of its teeth from the French port of Dunkirk. Every little yacht and steamer was pressed into service to bring the defeated army back across the Channel from Dunkirk's beaches. It must have been strange to return in a chirpy little pleasure boat named *Saucy Annie* while shells and bullets hurtled past.

In this dark hour Churchill stood for a new spirit of determination in Britain – the spirit of Dunkirk, as it came to be called. In his rasping, powerful voice, he told the people that he had nothing to offer but

*During air raids, people slept in Morrison shelters, which took the place of kitchen tables for extra protection. Windows were blacked out to prevent light showing.*

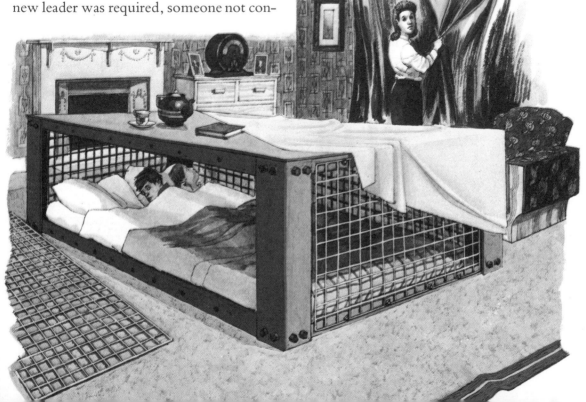

'blood, toil, tears and sweat'. But those who listened to his warning of the hardship and pain that lay ahead felt a new sense of resolution and confidence. The defeat of Dunkirk was. as inspiring as any victory.

Britain's spirited new political leadership was not matched in France. Marshal Pétain, who was called in to take charge of the government, asked the Germans for an armistice. The 'Free French', led by Charles de Gaulle, set up headquarters in London, where other conquered countries had 'governments in exile'. Britain remained as Hitler's one serious opponent.

Although Britain had suffered defeat on land, it still had the protection of the navy and air force. If the country were to be defeated, it had to be invaded, and that meant gaining command of the air. Between July and September 1940 a campaign was fought which is known as the Battle of Britain. The attack of the *Luftwaffe* (air force) was first directed at ports and ships, then at airfields, and finally at cities, chiefly London. But this campaign the Germans did not win.

All things considered, the odds were

*'D' Day: British troops clambering from their landing craft towards a Normandy beach in June, 1944. The last stage of the war had begun.*

*Soldiers standing guard over a German bomber, shot down during the Battle of Britain.*

advantage of radar, which gave early warning of the size and direction of attacks by 'bandits' (enemy aircraft). All the same, if the *Luftwaffe* had pounded the airfields for another week or two, the Royal Air Force would probably have been cleared out of the sky. As it was, a German invasion became impossible. The *Luftwaffe* lost more than 1,300 aeroplanes in less than three months, although heavy bombing attacks on London, Coventry and other cities continued.

The attack on cities involved ordinary men and women directly in the war. This was new. Civilians on the whole showed great courage: it is not pleasant to be in a fight when most of the weapons belong to the other side. People sheltered nightly in underground railway stations, and put up with discomfort and fear in a way that won the admiration of foreign journalists.

Those who could not serve in the armed forces found war jobs as air-raid wardens or in the Home Guard. Conscription for women was introduced. Taxation soared, and the government involved itself in every activity. There was rationing of food, clothes and petrol. Many ordinary things, like bananas, could not be bought at all. But

about even. Although the British were heavily outnumbered in aeroplanes and pilots (in spite of the Poles, Czechs, Belgians and French who flew for Britain), the Spitfire was superior to any German aircraft in British skies. Britain also had the great

*The scene in Coventry after a particularly heavy German raid on the city.*

people understood that sacrifices were necessary, although they did not always obey government restrictions. Efforts to prevent rail travel except for essential journeys were never very successful.

Far more civilians were killed or injured than in the First World War (but fewer soldiers). This time there was no false and silly patriotism: no women presented white feathers, they were too busy in the weapons factories. People were better informed, thanks to radio, and more realistic. Almost everyone recognized that the war was worth fighting. Propaganda could not make Hitler's regime more hateful than it was. (It was not until after the war that the true extent of the Nazi horror was known: of Jews alone, about six million men, women and children were murdered, mostly in the concentration camps.)

The spirit of neighbourly co-operation, heroic defiance and self-discipline was not so universal as the government pretended, of course. Crime did not stop during the wartime 'blackout' (no lights showing, to prevent enemy aeroplanes recognizing their targets). More work was lost through strikes in 1943–44 than in some peacetime years. All the same, the British had good reason to feel proud of themselves.

The *Luftwaffe* had been checked, but elsewhere German victories continued in 1941. British troops were forced out of Greece, and then Crete, while German tanks rolled through south-east Europe and German submarines preyed on Atlantic shipping. The British had a few victories against the Italians, and they sunk the big German battleship *Bismarck,* but otherwise were forced into a desperate defence.

Yet two events in 1941 made certain of Germany's eventual defeat. In June Hitler turned on Russia and in December the Japanese (allies of Germany) attacked the American naval base of Pearl Harbor, Hawaii. The two most powerful countries in the world were drawn into what had truly become a 'world war'.

Russia was supplied with equipment – not all of it the best quality – but had to defend herself alone, aided by a very severe winter in 1941–42. The Americans and the British became close allies. American equipment had been pouring into Britain since 1940 and in 1942, armour and men followed. The British found themselves almost a junior partner in the war against Germany.

On the whole, the Americans and the British got on extremely well. The Americans, even ordinary soldiers and airmen, had more money than the British were used to, and they were very generous with gifts. Their very generosity sometimes caused trouble in village pubs, where free distribution of nylon stockings and other rare luxuries gave 'the Yanks' great advantages in the eyes of local girls. Many British girls married American servicemen.

Military prospects soon improved. In North Africa, General Montgomery won a great victory over the Germans at El Alamein. This, with the German defeat at Stalingrad in Russia, was the turning point of the war. After Alamein, the news was of victories, not defeats. British and American aircraft began heavy raids on Germany which went on to the end of the war. The most horrible was the raid on Dresden in 1945, when the beautiful old city was almost completely destroyed and many thousands of civilians were killed.

Italy was invaded in 1943 and withdrew from the war. But the Germans prevented Rome being captured until June 1944. In that same month, the allied forces under the American General Eisenhower landed in France, thus opening the 'Second Front' which the Russians had long been asking for. It was obvious that Germany was heading towards defeat. Yet the allies met terrific resistance as they fought their way into France, while London was attacked by frightening new weapons – the V1 flying bomb and V2 rocket. In the Far East, the

*The terrible mushroom cloud rising over Nagasaki: the mind-freezing horror of nuclear war has been experienced only by the Japanese.*

Japanese were being forced out of Burma by General Slim, and were on the retreat everywhere.

In February 1945 the allied leaders met at Yalta. Stalin, the Soviet dictator and himself a mass-murderer on Hitler's scale, was promised control of much territory in eastern Europe. These promises were unnecessary, and the allied advance was deliberately held back so that the Russians could be the first to enter Prague and other east European capitals.

In April the first United Nations meeting took place in San Francisco, attended by representatives of all the allied countries. The war in Europe ended officially the following month. It continued in the Far East, and the Americans, in order to force the Japanese to surrender, dropped atomic bombs on Hiroshima and Nagasaki. Developed by a team which included British scientists, they were the first nuclear weapons to be used in war and – so far – the last.

# Chapter 15

## Welfare State

Britain and its allies had won the Second World War, but victory did not bring rich rewards. Like other Western European countries, Britain's economy in 1945 was in a state of collapse. Exports had been cut back, factories had been destroyed, and skilled workers lost. The war had been paid for partly by taxes (income tax was raised to 50 per cent in 1941), but also by selling foreign investments, and by borrowing.

Britain's debts to the United States especially were huge. But Britain and the rest of Europe could only recover from the destruction of war with the help of more American loans.

At the end of the war, Britain still seemed to be a great world power. But during the war, the United States had replaced Britain as the leading Allied nation, and after the war American power was even greater. American aid helped Germany, which was in a worse state than Britain in 1945, to become a vigorous and wealthy country by the 1950s, and without American loans, Britain would have been bankrupt. Since their partnership during the war, Britain and the United States had become very close allies. This 'special relationship' continued, but it was not a partnership of equals. At times, the

*War and its shortages introduced the British to the queue. They have gone on queueing ever since!*

country seemed to be little more than an American satellite. Even ideas on fashion, entertainment and the arts came from the United States.

Europe's recovery from the war was surprisingly quick. But no amount of American aid could cure the deeper problems in the British economy. These went back to the nineteenth century. The gravest of them was the balance of trade. Britain imported more goods than it exported and was therefore spending more than it earned.

The war had also resulted in economic advantages. In Germany, the destruction of industry was so great that it had to start again from nothing – with the result that German industry became the most efficient in Europe. In Britain, farming had benefited. The need to increase food production so much during the war left Britain a leader in modern farming methods.

The British people expected other results from the war. They expected a better, fairer society. In the general election of 1945 the Labour party, for the first time, won a majority. This was perhaps unkind towards Churchill, the victorious war leader, but while most voters would probably have voted for him personally, they did not want a Conservative government. They wanted reform.

Between 1945 and 1950 the Labour government under Attlee changed British society more than any other modern government. It made Britain into a 'welfare state', a state which looks after its citizens 'from the cradle to the grave'. These reforms were based on a report (1942) on the social services in Britain by the economist William Beveridge (who was actually a Liberal, and not a member of the Labour party).

The National Insurance Act (1946) provided new benefits for the sick, the old and the unemployed, to be paid for out of taxes. Even more adventurous, the

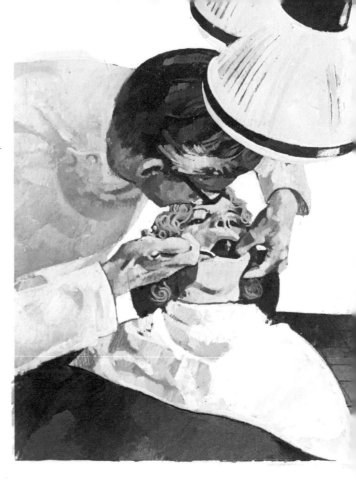

*'Open wide!' The National Health service meant that thousands of children's teeth were looked after.*

National Health Act, which came into effect in 1948, provided completely free medical care for everyone. The man behind it was the fiery, dynamic health minister, Aneurin Bevan. He had to fight against the fierce opposition of doctors, though they later became equally strong supporters of the National Health Service.

The National Health Service was very expensive. When small charges were introduced on things like spectacles and false teeth, Bevan resigned. But as time went on, the Health Service became more and more expensive and charges steadily rose. However, treatment remained free for those who could not pay.

The Attlee government made other social reforms, for example in education and public (council) housing, but its most

287

dramatic reforms were in economic policy. Labour's aim was to introduce a socialist society, in which industries are owned, not by private companies or private people, but by the state.

Most people agreed that nationalization of the coal industry or the railways, which were badly run under private ownership, was sensible, but strong opposition greeted the nationalization of some other industries, such as steel.

The nationalized industries were not, on the whole, very successful. However, people who complained about British Railways (often justly) forgot that if the old, bankrupt, railway companies had remained in charge, there would have been no trains at all.

The reforms of the Attlee government made Britain a different kind of society, based on the 'welfare state' and a mixed economy – part socialist (or nationalized) and part private. In spite of the quarrels over some acts, most people accepted this. When the Conservatives regained power in the 1950s, they 'privatized' steel again, but not the other industries nationalized by Labour (not even the Bank of England). Only much later, in the Thatcher era, did 'privatization' become government policy.

Conservative and Labour politicians still found plenty to disagree about, but both parties accepted that the basic system was about right. The policies of Gaitskell (Attlee's successor as Labour leader) and a Conservative like R A Butler (responsible for the reforming Education Act of 1944) were more or less the same. Someone invented the word 'Butskellism' to describe this closeness of views between political opponents, which lasted until the late 1970s.

In some ways, the late 1940s were rather dull and depressing years. There were shortages of almost everything: more goods were rationed than in wartime. The

*Britain's housing shortage was eased in the early 1950s through construction by local councils of houses for rent.*

*The Labour cabinet, 1945: Attlee (front row sixth from left) has Ernest Bevin (foreign secretary) on his right. Stafford Cripps is third from the left, front row, and Aneurin Bevan on the extreme left, back row.*

economy was struggling, and in 1949 the pound had to be devalued, from $4 to $2.80. People resented the growing class of government planners and civil servants, who seemed to interfere in so many activities.

On the other hand, living standards were higher than before the war, especially for working people. Wages rose and unemployment was very low (the Labour government was determined not to return to the dole queues of the 1930s). People had more holidays and more entertainments. Crowds of 60,000 filled the bigger football grounds every Saturday.

Britain's large debts forced the government to follow a policy of 'austerity', and the Labour government was blamed for the shortages and the economic difficulties. The Chancellor of the Exchequer, Sir Stafford Cripps, who was responsible for the austerity policy, happened to be a thin, rather strict-looking man. Unfortunately, he looked as if he had been designed for the part.

The austerity policy had some success,

increasing economic growth while keeping inflation down, but it did not save Labour from defeat in the 1951 election. The Conservatives returned to power and Churchill, at the age of seventy-seven, to 10 Downing Street. He suffered a stroke two years later and finally resigned in 1955, but the Conservatives remained the governing party until 1964.

## British governments 1945–92

| Year | Government | Prime Minister |
| --- | --- | --- |
| 1945 | Labour | Attlee |
| 1951 | Conservative | Churchill |
| 1955 | Conservative | Eden |
| 1957 | Conservative | Macmillan |
| 1963 | Conservative | Douglas-Home |
| 1964 | Labour | Wilson |
| 1970 | Conservative | Heath |
| 1974 | Labour | Wilson |
| 1976 | Labour | Callaghan |
| 1979 | Conservative | Thatcher |
| 1990 | Conservative | Major |

# End of Empire

In 1945 Britain still held a large world empire. It was obvious to most people that Britain could not keep it. For one thing, the people of the British empire wanted national independence. For another, Britain no longer had the power to defend its far-flung possessions, which was almost the only justification for keeping them. Both superpowers, the United States and the Soviet Union, were hostile to British imperialism, and so was the Labour government.

In twenty years or so Britain, along with other European imperial powers, shed almost all its colonies. On the whole, it was done in a reasonably peaceful, even friendly manner, although there were serious problems. In India, where independence had long been promised, it proved impossible for Hindus and Muslims to combine in a single state. At

*Gandhi showed that non-violence works: here he is fasting in protest against the delay in India's progress towards independence from Britain.*

the cost of great bloodshed and upheaval, the country was divided into India and Pakistan. Both countries remained in the Commonwealth, a group of about 50 independent states united only by their historic links with Britain. So did Ceylon (Sri Lanka), though Burma decided not to do so. Most former colonies in Africa joined the Commonwealth.

In Malaya, Communist guerrillas had to be defeated before the Federation of Malaysia was founded (1957), and in Kenya there was a fearful campaign by a Kikuyu organization, the Mau Mau. Other African countries reached independence peacefully. (Their new rulers were often men who, in earlier times, had been imprisoned by the British as rebels.)

The eastern Mediterranean was (and still is) a problem region. Under the authority of the old League of Nations, now replaced by the United Nations, Britain governed Palestine. It was a thankless job. The Arabs and Jews of Palestine were united in one thing only, hostility to the British. With no solution to offer, the British simply

announced that they were leaving Palestine (1947). As they left, war began between the newly declared republic of Israel and its Arab neighbours.

In Cyprus, the majority wanted union with Greece, but the minority of Turkish Cypriots opposed it. The British patched up an agreement that made Cyprus independent (1961) and though it soon broke down, Cyprus was then no longer Britain's responsibility.

The part that Britain had played as a kind of world policeman was being taken over by the United States. When the British government declared in 1947 that it could not continue to defend the Greek government from Communist rebellion, the American president announced the Truman Doctrine. The United States, said President Truman, would support free peoples everywhere against 'armed minorities or outside pressure'. By 'outside pressure' he meant Communism and the Soviet Union.

The 'Cold War' between the Soviet Union and the United States had begun when the Soviets took over the countries of eastern Europe after the war. They became Soviet 'satellites', under Communist rule and supervised by Moscow. In 1949 China, the biggest country in the world, also became Communist. Americans feared a Communist plan to take over the world. On the other side, Soviet Communists feared plots by the Americans and their allies in NATO (North Atlantic Treaty Organization) to destroy them.

As the closest ally of the United States in Europe, Britain was a leading member of NATO. Britain was also involved in the Korean War (1950–53), in which the main contestants were the United States, with UN (including British) support, and the Communist Chinese.

The British had surrendered their empire in a sensible manner, but in 1956 the government of Anthony Eden suddenly

*The United Nations was founded in 1945. Its Secretariat (administration) was housed in an impressive new building in New York. Britain became one of the five permanent members of the Security Council.*

acted as though Britain were still a great world power. Together with the French and Israelis, British troops invaded the Suez Canal Zone.

The Canal, which was owned by an international company, had been nationalized by the Egyptian government of Colonel Nasser. This was strictly against international law, but it hardly justified an invasion of Egyptian territory. Nasser was an anti-Western Arab nationalist with a strong appeal to Arabs everywhere, and the Eden government feared he would destroy British influence in the Arab world. Eden saw Nasser as another Hitler, who had to be stopped.

The invasion was condemned by the UN, and the United States failed to support it. The value of the pound fell sharply and Britain's gold reserves shrank alarmingly. The British and French were forced to withdraw, and UN forces took over in the Canal Zone.

# A Change of Mood

In the 1950s the British were more prosperous and pleased with themselves than at any time since the 1920s. Two events marked this change of mood: the Festival of Britain, with its spectacular fun fair, held in London in 1951, and the coronation of a new, young queen with a name that reminded people of a 'golden age' in the past, Elizabeth, who succeeded her father King George VI in 1952.

National recovery was underway. Economic growth was faster, wages were going up, while unemployment remained low. Some people made a lot of money rather easily in industries like advertising, entertainment and sport, as well as business. Many people bought their first television set to watch the Queen's coronation. Sales of cars, refrigerators, and other luxuries were also booming.

The arts were especially lively. Television reduced cinema audiences but it did not stop people reading novels by writers like Lawrence Durrell, Iris Murdoch, Evelyn Waugh, Anthony Powell and Kingsley Amis. Free public libraries and cheap paperbacks made reading a less expensive pastime.

Nor did television stop people going to the theatre, where a minor revolution took place. The plays of Samuel Beckett and Harold Pinter introduced a new kind of drama, while John Osborne's *Look Back in Anger* (1956) fiercely attacked the ideas and customs of welfare-state Britain. Osborne was one of the writers nicknamed 'Angry Young Men'. Plays, like films and novels, more often had working-class subjects.

Theatre and the arts received support from government through the Arts Council, founded in 1946. This enabled grand companies like the Royal Opera as well as small local companies to survive. New companies were founded, including the Royal Shakespeare and the National Theatre, though the National did not gain its own building until 1975.

The National Theatre, like some other new buildings in the cultural centre of the South Bank, was not beautiful to look at. Much new building took place in Britain at

*The splendour of the Festival of Britain brightened life for the British after the worry, gloom and depression of the 1940s.*

this period, and several 'new towns' were founded, but architecture was far less distinguished than other arts. Slabs of glass and dingy concrete spoilt many an old city centre. Some new housing developments were little better than the dreadful, prison-like suburbs being built under Communist rule in eastern Europe.

Music played a larger part in British life. Beside the work of internationally famous composers like Benjamin Britten, music was played more in schools, by local groups and at festivals such as the Edinburgh Festival (founded 1947). 'Pop' music, appealed mainly to teenagers. Until the Beatles pioneered a revolution in Rock music about 1960, the most popular stars were American.

As most families became better off, teenagers had more money to spend. Entertainment designed for them, especially pop music, became a big industry. Young people gathered at the coffee bars that sprang up in the larger cities.

Many young people were critical of British society. They especially disliked its selfishness and desire for money and success. Young people were active in

*Television was becoming the chief entertainment. Many people bought a set to watch the coronation of Elizabeth II in 1953.*

protest movements such as the Campaign for Nuclear Disarmament. The young supporters of CND were usually students. The number of students was growing: there were only 17 universities in Britain in 1945, but by 1975 there were 44.

*In the 1950s, many more families owned a car. Outings to the sea became more popular.*

FMC 987

# Winds of Change

The Suez disaster was a turning point in British history. It showed that Britain was no longer a great imperial power, and also that it could not take independent action in foreign affairs without the support of the United States. However, the effects of Suez were small. Good relations with the United States were soon restored. Though Eden, a sick man, resigned, the Conservative government did not fall.

The man chiefly responsible was Eden's successor as prime minister, Harold Macmillan. With his long experience, political skill and calm, easy-going manner, 'SuperMac' (as a pro-Labour cartoonist portrayed him) was the outstanding British prime minister between Churchill and Thatcher.

Personality alone does not keep a government in power, and the Macmillan government survived for other reasons. An election was not due until 1959, and by that time the wounds of Suez had healed. The country continued prosperous ('You've never had it so good,' was Macmillan's election slogan), with almost full employment. The unpopularity of the nationalized industries reduced support for Labour.

The Conservatives wisely did not attempt to undo the reforms of the Attlee government. They denationalized one or two industries, but did not oppose nationalization in principle. They merely criticized it for being inefficient: large subsidies had to be paid to the nationalized railway and coal industries. Most other differences between the main political parties were also about practical effects rather than principles.

One subject which did cause sharp and long-continuing argument was education. Under the Education Act of 1944, schoolchildren took an exam at the age of

*A post-war hospital. Free medical care proved expensive, so changes were soon introduced.*

eleven to decide whether they should go to a grammar school or a secondary modern. By the 1960s many people considered this system unfair, because secondary-school children had little chance to reach high academic standards. When Labour came to power, the government introduced comprehensive education, ending the division of children into bright and not-so-bright at the age of eleven. However, Labour never gained enough public support to abolish private or fee-paying schools (confusingly called 'public' schools in England). The public schools continued to exist side by side with the state's comprehensive system.

Another effect of Suez was to speed up Britain's surrender of its colonies. Although Britain was spared such horrors as the war in Algeria, which nearly ruined France before Algeria became independent, trouble was not avoided everywhere. Southern Rhodesia, like Algeria, had a large minority of Europeans, who controlled the country at the expense of Africans. Unwilling to give up their position, the Europeans under the government of Ian Smith declared their independence of Britain. Only after a long civil war with African nationalists did they surrender. In 1980 the country, renamed Zimbabwe, gained majority rule and independence.

As a result of its imperial past, Britain gained many new citizens from its former colonies. Until the 1930s, there were more emigrants leaving Britain than immigrants coming in. That changed when European refugees, many of them Jews, fled to Britain to escape the Nazis.

Twenty years later, a new wave of immigration began. This time the immigrants were Commonwealth citizens, who had the right of free entry. At first they came chiefly from the West Indies, later from South Asia. Many of them were lured to Britain by employers seeking labour.

About 100,000 people, mostly from the Commonwealth, entered the country every year in the 1950s and 1960s. By 1971 they made up 2.5 per cent of the

population. As immigrants they tended, naturally, to settle together in certain districts.

The changing nature of the British population caused social problems, especially when unemployment increased. Some of the trouble rose from ignorant radical prejudice. As immigration grew, the government introduced new laws to limit the numbers, ending the free entry of Commonwealth citizens. The 1971 Immigration Act treated Commonwealth citizens as foreigners, and made immigration almost impossible for anyone who did not have family connections in Britain. In 1981 serious riots broke out in run-down city districts, one cause of which was the resentment of young blacks (not immigrants but British-born) at racial discrimination.

*The children's ward of a modern hospital.*

# The Sixties

Every period of history has its own special atmosphere or 'flavour', although it may be hard to recognize the flavour until later. Some periods are especially distinctive. The 'Sixties' was one of those periods. Of course it did not last exactly ten years, and it had no clear end, or beginning. In Britain the 'Sixties' really began about 1957, with the beginning of the Macmillan government.

In this period people – especially young people – behaved with greater freedom. One small sign of that was in hairstyles. For 40 years or more all men had worn their hair cut short, well above the ears. Older people were shocked when the Beatles pop group appeared with their hair growing over their ears. Soon, much longer locks became normal. Young women's skirts were equally shocking to their parents. The 'mini-skirt', showing almost as much leg as a bathing costume, appeared in 1965.

Long hair and short skirts were only signs of changing behaviour. Britain was becoming more tolerant in matters of sex. A new law in 1964 made homosexuality among men legal (it was already legal among women). Easy methods of birth control ended the fear of pregnancy, and sexual relations became much freer – until the disease called AIDS reached Britain in the 1980s. More marriages ended in divorce, with a growing number of one-parent families.

London, with its boutiques and pop stars, became a kind of youth capital of the world. Thousands of tourists visited 'swinging London', where life seemed to be mostly entertainment. The satirist Jonathan Miller remarked that Britain seemed to be about to sink giggling into the sea.

But the sixties were not entirely a happy decade, and there was another side to the

*The Beatles appeared at the London Palladium in 1963 to the accompaniment of about 2,000 screaming teenage girls, who had besieged the theatre all day long.*

*CND (Campaign for Nuclear Disar-
mament) members took part in a series
of protest marches to the nuclear
research centre at Aldermaston.*

'youth culture'.

Beneath the rather flashy surface, British society contained deep divisions. Among the young, the same kind of people who supported CND took the lead in opposing the Vietnam war, in which tens of thousands of innocent Vietnamese people died. The war began as part of the United States' defence of democracy against Communism but became a dreadful, pointless slaughter, which ended in 1973 with American defeat. Although few British troops took part, the British government fully supported the Americans.

Youth leaders attacked society for its uncaring ways. Nuclear weapons, pollution of the environment, old-fashioned rules and regulations – these were some of the things that roused them to anger. In some universities in the late 1960s student protests developed into rebellion. Lecture halls were occupied and vice-chancellors insulted, but these outbreaks were brief and less serious than student revolts in France or the United States.

A few people showed their dislike of modern consumer society by 'dropping out'. They formed their own groups, living a simpler sort of life, even dressing differently. These hippies, as they were called, were usually gentle people, but they were widely disliked. Apart from being 'different', they were linked with the growing use of dangerous drugs among young people.

There were other reasons for division and revolt in British society. Nationalism grew stronger in Scotland and Wales, where the native traditions (and languages) were steadily disappearing. Many Scots and Welsh objected to the dominance of the London government, of English customs and English money which (for example) led to rich English people buying up Welsh cottages as holiday homes at prices that local people could not afford. Extreme Welsh nationalists even set off a few bombs, though without killing anyone. Minorities within England itself, especially Muslims, Hindus and other mainly black groups, also had cause to protest against discrimination.

# Britain's Place in the World

Soon after the end of the Second World War, many leading Europeans began talking about some kind of Western European union. The strongest reason in its favour was to link Germany more closely with its neighbours, especially France, which would make another European war impossible.

The British did not like the idea. They were much more interested in the Commonwealth than in Europe, and they were keen to keep up the 'special relationship' with the United States. They also disliked the idea of European officials interfering with British laws and government.

In 1957 the European Economic Community was founded by six Western European states. Britain was not one of them.

The EEC (later called the EC or European Community) was intended to form an economic union, or Common Market. Its members, acting as one economic unit, would be able to compete on nearly equal terms with other economic

giants, such as the United States. In its early years it appeared very successful; EEC members grew rapidly more prosperous, while Britain lagged behind.

Britain's first attempt to join the EEC was blocked by France, under President De Gaulle, in 1963. His reason was that Britain was too closely tied to the United States. Most British people were not greatly disappointed. Joining the EEC meant higher food prices, as well as threatening Britain's control of its own affairs. Labour and trade union leaders were suspicious of the EEC as a 'bosses'' club. Some Conservatives – 'Empire loyalists' – wanted to keep old Commonwealth links. Countries like Australia and New Zealand, which exported large quantities of food to Britain under a Commonwealth trade agreement, would lose their biggest market, because such agreements would be scrapped if Britain joined the EEC.

Ten years passed before Britain became a member of the Community in 1973. The economic advantages seemed greater than the disadvantages, and in 1975 a referendum was held (the first in British history) in which a large majority voted in favour of remaining a member. All the same, the British people did not become keen Europeans. The EEC's 'common

*In 1972 Edward Heath signed the agreement taking Britain into the EEC. On his right is the foreign secretary, Alec Douglas-Home; on his left Geoffrey Rippon, who negotiated the terms.*

*Britain's former colonies experienced mixed fortunes after independence. Some remained poor and unstable. One of the most successful was Singapore, which became a thriving world centre of business.*

agricultural policy', which was designed to help small German and French farmers, seemed ridiculous. It led to 'butter mountains' and 'wine lakes', while food prices in Britain rose sharply. The idea of a future 'United States of Europe', run by unknown civil servants from vast office buildings in continental cities, was very unattractive.

However, it seemed obvious that Britain's future lay in Europe, not overseas. The 'special relationship' meant much less in the United States than it did in Britain, and the British themselves were less attached to the United States in the 1970s, partly as a result of the Vietnam war and the presence of American nuclear missiles in British bases. Moreover, the Americans themselves favoured British membership of the EEC.

The links with the Commonwealth were also steadily fading. Trade with the Commonwealth since 1945 had shrunk, while trade with Europe had grown. The old dominions, such as Australia and Canada, were drawing closer to the United States, and depended on the Americans, not the British, for defence. A backlash against Commonwealth immigrants to Britain made the Commonwealth less popular, and quarrels broke out over British policy towards Rhodesia (Zimbabwe) and South Africa.

## Growth of the European Community

1957 Belgium, France, Italy, Luxembourg, Netherlands, West Germany

1973 Britain, Denmark, Ireland

1981 Greece

1985 Portugal, Spain

1990 East Germany (as part of reunited Germany)

# Pounds in Pockets

One reason for the growing dissatisfaction in the 1960s and 1970s was the economic situation. Although the British had become richer since the early 1950s, long-standing economic problems had not been solved. Throughout the 1960s the value of the pound in the international market remained fragile, and the government was forced into another devaluation in 1967 (from $2.80 to $2.40). Prime Minister Wilson insisted that devaluation would not alter the value of 'the pound in your pocket'. But of course it did. British exports grew a little, but devaluation did not cure all old problems and it helped create new ones. The rate of inflation began to rise, while at the same time unemployment grew. This was especially worrying because it was unexpected. Rising inflation should have reduced unemployment and increased production, but the opposite was happening.

Britain was gaining a bad economic reputation. Once the 'workshop of the world', it could no longer produce the goods to keep a healthy share of the world trade. As living standards went down, unions demanded higher wages (making British goods even more expensive in world markets). Strikes were frequent and manufacturing standards went down.

*Nationalization: the National Coal Board took over the mines from private owners to the relief of nearly everyone.*

British-made goods lost their reputation. If you wanted a reliable machine, you bought German, or Japanese – but not British.

As they often had in the past, the coal miners took the lead in demands for higher wages. In 1974, after two damaging coal strikes, the Heath government called a general election to answer the question, 'Who governs Britain?' The bluff failed. Heath lost the election and the miners got their wage rises.

The Labour government under Wilson and Callaghan reached an agreement with the unions, called the 'Social Contract', but it did not last long. In the 'winter of discontent' (1978–79) a series of strikes brought many public services to a halt and led to the defeat of Labour in the 1979 election.

Industrial distress was worst in the places on which Britain's prosperity had been built in the past – the regions of heavy industry in the Midlands, the north-east, and in Scotland and South Wales. Unemployment was high also whole communities were ruined when a big factory, like the famous steel works at Consett, shut down. At the same time inflation was still rising (it reached 25 per cent in 1975) and government spending was reduced, which meant that public services were cut back.

There was more violence in society. Crime increased; workers were threatened in industrial protests; football fans battled on the terraces; riots erupted in poor city districts. Was British society, as a few people thought, cracking up?

In spite of its troubles, Britain was still both more prosperous and more peaceful than most other countries, including many of its closest neighbours and allies. British industry was not only a story of strikes and falling standards, and more went on in universities than student demonstrations. In some areas of science and technology Britain was still a world leader. British skills played a large part in the development of computers. British engineers, in co-operation with French, built the first successful supersonic airliner, *Concorde*. British scientists often appeared among the annual Nobel prize winners.

Most British people were still content to be British. The monarchy was one British institution which remained extremely popular. Politicians were not so popular (they seldom are), but no one suggested abolishing parliament. Old traditions, both local and national, were still respected. British artists, writers and scholars were widely admired abroad, and, thanks to the BBC, Britain enjoyed the world's finest broadcasting service.

The troubles of the 1970s did not mean that British society was breaking down, but they did mean that changes were necessary.

*Strikes were a damaging feature of the British economy in the 1970s. Government tried to keep wage demands in line with inflation.*

*Unemployed men waiting for jobs. Industry went through a painful period of change in the 1970s, as traditional manufacturing declined and new, 'high-tech' industries demanded different skills. High unemployment was costly in financial as well as human terms.*

*British soldiers confront a civilian across a barbed-wire barrier in Belfast. Terrorist violence was confined to big cities and border regions, but all Northern Ireland was affected by the bitter conflict.*

# Northern Ireland

The British are not a single nation. When someone speaks about 'the English', when they mean 'the British', they offend three million Welsh and six million Scots. Although a referendum held in both countries in 1979 showed only small support for separate Scottish and Welsh assemblies, the Scottish Nationalists, who wanted total independence, held three seats in the House of Commons in 1992.

In the province of Northern Ireland, the situation was different. The Protestant majority there clung fiercely to their right to remain British. Most of the Roman Catholic minority preferred union with the republic of Ireland.

The troubles that tore Ireland apart in the early 20th century were the result of 700 years of British colonial rule which had

often been unjust and sometimes brutal. The Irish problem appeared to have been solved at last when Ireland gained independence in 1922. But, under pressure from the Protestants in Ulster, the British kept the six counties of Ulster that form the province of Northern Ireland.

Northern Ireland, which had its own parliament, was dominated by Protestant landowners and businessmen. The minority of Roman Catholics were 'second-class citizens'. Not only were they kept out of power, they were kept out of the best jobs as well. They were distrusted because they were Catholics and republicans.

During the 1960s there were movements in many countries to gain full civil rights for minorities (such as blacks in the United States). A civil-rights campaign began in Ireland. Though the protests themselves were peaceful, riots broke out, and British troops were sent in to keep the peace. At first the troops were welcomed by Catholics, who regarded the Northern Ireland police (nearly all Protestants) as enemies. But it soon appeared that the troops were on the side of the authorities.

The British government insisted on reforms to give Catholics equality. The Northern Ireland government was willing, but was under pressure from Protestant extremists. The Catholics found new defenders in the IRA.

The IRA (Irish Republican Army) had been founded in the 19th century to fight the British, but by the 1960s it had given up violence in favour of propaganda. The disorders of 1969 to 1972 produced a breakaway IRA group, the Provisionals, who began a campaign of bombings and murders to drive out the British. Protestant terrorist groups retaliated.

The Northern Ireland government took drastic steps, including the policy of internment (prison without trial). Hundreds of people were arrested, but practically all were Catholics. Such policies strengthened Catholic support for the IRA.

In 1972, the Northern Ireland government was suspended. The province came under direct rule from London, which brought the British government into direct conflict with the IRA.

Violence increased. Only nine people died in 1969; in 1972 the number was 474. It included 13 Catholics shot by British troops on 'Bloody Sunday' (30 January) in Londonderry. The IRA extended their campaign to Britain and even to British forces in Europe. Among their most notorious attacks were the murder of a member of the royal family (Lord Mountbatten) in the republic, and of a Northern Ireland minister inside the precincts of Parliament (1979); the bombing of a Brighton hotel during the Conservative party conference (1984); and a mortar attack on 10 Downing Street (1991).

The British government refused to talk to the IRA or its political wing, Sinn Fein, but failed to find a political solution. The Protestant majority refused to accept any settlement which threatened their position. They especially resented Britain's efforts to involve the Irish government in a settlement, although the regular Anglo–Irish conferences which began in 1985 continued, in spite of Protestant distrust.

The IRA obviously could not defeat the British army. But the army could not stop terrorism as long as the IRA held the sympathy of so many Catholics.

*Stormont Castle, the seat of the Northern Ireland government. In 1972 its function ended, when the Northern Ireland government was suspended.*

# Oil, Energy and the Environment

In the modern industrial world, no country can survive without a good, inexpensive supply of energy, or power. Britain's industrial success in the 19th century was based on coal. Large coal reserves still exist, but the coal industry was in decline in the second half of the 20th century, due chiefly to competition from cheaper, foreign supplies, and from oil.

The importance of oil in the world economy was brought home to everybody in the 1970s, when the Arab producers of the Middle East raised the price sharply, causing a severe recession. Britain suffered along with other countries, but its prospects were better than most because new reserves of oil – and natural gas – had been discovered in 1970 in the North Sea.

By the 1980s Britain was a net exporter of oil (selling more than it bought). This was one reason why the country grew more prosperous at a time when manufacturing industry was in decline and the balance of trade was still unfavourable. However, by 1990, North Sea oil production was already falling.

The so-called 'fossil fuels' – oil, natural gas and coal – will all run out in time. Therefore, all countries invested in the search for a source of energy that did not depend on fossil fuels. Britain was a leader in the development of nuclear power, which provided about ten per cent of electricity by 1980. But nuclear power is dangerous. In 1986 the event that many people feared – a serious accident at a nuclear-power station – actually happened. A reactor at Chernobyl in the Ukraine exploded. The effects were felt as far away as Scandinavia and north-west Britain. The nuclear-power industry became even more

*An oil rig in the North Sea. Discovery of rich new sources of oil gave Britain and some other countries a welcome boost. However, this only postponed the problem of world consumption of 'non-renewable' fuels.*

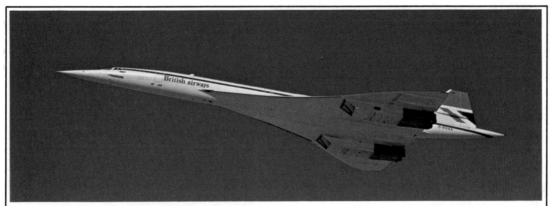

Concorde, *the only faster-than-sound airliner (a Soviet version was a failure), was a marvellous piece of engineering but, twenty years later, no successor was planned.*

unpopular: it no longer offered a sane answer to the energy problem.

Radiation was just one example of industrial pollution which, in the second half of the 20th century, became a growing worry in industrial countries. The concern of ordinary people for the natural environment dated from the publication of *Silent Spring*, by the American biologist Rachel Carson, in 1963, which attacked the use of chemical pesticides and weedkillers. People became aware of the damage being done by modern, industrial society to the natural world. Air made filthy by factory smoke and car exhausts, rivers poisoned by industrial waste and agricultural chemicals, seas and beaches fouled by spilling oil tankers – were human beings turning the beautiful green earth into a desert planet out of some science-fiction nightmare?

Individuals and organizations concerned with nature – even governments – became concerned. A rise in world temperature was explained by the 'Greenhouse Effect', in which waste gases such as carbon dioxide prevent heat being reflected from the Earth into space. If not stopped, the effect would be disastrous for farming, and would cause immense floods.

British scientists working in Antarctica discovered a gap in the ozone layer, which protects the Earth from harmful rays of the Sun. It was caused by the use of certain artificial chemicals in such things as hair sprays. Prodded by dedicated organizations like Friends of the Earth, governments made efforts to ban such things. But the damage could not be cured in a moment. The ozone layer is still getting thin. The 'victory' of human beings over nature may prove to be humanity's worst defeat. Even if disaster is avoided, a country like Britain has changed for the worse in the 20th century through loss of wild plants, animals and habitats. Since 1945, Britain has lost 30 per cent of its hedges, 95 per cent of lowland meadows, 80 per cent of chalk downs, and 60 per cent of marshes and wetlands. Many wildflowers, insects, birds and other animals have disappeared, or will soon disappear. Conservationists and 'green' groups have had some successes, but the general decline continues. Governments are aware of the dangers, but they are also dependent on votes, and most people are more interested in preserving their standard of living than preserving nature. Shocked by polluted rivers, the government created the National Rivers Authority to fight the problem in 1989. In 1992 an investigation showed that the state of Britain's rivers had grown worse since the NRA was founded.

# Thatcher's Britain

In 1979 the Conservatives returned to power under Margaret Thatcher. She was Britain's first woman prime minister. Her presence in 10 Downing Street was a sign of the much larger part that women had come to play in public life, as well as in the professions and even in business. Most women wanted a career, like men, and this was becoming easier, even for mothers. Margaret Thatcher herself was a self-made woman, who owed little to the feminist movement. Daughter of a grocer, she was intelligent, courageous and very determined. Under her, the Conservative party moved further to the Right, while at the same time Labour was moving to the Left. Consensus (or 'agreement') politics came to an end. 'I'm not a consensus politician,' said Thatcher, 'I'm a conviction politician.' She strongly disliked socialism, which she believed was responsible for Britain's poor economic performance since 1945. Thatcherites thought the welfare state had made the British feeble. People should stand on their own feet, they said, not rely on state benefits. They believed in a capitalist free market, in which prices are controlled by competition, not by government subsidies. Businesses that could not survive should be closed down.

The first task was to reduce inflation. This was done – by 1985 it was down to 5 per cent – but at a price. Government spending on housing, education and health was reduced, and unemployment rose sharply. By 1983 over 3 million people were out of work.

Nationalized industries such as gas, electricity and telephones were sold to private companies, and new laws were passed to control the powers of trade unions. It became impossible for political extremists to use industrial disputes as a means of damaging the economy. Earlier govern-

*Margaret Thatcher with U.S. foreign minister, James Baker.*

ments, both Conservative and Labour, had tried and failed to end the misuse of union power. Yet the Thatcher government's trade union reforms were popular even among many trade unionists.

Cuts in public services and high unemployment made Thatcher, nicknamed 'the Iron Lady' by a Soviet newspaper, unpopular. Yet her party won the 1983 election easily. One reason for its success was a British victory in war.

Among the remains of the British empire, places too small to become independent states, were the Falkland Islands in the South Atlantic. They had no value for Britain, but the population (less than 2000) was entirely British. Argentina had an ancient claim to the Falklands (or Malvinas), and in 1982 Argentine forces suddenly invaded the islands. This was an illegal act by a brutal and unpopular Argentinian dictator, and it was condemned by the United Nations. A large British force was sent to the Falklands and in less than two months the islands were recaptured. Several British ships were destroyed and an Argentine cruiser sunk with the loss of its crew of 350. Altogether, about 1000 Argentinians died in the brief war and 250 British. It was a risky but successful operation, and caused an outburst of patriotism in Britain from which the government benefited. The 'Iron Lady' won international respect for her steely defence of British interests.

The armed forces were involved in another international conflict, the Gulf War, in 1991. They provided the largest European contingent in the U.S.-led force which compelled Iraq to withdraw from Kuwait. That campaign was sanctioned by the UN, and British troops also helped in UN policing and relief operations, for example in Bosnia (Yugoslavia) in 1992-93. Together with commitments in other parts of the world, such as Belize and Cyprus, and above all in Northern Ireland, British forces were fully stretched. Cuts in defence spending, which were expected after the collapse of the Soviet Union, were smaller than planned.

In 1988 Margaret Thatcher became the longest-serving prime minister of the century. The sale of shares in privatized industries, and of council houses to their tenants, were part of her mission to involve more people in capitalist society. Abroad, she reinforced the 'special relationship' by her close alliance with U.S. President Ronald Reagan, another admirer of free-market forces, and supported the reforming ruler of the Soviet Union, Mikhail Gorbachev. Other countries adopted 'Thatcherite' economic policies, even France (under a socialist president), and she was admired in the countries of Eastern Europe, which in 1989 escaped from the grim and inefficient rule of Communism to become democ-

*Growing criticism of the royal family made the Queen agree to pay taxes on her private income in 1992 (her 40th anniversary). The marriage problems of her children reduced people's respect for the monarchy.*

racies. She was less popular with fellow-leaders of the European Community. Her powerful personality and plain speaking made enemies as well as friends, but her admirers boasted that she had put the 'Great' back into Great Britain.

Britain was enjoying its biggest economic boom since 1945. The Thatcher government claimed the credit, but deserved only some of it. In the 20th century, economic 'booms' and 'recessions' in the capitalist world are international. The policies of national governments usually have only minor effects. The rise in government income was due partly to lucky – and temporary – events.

Most important of these was income from the new oil industry. Also valuable was the sale of nationalized industries. But the oil 'bonanza' could last only a few years, while public companies could only be sold once (the government was 'selling

the family silver', complained the elderly statesman, Harold Macmillan). A third factor was the reduction in spending on public services such as education and health. Thatcher was so unpopular among educationalists, who believed that schools and universities were being badly damaged by the cuts, that her old university, Oxford, refused her an honorary degree.

The Thatcher 'revolution' had some other dark spots. The sharp rise in prosperity was limited mainly to southern England. The old centres of manufacturing industry in the north and in Scotland and South Wales continued to decline. By 1990 the Conservatives held only ten of the 72 Scottish seats in the House of Commons. As the social division between 'North' and 'South' in Britain grew deeper, so did the division between rich and poor. Reductions in taxes favoured the well-off.

Another unpleasant effect, harder to

*Everyday activities like shopping changed enormously between the 1940s and the 1980s. After the super-market came the 'hypermarket' and elegant indoor shopping centres, like this one in Gateshead.*

measure, was the mean and aggressive pursuit of money by people who had a great deal of it already. This was the age of the Yuppies ('young, upwardly mobile people'), whose only object in life seemed to be to get richer. By encouraging more competition, the government also encouraged selfishness and sharp practice.

By 1989 the prime minister's popularity was low even among close colleagues. She was forced to resign as Conservative leader and therefore as prime minister. Many Conservatives resented her domineering leadership. Many more were worried by government spending cuts. Pro-Europeans despaired at Thatcher's hostility to the European Community. The government also made a serious error by introducing a new tax to pay for local government. The 'Poll Tax' replaced the old tax on property known as the Rates. But the Poll Tax appeared very unfair, biased in favour of the rich. It was so unpopular that, after Thatcher's resignation, the government abandoned it.

A final reason for Thatcher's downfall was the end of the boom of the 1980s. Britain was entering another recession, which was to last well into the 1990s. In spite of economic gloom, the Conservatives under John Major won their fourth successive general election in 1992. Though narrowly defeated, the Labour party had revived under Neil Kinnock, adopting less divisive and less socialist policies. After his defeat, Kinnock resigned and was replaced by an energetic Scots Lawyer, John Smith.

Recession deepened under the Major government. Though inflation fell, unemployment rose, passing 3 million again in 1993, and many businesses went bankrupt. Lack of jobs was blamed for rising crime. Relations with the EC, expected to improve after Thatcher, proved troublesome. Though the EC became a single market in 1993, the next step towards union, the Treaty of Maastricht, proved

*Canary Wharf, centre of London's docklands development, proved a white elephant in the 1990s. Tenants could not be found to fill it.*

unpopular. The Danes rejected it in a referendum, and the French almost did. The government refused a referendum in Britain, fearing a 'No' vote. Another EC institution, the ERM (Exchange Rate Mechanism), was failing. It was designed to link the value of members' currencies and prevent large changes in exchange rates. By 1992 the pound was obviously too highly valued against the German mark – the dominant European currency. International dealers began to sell sterling. The Bank of England, though spending millions in an attempt to support its value, could not prevent the pound falling below its permitted minimum. The government was forced to withdraw from the ERM – in effect devaluing the pound.

In the 1990s Britain still seemed more prosperous than most countries. The British had come to terms with their smaller role in the world. Their history and culture earned them more respect than their numbers or their wealth warranted. Large problems loomed, however, especially the large gap between rich and poor.

# Table of Events

310

## BC

- **1900** Stonehenge building begins
- **55** Invasions of Julius Caesar begin

## AD

- **30** *Crucifixion of Jesus*
- **43** Roman conquest begins
- **61** Boudicca's revolt
- **127** Hadrian's Wall completed
- **406** Roman troops leave
- **535** Arthur dies about this time
- **550** St David converts the Welsh to Christianity
- **563** St Columba at Iona converts the Picts
- **580** Anglo-Saxons settle in most of England
- **597** St Augustine arrives at Canterbury
- **622** *Flight of Muhammad from Mecca (the Hejira); first year of the Muslim calendar*
- **660** Approximate date of Sutton Hoo burial
- **663** Synod of Whitby; English Church follows Roman, not Celtic, practice
- **700** *Beowulf*, first long epic poem in English
- **700** Lindisfarne Gospels produced
- **735** Death of Bede at Jarrow
- **782** Offa's Dyke under construction
- **793** First Viking Invasion
- **843** Scots and Picts united under Kenneth MacAlpin

- **1263** Simon de Montfort leads revolt against Henry III
- **1278** Edward I's inquiry to discover rights of landholders
- **1284** Wales finally conquered by English
- **1290** All Jews expelled from England
- **1295** 'Model' Parliament, including Commons
- **1296** Edward I takes Stone of Scone to England
- **1304** Capture of William Wallace
- **1306** Robert Bruce crowned at Scone
- **1314** Bruce defeats English at Bannockburn
- **1337** Edward III claims French crown: beginning of Hundred Years' War
- **1340** Sluys: English naval victory
- **1346** English victory at Crecy
- **1346** David II captured at Neville's Cross
- **1348** The Black Death (plague)
- **1356** English defeat French at Poitiers
- **1377** Wyclif's preaching creates Lollards
- **1380** Chaucer at work on *Canterbury Tales*
- **1381** Peasants' Revolt
- **1385** St Giles's, Edinburgh, under construction
- **1400** Welsh War of Independence
- **1415** English defeat French at Agincourt

- **1560** Treaty of Edinburgh: English alliance with Scots
- **1567** Mary Queen of Scots abdicates and flees to England
- **1569** Rising in the north against Elizabeth
- **1570** Elizabeth excommunicated by Pope Pius V
- **1577** Drake sets sail around the world
- **1582** Raid of Ruthven: James VI kidnapped by Protestants
- **1587** Execution of Mary Queen of Scots
- **1588** Defeat of Spanish Armada
- **1600** East India Company founded
- **1601** Essex executed
- **1601** Poor Law Act
- **1605** Gunpowder Plot
- **1607** First permanent colony in Virginia
- **1611** Authorized Version of the Bible
- **1616** Death of Shakespeare
- **1620** Voyage of the *Mayflower* to New England
- **1629** Start of 'Eleven Years' Tyranny'
- **1638** Scottish Covenant
- **1641** Grand Remonstrance passed by Long Parliament
- **1642** Outbreak of English Civil War
- **1643** Solemn League and Covenant: agreement between Scots and Parliament
- **1649** Execution of Charles I
- **1650** Battle of Dunbar; Cromwell takes Edinburgh Castle

- **1756** Outbreak of Seven Years' War
- **1765** Watt's improved steam engine
- **1766** Stamp Act repealed
- **1768** Wilkes elected MP; rejected by Commons
- **1768** Cook's first voyage
- **1773** Boston 'Tea Party'; protest against British trade policy
- **1776** American Declaration of Independence
- **1783** Younger Pitt prime minister
- **1785** Cartwright's power loom patented
- **1788** First convicts to Australia
- **1789** *The French Revolution breaks out*
- **1790** Forth-Clyde canal opened
- **1793** Beginning of French wars
- **1798** Wolfe Tone's rebellion in Ireland
- **1799** First British income tax
- **1800** Act of Union with Ireland
- **1805** Trafalgar: Nelson killed during naval victory over French and Spanish
- **1807** Slave trade abolished
- **1812** Assassination of Prime Minister Spencer Perceval
- **1812** War with United States
- **1815** Waterloo: final defeat of Napoleon
- **1819** Peterloo 'Massacre'
- **1826** Menai Bridge opened
- **1829** Catholic Emancipation Act
- **1829** First regular police force ('bobbies')
- **1830** Liverpool–Manchester Railway opens

- **1875** Britain gains control of Suez Canal
- **1884** Third Reform Act
- **1885** General Gordon killed in Khartoum
- **1886** Irish Home Rule bill defeated
- **1889** Great London dock strike
- **1890** Fall of Parnell as Irish leader
- **1894** Retirement of Gladstone
- **1895** First Promenade concerts, London
- **1898** Fashoda Incident: Britain and France avoid clash in Africa
- **1899** Outbreak of Boer War
- **1900** Modern Labour Party founded
- **1908** Old Age Pensions introduced
- **1912** *Titanic*, biggest liner ever, sunk by iceberg on maiden voyage
- **1914** Outbreak of Great War
- **1916** British Summer Time starts
- **1916** Easter Rising in Dublin
- **1916** Lloyd George coalition government
- **1917** *Revolution in Russia*
- **1919** Treaty of Versailles ends World War
- **1922** Conservative government of Bonar Law
- **1922** First radio entertainment broadcasts
- **1923** Baldwin succeeds Bonar Law
- **1924** First Labour government under Ramsay MacDonald, lasts nine months
- **1926** General Strike, May 1 to May 12

866 Major Danish invasion of England

878 Alfred defeats Danes; Danelaw created

899 Death of Alfred

900– Creation of united English
950 kingdom under Edward and Athelstan

1016 Danish king, Cnut, king of England

1018 Malcolm II gains Lothian

1040 Duncan murdered by Macbeth

1042 Edward the Confessor king of England

1066 Norman Conquest begins

1086 Domesday Book finished

1095 *First Crusade proclaimed*

1153 Treaty of Wallingford ends civil war

1154 Nicholas Breakspear becomes Pope Adrian IV, the only English pope ever

1167 Foundation of Oxford university

1170 Thomas Becket murdered

1170 Strongbow captures Dublin

1174 William the Lion captured at Alnwick

1192 Richard I and Saladin make truce ending Third Crusade

1204 Loss of Normandy

1206 John quarrels with Pope Innocent III

1209 Foundation of Cambridge university

1215 John forced to accept *Magna Carta*

1220 Salisbury Cathedral begun

1429 French, inspired by Joan of Arc, defeat English

1450 Rebellion of Jack Cade against bad government and high taxes

1455 Beginning of Wars of the Roses

1471 Warwick killed at Barnet; end of Wars of Roses

1471 James III annexes Orkney and Shetland

1476 Caxton sets up printing press

1485 Battle of Bosworth; Richard III killed

1492 *Columbus discovers West Indies*

1497 John Cabot's voyage to Newfoundland

1513 Scots defeated at Flodden

1517 *Luther attacks the pope: beginning of the Reformation*

1529 Fall of Wolsey: English Reformation begins

1536 Beginning of suppression of monasteries; Pilgrimage of Grace

1540 Thomas Cromwell executed

1541 Welsh members in English Parliament

1544 English capture Edinburgh

1549 Ket's rebellion in Norfolk

1553 Lady Jane Grey queen for nine days

1554 Protestant revolt against Mary

1555 John Knox returns to Scotland

1558 England loses Calais

1559 Acts of Supremacy and Uniformity restoring Protestant Church

1651 Charles II crowned king of Scotland

1651 Navigation Acts against Dutch shipping

1655 Capture of Jamaica

1660 Royal Society founded

1665 Milton finishes *Paradise Lost*

1665 Last bad outbreak of plague

1666 Great Fire of London

1675 Wren begins work on St Paul's

1687 Newton publishes his major work

1688 Glorious Revolution

1690 Battle of the Boyne: James II defeated

1692 Massacre of Glencoe

1694 Bank of England founded

1698 Failure of Scottish Darien Scheme

1701 Act of Settlement ensures Protestant monarchs in England

1702 War of Spanish Succession begins

1707 Act of Union

1713 Treaty of Utrecht

1715 Jacobite rising in the north

1720 'South Sea Bubble' bursts

1730 Methodist Society founded

1736 Porteous Riots in Edinburgh

1739 Outbreak of War of Jenkins' Ear

1745 Jacobite rebellion led by Prince Charles Edward

1746 Culloden: final Jacobite defeat

1755 Publication of Dr Johnson's *Dictionary*

1832 Great Reform Act

1834 Slavery abolished in British Empire

1834 Reform of Poor Law

1836 Great Trek: Boers found Orange Free State

1839 Chartist Petition rejected by Parliament

1839 Outbreak of Opium Wars with China

1840 Marriage of Queen Victoria and Prince Albert

1841 Peel prime minister

1843 Establishment of Free Church of Scotland

1843 SS *Great Britain*, screw-driven steamer, crosses Atlantic

1846 Irish famine: Corn laws repealed

1848 *Revolutions in Europe*

1848 Pre-Raphaelite Brotherhood founded

1851 Great Exhibition, Hyde Park

1854 Outbreak of Crimean War

1855 Livingstone crosses Africa, east-west

1857 Indian Mutiny: native soldiers revolt

1859 Darwin publishes *Origin of Species*

1861 *Outbreak of American Civil War*

1867 Second Parliament Reform Act

1868 First Trades Union Congress

1870 Death of Charles Dickens

1870 Elementary Education Act

1871 Trade Unions legalized

1875 First Gilbert and Sullivan opera

1926 Television demonstrated by Baird

1927 BBC founded

1928 Penicillin discovered by Fleming

1928 All women over twenty-one gain right to vote

1929 Second Labour government

1929 *Wall St crash*: economic slump

1931 Statute of Westminster: independence of the Dominions, under the Crown

1931 National (coalition) government

1933 *Hitler gains power in Germany*

1937 Chamberlain succeeds Baldwin as premier

1939 Outbreak of Second World War begins

1940 Churchill prime minister of national government; food rationing begins

1941 Conscription for women and men

1942 Beveridge Report published

1944 *Dumbarton Oaks conference: United Nations established*

1945 *Atomic bombs dropped on Japan*

1945 Labour government under Attlee

1947 Independence of India: other countries follow

1948 Olympic Games held in London

1950 *Korean War: UN v. North Korea and China*

1951 Conservative government under Churchill

1951 Festival of Britain

*Table of Events continued on page 312*

# Table of Kings and Queens

*continued from page 311*

| Scottish Monarchs 1124–1625 | English Monarchs 1066–1603 | British Monarchs since 1603 |
|---|---|---|
| David I 1124–53 | William I 1066–87 | James I 1603–25 |
| Malcolm IV 1153–65 | William II 1087–1100 | Charles I 1625–49 |
| William I 1165–1214 | Henry I 1100–35 | Charles II 1660–85 |
| Alexander II 1214–49 | Stephen 1135–54 | (Scotland from 1651) |
| Alexander III 1249–86 | Henry II 1154–89 | James II 1685–88 |
| Margaret 1286–90 | Richard I 1189–99 | William 1689–1702 |
| John Balliol 1291–96 | John 1199–1216 | (and Mary d.1694) |
| Robert Bruce 1306–29 | Henry III 1216–72 | Anne 1702–14 |
| David II 1329–71 | Edward I 1272–1307 | George I 1714–27 |
| Robert II 1371–90 | Edward II 1307–27 | George II 1727–60 |
| Robert III 1390–1406 | Edward III 1327–77 | George III 1760–1820 |
| James I 1406–37 | Richard II 1377–99 | George IV 1820–30 |
| James II 1437–60 | Henry IV 1399–1413 | William IV 1830–37 |
| James III 1460–88 | Henry V 1413–22 | Victoria 1837–1901 |
| James IV 1488–1513 | Henry VI 1422–71 | Edward VII 1901–10 |
| James V 1513–42 | Edward IV 1471–83 | George V 1910–36 |
| Mary 1542–67 | Edward V 1483 | Edward VIII 1936 |
| James VI 1567–1625 | Richard III 1483–85 | George VI 1936–52 |
| (James I of England) | Henry VII 1485–1509 | Elizabeth II 1952– |
| | Henry VIII 1509–47 | |
| | Edward VI 1547–53 | |
| | Mary 1553–58 | |
| | Elizabeth I 1558–1603 | |

**1953** Hilary and Tensing climb Mt Everest

**1954** Bannister runs a mile in under four minutes

**1955** Eden succeeds Churchill as premier

**1955** First commercial TV

**1956** Suez crisis

**1957** Macmillan succeeds Eden as premier

**1958** Computers in use in industry

**1959** Part of M.1 motorway open

**1962** First Beatles record

**1964** Labour government under Wilson

**1965** Rhodesia declares independence

**1966** England wins World Cup (football)

**1967** First colour TV broadcasts

**1969** British troops sent to N. Ireland

**1970** Heath Conservative prime minister

**1970** Oil discovered in North Sea

**1973** Britain joins European Economic Community

**1974** Labour government under Wilson

**1979** Thatcher first woman prime minister

**1982** Unemployment exceeds 3 million

**1982** Falkland Islands crisis

**1987** Channel Tunnel begun

**1987** Thatcher government wins third election

**1992** Fourth Conservative government under John Major

Wellesley, Sir Arthur, later
    Duke of Wellington 193,
    **193**, 209, 220, 225, 231
Wells, H. G. 235, 263, **272**, 273
Wentworth, Thomas, 1st Earl
    of Strafford 133, 136
Wesley, John 190, 212–12,
    **212–13**
Wessex 24, 33, 36
West, Benjamin 181
Whistler, James 234, 235, **235**
Whitgift, Archbishop John **117**
Wilberforce, William 191, 213,
    240
Wilde, Oscar 233, 235
Wilkes, John 171, 187, 190, 224
Wilkinson, John 205–6
William II, Kaiser of Germany
    267
William I, King of England
    (William the Conqueror)
    family tree **48**

invasion of England 38, **39**
policies 40, 42, 56, 66, 80
William II, King of England
    (William Rufus) 40, 41
William III, King of Great Bri-
    tain, and William III,
    Prince of Orange 149,
    153–5, **154**, 156, 160
William the Lion, King of Scot-
    land 54, 61
William the Silent, Prince of
    Orange 125
William of Doncaster 85
Williams, Roger 143
Wilson, Harold 289, 300
Wilton Diptych 102–3, **103**
Winchcombe, John 118
Winchelsea, George Finch-
    Hatton, 9th Earl of 225
Winstanley, Gerrard 144
Winthrop, John 143
Wolfe, General James 169, 181

Wolsey, Thomas 112, 113, 114
Wood, Henry **233**
Woolf, Virginia 273
Worde, Wynkin de 109
Wordsworth, William 194
Wren, Christopher **149**, 150
Wright, Joseph 181
Wright, Michael **159**
Wright, Orville and Wilbur
    263
Wyclif, John 75–6, 105, 114
Wyninge, Matilda 72

Yeats, W. B. 254
York, House of 100–1, **101**
York, Richard, Duke of 101
Young, Arthur 196
Young Ireland Movement 252
Young Pretender *see* Charles
    Edward, Prince

Zwingli, Huldreich 114

*Acknowledgements*

The Illustration on page 157 is reproduced by gracious permission of Her Majesty the Queen.
Ashmolean Museum, Oxford 35; J. Bartholomew & Son Ltd., Edinburgh 77; J. Bethell 66, 149, 180, 208, 209; British Airways Corporation 305, British Museum, London 10, 15, 20, 22, 30, 59, 82; British Petroleum Company 304; British Tourist Authority 21; Camera Press London 306, 307; Central Press Photos 276, 280, 281, 292, 297, 298; City Art Gallery, Bristol 122, W. F. Davidson 78; Department of the Environment 64, 257; R. Estall 134; Mary Evans Picture Library 128, 130, 220, 221, 229; Freer Gal-

lery of Art, Washington, D.C. 235; Greater London Council 237; Guildhall Library, London 185; Hulton-Deutsch Collection 288, 289, 297, 301 (both), 302; A. F. Kersting 28, 41, 86, 107, 127B; Keystone Press Agency 277, 297, 300; Mansell Collection 29, 85, 104, 108, 152, 153, 156, 172–173, 243, 245, 269; Mei Lim 299; Metrocentre, Gateshead, 308; Museum of the History of Science, Oxford University 109B; National Coal Board 300, National Gallery, London 103L; National Maritime Museum, Greenwich 125; National Portrait Gallery, London 114, 133, 242; National Trust (John Bethell) 178; Public Records Office 42; Reed International Books Ltd., 38, 78–79, 98, 102, 103R, 109T, 164, 166B, 181, 192, 194, 217, 260,

261, 268, 272, 285; Scottish National Portrait Gallery, Edinburth 159; Sir John Soane's Museum, London 166T, 167, 182; Spectrum Colour Library 291, 294, 303, 309; Tony Stone Associates 2–3, 6–7; Tate Gallery, London 218–219; E. Tweedy 215; Victoria and Albert Museum, London 103B, 127T, 160, 161; Woodmansterne Ltd. 61.


The publishers would like to thank the following for providing photographs which have been used as artists' reference: British Film Institute (Kevin Brownlow and Andrew Mollo): 144; Sussex Archaeological Trust: 17.